CONVERSATIONS
ON *Success*

Dr. Sharon —
Live with
Purpose & Passion!

INSIGHT PUBLISHING
SEVIERVILLE, TENNESSEE

9/14/06

Published by Insight Publishing Company
P.O. Box 4189
Sevierville, Tennessee 37864

10 9 8 7 6 5 4 3 2

Printed in Canada

ISBN: 1-932863-42-7

Table Of Contents

A Message From The Publisher

Some of my most rewarding experiences in business, and for that matter in my personal life, have been at meetings, conventions, or gatherings after the formal events have concluded. Inevitably, small groups of ten to fifteen men and women gather together to rehash the happenings of the day and to exchange war stories, recently heard jokes, or the latest gossip from their industry. It is in these informal gatherings where some of the best lessons can be learned.

Usually, in informal groups of professionals, there are those who clearly have lived through more battles and learned more lessons than the others. These are the men and women who are really getting the job done and everyone around the room knows it. When they comment on the topic of the moment, they don't just spout the latest hot theory or trend, and they don't ramble on and on without a relevant point. These battle scarred warriors have lessons to share that everyone senses are just a little more real, more relevant, and therefore worthy of more attention.

These are the kind of people we have recruited to offer their insights and expertise for *Conversations On Success*. The book is filled with frank and powerful discussions with men and women who are making a significant impact on their culture, in their field, and on their colleagues and clients. It is ripe with "the good stuff," as an old friend of mine used to always say. Inside these pages you'll find ideas, insights, strategies, and philosophies that are working with real people, in real companies, and under real circumstances.

It is our hope that you keep this book with you until you've dog-eared every chapter and made so many notes in the margins that you have trouble seeing the original words on the pages. There is treasure here. Enjoy digging!

Interviews conducted by:

David E. Wright
President, International Speakers Network

Chapter 1

DEBORAH MOSES

THE INTERVIEW

David E. Wright (Wright)

Today we are talking to Deborah L. Moses. With more than twenty years experience in information technology and management, Deborah brings a vast array of knowledge to her audiences and seminar participants. She manages the businesses, but is frequently still the leader in front of the room entertaining the audiences she speaks with and trains. Deborah practices what she preaches and continues to learn as much from others as they learn from her. With a blend of facts and figures, real life examples and humor, she lives up to the tag line "Training That Transforms." Deborah, welcome to *Conversations on Success.*

Deborah L. Moses (Moses)

Thank you David, and I appreciate the chance to be part of this project.

Wright

Could you tell us about your company Veris Associates, and how it came to be?

Moses

Veris Associates is a consulting company, specializing in training and development. It came to be, because to be perfectly honest, I was tired of the corporate world. I had been in corporate America most of my career, in information technology and management, and decided that it was time to get out and follow my heart. The lack of ethics, morals, and values in corporate America today are so troubling. I decided that I wanted to create a company I would be proud to own and that people would be proud to work for and with.

Wright

I know you have another business as well, Transforming U Seminars. How did that come to be?

Moses

Transforming U Seminars is an offshoot. Veris Associates, as we said, is a training company. We specialize in corporate training and development, and so many people that I spoke to would say to me, in a somewhat envious tone, "I'm so impressed. I can't believe what you did. I could never do what you have done." They just couldn't believe that they could do it themselves, and I would ask them, "What is it you think I did?" Their answers would be things like, "Well, you know, you took a leap of faith, you jumped off the corporate bridge, gave up a stable income." People seem to think that having that steady, stable income will be the end to all their problems. I don't believe that. I really didn't believe other people, who wanted to get out of corporate America and follow their passion, couldn't do it, too. So I started thinking about what it was that I had done, and what characteristics I had that allowed me to move forward and take that leap of faith and start the business. As I thought about that, it became clear that I could teach other people how to do this—how to create the life they want.

So, in addition to the corporate training, we decided to go forward and provide personal development as well. It really didn't work having it in the same business, because it just didn't make sense to people. They didn't get what we were trying to do. So we decided to split it off and have a separate company, which we called Transforming U Seminars. We wanted to have what we do in the name, to make it clear to people what services we provide.

Wright

So Veris is corporate, or business training, and Transforming U is for individuals?

Moses

Correct.

Wright

The title of your new book is *Change Your Life, The CORE Approach™ to Creating the Life You Want.* What was the catalyst for putting your thoughts into the book form?

Moses

The catalyst was partly getting my own thoughts in order. As we began to talk about Transforming U Seminars and the seminar content, it started to become clear to me that I needed a methodology with which to teach this concept. I have an information technology industry and management background, where there are methodologies and process flows for pretty much everything that you do. I wanted to make sure that I had something to give to others, to help them easily understand the approach that we were putting together. The other reason is that not everyone can come to a seminar; I wanted a way for people to have this information, relatively inexpensively, and be able to take it, read it, understand it and then hopefully integrate it.

Wright

And The CORE Approach™ stands for?

Moses

The CORE Approach™ stands for Choice, Opportunity, Responsibility and Expectation. The theory is that we can and should make conscious choices in our lives. Did you ever talk to someone and ask them, "How did you get in the line of business that you're in?" Their answers frequently sound something like, "Well, I met a guy who offered me a job doing such and such, and it wasn't what I went to school for. But I thought, oh, what the heck, I'm not getting paid to do that right now. And one thing led to another and here I am." Most of us end up in these roles and positions in a sort of happenstance, or round-about way. I believe that we need to make conscious choices about what we want, where our passions lie, and about our belief systems, in order for us to be happier in our lives and more fulfilled.

The Opportunity segment has to do with what happens once we make those choices. We need to go and seek out opportunities or create them. There's a motto that I use. "I will find a way or make one." We need to go find those opportunities to make those choices become reality.

Responsibility has to do with the segment that its faith-based, for me at least. I think a lot of people have a strong faith, regardless of who or what they put their faith in—they do believe in a higher authority. Responsibility has to do with getting to a place of peace with yourself and the world. We all have talents, gifts, and blessings that we're provided and we're supposed to give those things away. They're given to us as spiritual gifts, and the more we give them away to others, the more good things come to us. I believe there's an immutable law of reciprocity in the universe, and that the more we give, the more we get—especially when we give without intent to receive. So, responsibility is about giving back. Once your choices have been made, and you're out there actively seeking opportunities, you have to act on what comes your way. Taking the action is the key. My belief is that you can't just have these thoughts and beliefs, you actually have to go out and act on them, because God helps those who help themselves.

The last segment of the methodology is Expectation. Expectation has to with setting our own internal expectation for success first. Many people have wonderful ideas, and they may even begin to act on those ideas, but they begin to act on those ideas with an underlying belief that they are not going to be successful. They really don't believe in themselves strongly enough to be able to put the plan they have created into practice in such a way that they can achieve the success they desire. The flip side of the expectation segment is that once we set our own internal expectation for success, and we make our choices, and we're out there beginning to seek opportunities and give responsibly, there are other people around us who are going to be affected by the changes we're making. We need to set their expectations appropriately too, rather than acting in a void or as if we're alone on an island. If we don't set others' expectations, they are not going to understand or be able to be on board with supporting our success.

Wright

It's odd, that while you were talking, I was thinking that characteristics such as love and caring are all hidden down within us and do not exist until they are given away.

Moses

You are absolutely right, David. These are the gifts we need to give away. It doesn't always have to be material—our best gifts are the spiritual ones, as far as I'm concerned.

Wright

You seem to be a busy lady. Two businesses, the book, and I know you do a lot of speaking engagements. When you go around the country speaking, what are your major topics and what do you try to say to the people?

Moses

Lately, I've done a lot of speaking about The CORE Approach™. The book came out a couple of months ago, so I've been doing a lot of talking about that and bringing that message to people. I seem to speak to a lot of women's groups. Not exclusively, but especially lately there have been a lot of women's groups. One of the topics I used in the last few weeks was "No Guilt Allowed." As working women we tend to experience a lot of guilt around making time for our families and our work. This country is divided; if you're a working woman there are people who think you are a hero. And if you're a working woman there are people who think that you're some cold-hearted materialist because you're not home with your family. And if you are a stay-at-home mom (also a hard-working woman!), there are two factions on either side of whether that is good or bad as well. So, there is this division, and no matter where you "land," there tends to be guilt involved. We need to get rid of the guilt.

I come at this from the perspective of being a working woman (outside the home), and I see that more and more men are getting into the guilt trip, too, to tell you the truth. It seems to me that since the year 2001 when September 11th events hit us, a lot more people—men and women—are reevaluating their lives. For instance, I know men who have turned down promotions in the corporate world, because the promotion would entail more traveling and they didn't want to be away from their families so much. They decided to reevaluate the balance in their lives and be home more. And as a result they are more in tune and more involved with their families. Women have the same issues; many want to be home more. They want more balance in their lives. So the "No Guilt Allowed" message is about giving people who are working permission, so to speak, to not feel guilty. Other topics for speaking engagements include women's issues, leadership, organizational change, having a career as a speaker, empowerment, time management and balancing your life, just to name a few.

We tend to have a sense of, "If I'm at work, I should be home," especially if it is that mid-afternoon range and you still have children in school. At three o'clock in the afternoon you know your kids are getting out of school and they're being taken care of by other care givers. There is frequently guilt about that. Then we get home, and on the rare occasions that we do get a chance to make dinner, while we're cooking, we're usually thinking about all of the things that need to be done in the house and whether we can get help doing them from our spouses or our children. And while we're thinking about all of those things, we're thinking about the report that needs to be completed by the morning or the budget that needs to be submitted by next week and, "Gee, I really should get the laptop out and work tonight, but the kids need help with homework." There are so many conflicting responsibilities that no matter where we are, we feel guilty about something. We need to stop feeling guilty, and arrange our lives with conscious choices in such a way that we can do as much as we can do and then not feel guilty about not being able to do everything for everyone.

Wright

Well, I'm sure the men join you in the balancing dilemma; I know I do.

Moses

I do believe that, especially now, more and more men are wanting to achieve a better balance in their lives. They are not so wrapped up in their work that they don't know their family.

Wright

It's a shame that we have to have two income families just to live nowadays.

Moses

It's true, a lot of people think they do. It's amazing what you can do with a single income, when you decide to try it, but a lot of people do want to have the things that they want to have, and there's nothing wrong with that. A dual income choice, with more disposable income, is nice to have, but some people who have this feel guilty about having too much. And when the choice of a single income is the choice that's been made, then you have to accept it and not feel guilty. Many people make this choice, and then feel a need to apologize or feel guilty that they can't provide all the "stuff" that the Joneses have.

Your question had to do with the topics for my speaking engagements. The other frequent subject for my talks is the challenge of positive change. Overcoming the obstacles caused by our own fears. Fear really is the biggest obstacle to change and The CORE Approach™ is all about change. So, in order to make changes, in order to use the Approach, we have to understand our own fears, and how we put obstacles in our own way. People don't even realize when they are being controlled by fear. They say, "Well, I can't do that, I can't change my life right now because I have a family to support." Or, "I can't make a career change, because what will happen if I don't succeed or if I don't have the knowledge?" Most of the fears are created by the unknown and some are caused by circumstances earlier in someone's life that didn't go quite well for them. They believe that those circumstances are what they are in the midst of, when ninety-nine percent of the time the current situation is a completely different set of circumstances. If they would take the time to analyze the current situation compared to the past, they would find out that their fears are unfounded. It's like you mentioned earlier when your first business didn't do well, but the second one did. Obviously, you didn't let the fear hold you over from the first experience—you learned from it, and made the appropriate changes to succeed the next time.

Wright

You spoke a few minutes ago of balance, and I was wondering how you do all that you do? I, of course, know from reading about you that you have a family and that you also run a couple of serious fund raisers each year, so how do you balance it all?

Moses

Well, that is a problem sometimes. I have had to learn to practice what I preach, that's for sure! I have three boys and a girl. My children are Michael Jr., currently 23 years old, who just graduated from Rutgers, and Kevin, who is 18 years old. Those two are my stepsons, but I think of them very much as my own. My seventeen year old is Jason, and my daughter, Christina, is almost fifteen. Her year-round basketball leagues make for a busy schedule. That, coupled with the emotional roller-coaster of the teenage years, makes life interesting. The teenage things are the biggest challenge, right now, to tell you the truth.

Wright

Yeah, tell me about it, I have a sixteen year old; she was sixteen, two weeks ago.

Moses

I'll offer my sympathies now...(laugh). It's interesting, the fact that they are more independent helps me have more time for the businesses than I would have if they were very dependent kids. I probably wouldn't have quite the freedom that I have, but they all understand what we're trying to build.

You asked about balance and also the fund raising. The way I handle that is to make sure each campaign is of short duration. Each event is a whirlwind, but it's only for a few weeks at a time. So it's manageable, because I can schedule those weeks in advance. It's something that I feel is important, it is one of my ways of being responsible and giving back.

The glitches in the balance come from the unexpected events. Things like an illness in the family, especially if it's my own, or last minute client date changes, those are unavoidable things that create an imbalance, but fortunately the imbalance is generally temporary. But mostly, I'm organized and that's what makes it all work. If I ever lose my schedule, look out.

Wright

So, what groups do you raise funds for, and what types of fundraisers do you use?

Moses

Mostly, we raise money for local social services agencies. I feel that it is important to be strong in the community where we live, so although I do business around the country, I do most of the fund raisers close to home. One of our local agencies is Manna on Main Street, in Lansdale, Pennsylvania and we do fund raisers for them each year. Manna is a local food kitchen. They help out indigent families in the area. I also want to provide funding for our church's mission groups and youth missions. One of my goals, and one reason I started the business, is to be able to fund mission trips. I've done lots of fund raisers and volunteer work over the years, such as charity auctions for groups like the Respiratory Distress Syndrome Foundation, groups that promote cancer research, March of Dimes, local community housing agencies and groups like that.

Wright

As I'm listening to you, I'm hearing The CORE Approach™ all come together. You live your approach. I thought when you spoke of it in the beginning it was a methodology for change.

Moses

It is a methodology for change, that's the way it was created. It was used to make the major change in my life. But our lives change all of the time. Really, we are constantly in a state of change, and hopefully, we're always doing something new. We're learning, we're taking on new areas of service. We are changing our jobs, our kids are growing up and we are in different stages of parenting or being a parent to our parents sometimes. Our lives are changing all of the time, so if I can manage my life according to The CORE Approach™, I can at least stay one step ahead. I don't know if I always do, but if not, I'm doing a good job of fooling myself into believing I am!

Wright

When you've considered the decisions that you've made all through the years, we've talked about some very serious decisions. Jumping off the corporate ladder—that is something that can scare a person to death. However, I did the very same thing and when I did, it wasn't as scary as I thought it would be. So, as you look back at the decisions you've made, what role, if any, has faith played in those decisions?

Moses

Faith has played a huge role in my decisions. Probably the largest role of anything as I consider the question. You talk about jumping off the corporate bridge. It's a little bit like terror mixed with excitement. That's how I explained it to someone recently. It's exciting, it's new, and different, but it is pretty scary. The way that I was able to keep moving forward was by having a strong faith in God and knowing that I had spent a lot of time in dialogue with Him. I didn't do this in two weeks; I spent a lot of time talking about this with my husband, with a close friend, with the Lord. Prayer came into it big time, I spent a lot of time meditating and listening. I think one of the things we learn on our faith journey is to listen. We constantly want to pray and to talk, but we have a tendency not to stop and listen to the answers that we are being given and not be aware of how those answers come into our lives. That's part of the Opportunity segment of The CORE Approach™. We all need to be aware of the answers we're being given, look at the opportunities that are around us, that are being presented to us. Sometimes they're right in front of our face and we don't recognize them. So faith was a big deal for me. I needed to know before I embarked on starting this business that I was on the path that was His will, not mine, and I was moving in a direction that was the right one for my purpose in life. That direction changes occasionally. I have found that we're not always on the extremely straight path, we veer off here or there and have to figure out where the changes come in. Every decision I make is only made once I know that I am on the right track.

Wright

Well, I was really concerned about something that I shouldn't have been concerned about when I jumped off of the corporate ladder. I went into business for myself and within a very short period of time, failed absolutely miserably. I was really a success in corporations and in my first business, I failed. But I learned a lot and I never regretted it. The second business was better than anything that I had ever done before. I tell my friends that even failing, you learn.

Moses

I don't think failure is really failure. I think failure is just a lack of success right then and there; it's a learning experience as you say. Sometimes we have those experiences for the very sake of learning from them. That's why He gives them to us sometimes, I think, so that we can learn and be ready for the next thing.

Wright

So what's next for you?

Moses

Well, some more of the same; speaking, teaching, continuing with the training business, adding seminars on, learning to use entertainment more to enlighten and present my work. I'm working on perfecting my craft all of the time, obviously. The next book we're talking about is *The CORE Approach™ to Business*. I'm currently trying to convince my husband to co-author it with me.

Wright

What advice do you have for others, who are not yet the picture of success that you paint?

Moses

Well, my advice would be to decide what your purpose is, and what your dreams are, and then follow them. Obviously, I have to say, use The CORE Approach™. It worked for me and I truly believe it can work for anyone. Make conscious choices, write down your goals, be specific about your goals. One of the problems that people have is that their goals are non-specific. You need to be specific about your goals; time frames, dollar amounts, the size and shape of the house you want, those types of things. Certainly the motto, "I'll find a way or I'll make one" has worked for me. I would expect that would also work for other people. They have to persevere and not give up. They have to be responsible, figure out what and where their giving plan is directed, and set their expectations for success. My advice would also include encouraging others to communicate with people about what their dreams are, and let others' help find the needed resources they don't have within themselves. Frequently, what we don't have can be found in others around us. This communication also helps set others' expectations. I think that if you set out knowing that you can succeed, you can't help but succeed.

Wright

Well, what an interesting conversation. I've learned a lot here today. The readers who will be reading this book will probably want

Change Your Life! The CORE Approach™ to Creating the Life You Want. Can they get it at Amazon.com or by getting in touch with you?

Moses

They certainly can. Amazon is carrying the book right now, and hopefully the other major booksellers will be picking it up as well. The major book distributors have it available. It is also available on my web site, or by contacting me using the contact information here in this book.

Wright

I really do appreciate you taking this much time with me today, to discuss this exciting subject.

Moses

No problem, David, I am honored to be part of this project. I think it is a wonderful way to get the message out to other people, the message that they too can be successful.

Wright

Today, we have been talking to Deborah L. Moses. Deborah practices what she preaches, as we have found out today, and she says she continues to learn as much from others as they learn from her. She presents her message with a blend of facts and figures, real life examples and humor. Thank you so much, Deborah, for being with us today on *Conversations on Success.*

Moses

Thank you, David.

About The Author

Deborah Moses is the founder and President of Veris Associates, Inc. and Transforming U Seminars. Her mission, "..to discover, affirm and promote the divine illumination in others" is directly related to the mission of the company. She attended Montgomery County Community College (Pennsylvania) and Temple University, and has furthered her career with certifications in management, leadership and information technology areas. She holds memberships in the National Association of Female Executives, National Association for Women Business Owners, and American Society for Training and Development (ASTD), is a past committee chair for the March of Dimes' WalkAmerica, and is a recent recipient of the Florence Nightingale Award. She's listed in Manchester Who's Who of executives and professionals.

Veris Associates is a consulting company specializing in training and development. Creating Transforming U Seminars was a natural extension, focusing on the individual rather than corporate teams. Deborah developed and trademarked The CORE Approach™ and has created a whole line of seminars based on this approach, which uses the elements of Choice, Opportunity, Responsibility and Expectation to enable change. The business is also managed using The CORE Approach™. Deborah practices what she preaches. Her book, Change Your Life! The CORE Approach™ to Creating the Life You Want, is also the basis for the seminars. She has already begun work on the next book, The CORE Approach™ for Business.

Deborah's schedule includes business management, development and delivery of training programs and seminars, speaking engagements at conferences, seminars and trade shows, and consulting and coaching. Her schedule can be hectic, but she works at staying grounded, making time for her family. Deborah is married and lives with her husband and four children in suburban Philadelphia. She is an active church participant and committee member, and a leader in local community and fund-raising events.

Deborah L. Moses

Veris Associates, Inc.

600 Collins Avenue

Lansdale, PA 19446

610-283-0948

Email: debmoses@verisassociates.com

www.verisassociates.com

www.transformingUseminars.com

Chapter Two

JOHN CHRISTENSEN

THE INTERVIEW

David E. Wright (Wright)

Today we are talking to John Christensen. John's story begins in the shipping department at Chart House Learning where he began working as a teenager for his father, Ray. He worked his way to the top the old fashioned way, having to prove to his father and the company that he was a real film maker who could tell moving stories. Today Mr. Christensen guides Chart House as playground director, which is business talk for CEO, with an inspiring vision of an engaged workplace that can be developed through the *Fish Philosophy*. Chart House Learning is changing the way business is done worldwide. Like his dad before him, John created an eloquent language to transform lives. In 1997, he translated what happens daily at Seattle's world famous Pike Place Fish Market's culture into a vital global learning program called *Fish* and changed the entire business film industry. In the process, John also achieved his lifelong dream of how to turn workplaces into energetic, creative, and whole hearted endeavors with the four simple principles embodied in the *Fish Philosophy*. John Christensen, welcome to *Conversations on Success*.

John Christensen (Christensen)

Thank you, David. I appreciate that.

Wright

John, obviously, my first question is what are the four simple principles of *Fish Philosophy?*

Christensen

The four simple principles are play, make their day, be there, and choose your attitude.

Wright

Play? In other words we're supposed to play at work?

Christensen

Yes. Play is the basis of where creativity and innovation happens. And if you look back into your own life and see where you were most creative, it was in those moments of play and inspiration where you got lost in the moment. We call that play. Now if corporations are scared by that, think of it as lightheartedness. Think of it as taking your work seriously, but yourself lightheartedly.

Wright

So tell us a little bit about what you do at Chart House Learning.

Christensen

We are kind of like cultural anthropologists. We study things that are out in the world, then we help put a language to it. For instance, that's what I saw at the fish market. I saw these fish mongers being totally engaged in their work and said, "Wait a minute. Wait a minute. There's something deeper going on than just play and all this craziness that I see on the shop floor." So we interpret that, then put a language around things and help get that out into the business world. Not only the business world, schools are using it, too.

Wright

When you say language, you're talking about terms that can be understood universally?

Christensen

Yes, absolutely. In *Fish,* it's ancient wisdom that's been resurfaced and brought to you in a new way and in an unlikely place, a fish market.

Wright

While preparing for this interview, I read that the first film in your series titled, *The Business Paradise* is the best selling film of all time. Is that true?

Christensen

Yes.

Wright

My goodness!

Christensen

Yes. That was first created in the '80s, with my father and a futurist. It's been translated in many, many languages. *Fish* is creeping up there, though. It's going to surpass *The Business Paradise* someday.

Wright

When you speak and train, how do you motivate people to create workplaces that are joyful and innovative, lighthearted and wholehearted?

Christensen

The interesting part of all this is when we tell them and they see the film or read the book, there's something that connects inside them that says either they had this in them or they were searching for this... this lightheartedness, this engagement of being at work and being engaged in what you do. We've made a film series with a poet named David White. David talks about being wholehearted. He has a friend, a monk friend, who said, "The way around burnout isn't necessarily burnout. It's being wholehearted in what you do." Now that's incredible. That says, if you come to work and you're totally engaged and enjoy what you are doing, the day goes by much quicker and you're going to be connected to it.

Wright

Do you find many CEOs, or especially upper management people, that are a little...

Christensen

Apprehensive of this?

Wright

Yes.

Christensen

Yes, there is. But the one's who embrace it and get it, stand back. Watch out for their organizations! For instance, the CEO of Aspen Ski Co., a ski company in Aspen, Colorado, who has embraced it said, "This is the pull; this is what we're going to be. This is the way we're going to service our employees. We're going to be engaged with what we do." They have 3500 seasonal employees. They teach them every year. They teach them the *Fish Philosophy* when the new group comes in, or even part of the old group comes in. They resurface this and say, "Remember, be engaged." And when they open that playing field and they give them the boundaries of saying, "Okay, safety is first in any business; here's the playing fields. Be safe. Don't do anything that's rude or crude." They saw things happening. For example, like a guy, a young man, created his super hero called *Captain Iowa*. And he'd fly kids through the lift line up to the front and he'd help create an atmosphere in the lift line. When they're standing there for 25 minutes, that was engaging. They started karaoke in the waiting lines, and they do limbo in the waiting lines for the lifts. Now that created an atmosphere because, again, the CEO is saying, "Look , we have great snow and the same mountains as the other resorts. What separates us from the other people? What separates us from our other ski friends?" It was the way they engaged with customers. That's the way, first and foremost, to have people engage in their work and be happy with where they're at. I'm not just talking about making a "Pollyannaish" happy, happy workplace. I'm talking about people being engaged in what they do. Now if you have that and you create that kind of atmosphere, watch out! Your bottom line is going to go up. Your retention is going to go down.

Another thing that we find that's just really amazing is when you step back and analyze it, we're in our places of work more than we are in our places of worship, more than we are in the great outdoors, and more than we are with our families. Now if we can't connect to that, be engaged and have a joyfulness to what we do, that's a sad statement saying, "Look at your life." The hours that you spend there, what are you giving it to? What are you spending your life's energy on? What are you giving, where are you giving your energy, your life energy too? Is this the place that you really want to be? Is this the place that's going to make you flourish?

Wright

What do you mean by "make their day?" Is this management theories that apply to employees, or are these employee theories that apply to customers?

Christensen

It's absolutely everyone. It's employee to employee. It's employer to employee. It's employee to customer. It's the whole thing. I'm saying, if you come with that attitude, again, your life is about what are you giving to people? Make their day is just a new term of saying, be it, make people's day.

Serving others is when we really find joy. No matter if the CEO is talking to a vice-president or a president, or an employee is talking to a guest in a hotel, I'm saying make people's day! And it doesn't take much. It's really amazing the stories that we hear about the little nuances of what makes peoples' day. I mean, just being with a person, that moves into being there. What does being there mean? Just being in the moment with a person. For example, if you're trying to talk to somebody in your office you've got the phone ringing and you've got a message on your cell phone, put all that other away. Let voicemail answer it, put the cell phone away and be with the person. When you're in the presence of a person, they can feel it. Do I have time to share a story with you?

Wright

Sure.

Christensen

There was a policeman who was in the service area of a jail, the booking agent shall we say. The police department he worked for went through the *Fish Philosophy* teaching, and he got aware of being present and making people's day. The prison guard was totally in the moment with a shoplifter, who was being booked for shoplifting. He gave the person dignity and respect. The prisoner started to weep, saying, "I've never been treated this way in my life, much less I'm being booked for a crime I know I did." That's being present. That made that guy's day! That made that guy's life, maybe. Who knows?

Fish brings to the surface what people have in them. It gives them a way to say, "I can do this. I have permission. My organization has shown me the light of being "a day maker." Be private with people. When you're choosing your attitude, making people's day, and being present for people, guess what? The appropriate play comes out.

Wright

In reference to the third principle, choose your attitude, we're publishing a book for a man now about attitude. One of his favorite sayings is, "The difference between a good day and a bad day is your attitude."

Christensen

Absolutely. We all have magnificent stories about our lives. But if you look at people that have tragedies in some respect, and they come whistling in, what is that? How would we face some of these tragedies if they would happen to us? That is what we mean by choose your attitude.

Wright

John, I'd like to quote something you said referring to business. The quote is: "We need people who are passionate, committed, and free to live the organization's vision through their personal value." Could you explain what you were talking about?

Christensen

Yes. When you have an alignment with what you stand for as an individual and what the company, the organization, is standing for, step out of the way. Watch out! Watch the power that happens to that.

Wright

When you talk about businesses, you use words like love and soul.

Christensen

Right.

Wright

Most people would think that spiritual values would not be appropriate in a business setting. Do companies accept your spiritual values as necessary ingredients to success?

Christensen

It's a whole new movement out there about spirituality. I want it to be clear. We're not talking religion. We're talking about the spirit and soul of people. And that brings the soul of a business alive. We made a film with Southwest Airlines. Southwest Airlines was founded on the statement by Herb Kelleher and his two buddies saying, "We wanted to create a workplace based on love rather than fear." Now, if Southwest Airlines with 33,000 employees is based on love and is doing incredibly well in the airline industry, is that not a valuable statement to everybody in business?

Wright

Is there anything or anyone in your life that has made a difference for you and helped you to become a better person?

Christensen

I have a lot of mentors in my life. My parents have been incredible mentors. My mom was a social worker and a very incredible people woman, and my dad was an artist. And when you combine those two, they've been wonderful mentors for me. I've also had the blessings of having Ken Blanchard as a mentor and Spencer Johnson. So I've had great mentors in that respect, too.

Wright

I was talking to Jim Cathcart the other day. I told him that one of my mentors had no knowledge of his being a mentor, and that was Bill Gove from Florida who I have been listening to his talks and tapes and reading his books for probably 40 years.

What do you think makes up a mentor? In other words, are there characteristics that mentors seem to have in common?

Christensen

I believe they're different for everybody. I mean everybody finds a different mentor. I think some of the beautiful mentorships happen when a person takes you under their wing.

Another inspiration for me is Norman Vincent Peale. Okay, he's got religion in there, but his being was a mentorship for me. His presence, the way he spoke so eloquently and so much passion, that's what mentored me. You can get inspired by many different things. If a tape or a book inspires you and becomes your mentor, fabulous. When it opens you up to the possibilities in your life, be it a book, a mentor, a tape, a film, they are all wonderful aspects of opening you up to possibilities.

Wright

I remember when I was in Seattle a few years ago and saw the people working in the company that you wrote about, I remember two feelings. One is a feeling that this would be a nice place to buy something. But the biggest feeling was these guys are really happy and fun. And they've got a tough job too. That's not one of your bank presidents type jobs.

Christensen

No. Hey, they don't work in air conditioning and heat. They work with dead fish, ice and cold cement floors. I've wiped out there many a time. It's just showing you the possibilities that if they can do it with their hands in dead fish, cold ice, 12 hour days, that's what's so powerful about it. That's why we call it the *Fish Philosophy*. It's based on the fact that if the fish market can do it, you can do it. But the philosophy is ancient wisdom but it's coming alive on a fish market. And if a fish market can do it, we all can do it.

Wright

We've talked about three out of four of the principles; the last one I'd like to ask you about is the principle "be there." Do you mean come to work on time and be there? Or be there for people?

Christensen

Be there for people. I mean absolutely be in the moment. Like I was saying, when you're with somebody, put the other things down. I catch myself so many times sitting at my desk when people come in, and I'm reading something, or half with them or not. You have to take that moment and put what you're doing down and be there for them. Another good little exercise to do is when the phone rings, take a moment before you pick it up and just pause. Think about what you're going to do on the phone. It doesn't matter if it's a sales person or whatever, just remember to be there in the moment when you're on the phone with a person. It's an interesting little exercise of being present.

Wright

Most people are fascinated with these new television programs about being a survivor.

What has been the greatest comeback you have made from adversity in your career or in your life?

Christensen

Wow! The biggest adversity? Well, there's two. We went through a stint with a company where some people tried to take over our business, and I made it through that. But one of the things was living up to my mentor, my father, and having knowing in my heart and my gut that I had the capacity to leave the company and to be a great filmmaker like my father. And I don't mean great in a cocky way. I'm saying bringing what we bring to the table of documentaries. Showing the world what possibilities are. That's what I mean by great. That was a high. That was a hurdle to work through.

Wright

When I was researching for this interview, I noticed on your website they also referred to Joel Barker, the futurist who helped your father.

Christensen

Futurist, correct.

Wright

And so your father started making what? Documentary films?

Christensen

Yes. He started off in advertising just when television was getting started in the late '50s. He happened to be in love with the documentary approach. He pursued the documentarian lifestyle and would go off and make films. What he brought to the table was this uniqueness, this anthropological aspect into looking at things, studying it, and saying, "What can we do to show that?" For instance, when his career started off in Omaha, Nebraska, he made a film about the city of Omaha. But through the whole film, you didn't know where you were until the end of the film, *Come See Our City, Omaha*. But it showed you who the people were, what the organizations were like in Omaha, and you'd like to come and live here and build your business here. So he brought that approach to it. Let's study it. Let's bring it. Let's show people what it's about instead of telling them, Again, that's what happened with the paradigm idea. Let's look at a paradigm. Let's look at it all these different ways. If it doesn't get you this way, look at it this way. Look at it this way. If this story doesn't connect with you, look at it this way. Ah, and then you can relate to that.

Wright

The free-wheeling workplace of the 1990s is long gone. Companies are cutting perks. Employees are reverting from casual attire to business wear. How can employees really play at work when the reins are being pulled back so tightly?

Christensen

Well, that's our point. The reigns shouldn't be pulled back so tightly. Ken Blanchard calls it the tight underwear syndrome. We need to get rid of that. We need to free people up because when you're free is when creativity and innovation happens. I don't know where the quote comes from, but it was said, "If works were plays, Silicon Valley would not have been created." Because it would out the play. Two guys in their garage, I mean how many guys were in their garage playing, tinkering around, right? H.P., Apple, I mean how many more can we list. They were playing!

See, it's the playfulness in which they react to each other and react to customers at the fish market. You can see what they're doing and make your own style. It opens you up to say, "What can *we* do that is about playfulness?"

Wright

I've heard about the impact that *Fish* is having on corporate America. Has it been used outside the business world?

Wright

Schools are one of our biggest clientele. It's amazing. We are now creating a curriculum for schools. We're working on creating how to bring this in. If you could talk about being present to what you are doing and making people's day to elementary students, imagine what possibilities lie in the future for that.

Wright

Are you having more success getting it into the private schools or public schools?

Christensen

Public schools are embracing it. First and foremost, what's happening is that the administration and the teachers are being brought into this, talking about how they can engage with their work. Again, you said the budget crunches and the tightening of the ropes, and with all that, how are we going to? It goes back to saying, "What kind of organization can we be that is going to help people be engaged in what we're here for?"

We have a roofing company that used this that turned their entire company around into roofing, and now they're a world famous roofing company. They get roofing jobs in different places in the world. They just showed up in a different way. They were being something different.

Now, back to education. If you are being present in the classroom for your kids, and saying, as a participant, not even as customer—they're the customers, "I have to serve them." They're there to teach you as much as you are to teach them. My goodness! That was my first love. I wanted to be a teacher saying, "What can you bring to the table."

Dead Poets Society, that's the kind of teachers we need. People engaged in the minds of our youth saying, "How do I get to them? How do I reach them? How am I there with them? What do I do to make their day?" We're actually working on the concept of saying the four principles of *Fish* are the rules of the classroom. What am I doing today to play, be playful. This works both ways. This is teacher and student, partner to partner. What are we doing to make the classroom fun? What are we doing to make each other's day? How am I being there for you? How are you being there for me? How are you being there for your other your peers? And first and foremost, how are you choosing to come to school? How are you choosing to be today?

Wright

Very interesting. Boy, this has been a fast, fast 30 minutes, and I really do appreciate you being a guest today on *Mission Possible*. I really appreciate you taking the time.

Christensen

David, thank you, and thanks for helping spread the word.

Wright

Today we have been talking to John Christensen whose story began work as he said working with his father as a great role model. And you've heard the intelligent statements and how the *Fish Philosophy* can literally change you and your company's future, as it's changing some in America. So, let me ask you before we leave, I'd like to shamelessly advertise the book. I think everyone should read it. I know you're making good at Amazon.com. Can they get it direct from you or can they find out more on your website? If you'll give us that information, I would appreciate it.

Christensen

Absolutely, it is charthouse.com. Inside of charthouse you can go to fishphilosophy.com, which is a whole website with all the fish information. You can purchase all sorts of our films on there and our ancillary products, our fishing gear and you can purchase the books. Now there's two books on the market, David. There's *First Fish!*, and our second one that came out in April is called *Fish Tales*.

Wright

I hope our readers and our listeners will rush to the website and get this book. I've got *Fish Tales*. I'm going to get the first one.

Christensen

Thank you, David. Thank you so much. I really appreciate your time.

About The Author

John Christensen's story begins in the shipping department at ChartHouse Learning where he began working as a teenager for his father, Ray. He worked his way to the top the old-fashioned way, proving to his father – and the company – that he was a real filmmaker who could tell moving stories. Today Christensen guides ChartHouse as "Playground Director" (CEO in business-speak) with an inspiring vision of an engaged workplace that can be developed through the FISH! Philosophy. The rest of the story is that ChartHouse Learning is changing the way business is done worldwide.

Like his dad before him, John's created an eloquent language to transform lives. In 1998, he translated what happens daily at Seattle's world famous Pike Place Fish Market's culture into a viable global learning program called FISH! and changed the entire business film industry. In the process, John also achieved his lifelong dream of how to turn workplaces into energetic, creative and wholehearted endeavors with the four simple principles embodied in the FISH! Philosophy: • PLAY• MAKE THEIR DAY• BE THERE• CHOOSE YOUR ATTITUDE

"The ChartHouse vision is an invitation to people to become fully immersed in their lives, using these four seemingly simplistic ideas," he says. "In many ways the FISH! Philosophy is really ancient wisdom for modern times, a lifestyle choice to engage in life-long learning and self-improvement. The products we offer are really learning tools, from some of the best mentors one could have – real-life experiences that ultimately speak to the human spirit."

Growing up around a filmmaking father and a supportive mother who shared the same values captured in many of Ray Christensen's films, John initially pursued a degree in Park and Recreations Studies from the University of Minnesota. But it was a post-college stint, working with kids as a summer Camp Director, where he first understood the value of artistry and teaching

Today John speaks to vastly different organizations about his journey – the serendipitous discovery of the fish market – and how that simple FISH! Philosophy he and his team poetically articulated on film four years ago can dramatically change the stories of companies and individuals.

John Christensen

www.charthouse.com

www.fishphilopophy.com

27

Chapter Three

SCOTT SCHILLING

THE INTERVIEW

David E. Wright (Wright)

Today we are talking to Scott Schilling. Scott has twenty-eight years of sales, marketing, speaking and training experience through a range of industries. He is known for his conceptual selling expertise. Scott is a dynamic presenter that gets the message across while addressing issues like maximizing performance, presenting valued added offerings, developing strategic plans and implementation until the task is completed. Many of the same principles used to maximize business situations are easily translated to any selling situation with his guidance. Teaching how to maximize the potential of any opportunity is Scott's specialty. Scott has created, developed had enhanced sales and marketing presentations for numerous organizations. As an accomplished professional speaker, Scott has appeared on TV, radio; satellite broadcasts, and regularly shares his ideas on how to maximize potential through speaking engagements worldwide. Scott, welcome to *Conversations on Success*.

Scott Schilling (Schilling)

Thank you very much. I'm excited to have the opportunity to share some time with you!

Wright

You've been personally successful across a broad range of industries. How have you been able to accomplish this?

Schilling

The success I've enjoyed across several industries comes from having a solid foundation of the basics and developing the expertise of a value-added conceptual salesperson. Early on, my mentors taught me that everything needed to be looked at from the customers' perspective. That means always creating an environment around the sale that insures the transaction is beneficial to them. When you present products or opportunities in that way, to a certain extent, the product itself becomes irrelevant. It simply becomes the vehicle to solve the problem. The task is to satisfy the needs, wants and desires of the potential customer with the benefits your goods and services provide. The vast majority of salespeople spend their time presenting the features of what they have to offer. The customer, however, really only cares about the benefits that they will derive from the features and the product offered. Once you understand this tenant completely, and how to present in a value added conceptual way, you gain tremendous flexibility to be able to work across various industries. It's really the process, not the product, that is the key to success. My experience comes from having wonderful opportunities to learn across many industries. With the knowledge that has been available to me, it is possible to apply that conceptual presentation expertise and have a great deal of success no matter what the industry.

Wright

So what are the keys to success as you see them?

Schilling

There are a number of real keys to success that anyone can implement. First, you have to have real passion for what you're doing. Too many times people don't live their passions so they come up unfilled, both personally and professionally. When you pursue your passion, when you truly have that burning desire for doing what you're doing, it spurs you to be successful. You will ultimately manifest success because success in that particular area of your life is tremendously important to you. When something makes you ache and you want it badly, you will make it happen. It's your purpose; it's where you're going. For me, the love of speaking, writing and training is natural because of my passion about helping others and having them succeed. To see others succeed in part because of my efforts, fuels the fires within me to continue giving it my all.

Secondly, you have to work to gain as much knowledge as you possibly can about your area of expertise and passion. Not long ago, someone stated that the definition of an expert is the person in the room that knows one more thing than everyone else in the room. That's kind of simple, yet true. He who has the most knowledge in any situation usually wins. The more knowledge you can gain, whether it is across a range of industries or on a specific topic, the better reservoir you will have to draw upon when needed. It is extremely valuable to have that knowledge at any time. To recognize this fact, simply think of any profession that requires a significant amount of education (Doctors, Lawyers, Accountants, etc.) and then think about the compensation they receive for their services. They have greater expertise in specific areas and are rewarded appropriately. Let me briefly touch on two other points about gaining knowledge. First, knowledge ultimately gives you confidence in any situation and confidence breeds success. Secondly, the knowledge you hold in your head is something no one can ever take away from you. Whether due to job loss, divorce, you name it. It's yours and both of the confidence and base knowledge stay self-contained.

The next key to success is that you have to be internally inspired, having a goal orientation, you have to have your purpose, and you have to live your purpose. Motivation is a wonderful thing, but motivation is an outside-in activity that fades with time. Inspiration is inside-out, always there for you to draw from within. Only you can set your own goals, know where you want to go and create your vision. We have all seen "outsiders" create expectations for others only to have the targets fail miserably. It's because the individual executing that activity did not "own" the goals. True success is driven from within, being entrepreneurial and enterprising. When someone has this internal drive, they really want to make things happen so in fact they do!

The next characteristic that is really essential is you have to make decisions. Whether the decisions are right, wrong or indifferent, you have to make one after another. The fact that in many cases, people don't make decisions is in reality making a decision. By putting something off and not addressing it immediately simply impedes their ability to grow. Being decisive, actually going toward something, gives anyone the opportunity to refine and improve his or her status

31

in anything. The reality is very rarely do we pick the exact right avenue the first time. But because we have taken action, made a decision, we can modify that decision using the newfound information and feedback we receive as a result of that decision. To get to the right avenue, venue or the right opportunity, you have to have disqualified the present one first. It becomes simple, make a decision and go after it, learn from it and modify your position later if need be and recommit.

The final characteristic is being willing to take input from others. There are so many wonderful mentors, so many amazing masterminds, and so many people who have far more experience than any single individual. The difference in the truly successful comes in their willingness to accept and contribute to mastermind groups. Multiple brains and peoples' experiences working together are far smarter and more efficient than any single brain or experience set. When groups of people come together with a common purpose, drawing on their collective expertise, it's amazing what can happen. Working with others, picking their brains, recognizing that we all have varied areas of expertise can be invaluable in our personal growth. Subordinating your ego, sharing as a mastermind group and being willing to give and take input can quantum leap individual success. In my mind, these five characteristics are critical to anyone's success.

Wright

One fellow told me a couple of days ago; all of us are smarter than any of us.

Schilling

A good friend of mine, Mark Victor Hansen, holds up the index finger on his left hand and puts it next to the index finger on his right and says one plus one equals eleven. That concept alone gets you thinking about the value of sharing expertise.

Wright

That gives us a great foundation to look at success. With your background in sales, can you share with us your definition of selling?

Schilling

Selling is absolutely essential in everything that we do; in fact everybody is a sales person at some point each day. Many, if not most people may not necessarily look at themselves that way, but in reality we are all salespeople every minute of every day. My definition of selling is quite simple—selling is education through communication without manipulation. A sale is nothing more than a transaction. It's an exchange of a product, service or idea for an amount of money or its equivalent. The key to the selling process is to educate the consumer or the prospect on the value of what it is you have to offer and how that value satisfies their wants and desires. When that happens, the transaction takes place. That transaction could result in selling a product, getting your kids to bed, or getting a date. Those are all sales in my book.

Wright

Right. If you ever met my wife you would know that I'm a great salesman.

Schilling

I say that all of the time in my training—"If you've ever been on a date, you have made a sale. If you have ever been married, you are a super salesperson!"

Wright

That's right. What is a conceptual value-added presentation?

Schilling

Many years ago I was taught that there are two types of selling. The first is "price" selling and the other is "brand or conceptual" selling. Price selling is pretty simple, this widget costs about five dollars from one supplier and someone else sells the same widget for four fifty. The one with the lowest price wins because that was the only thing presented—the price. There is no other information delivered to differentiate between suppliers. That approach doesn't really suit me very well so I've worked my entire career to gain as much expertise on conceptual value added (brand) presentation as possible.

Conceptual (brand) presentations revolve around understanding the benefits the goods or services offer and environment the consumer would like to have from the product or opportunity that they are being presented. In other words, you don't sell what it is—you sell what it does. You don't sell the steak; you sell the sizzle, the taste, and the glorious experience. You see this a tremendous amount in advertising, most people just don't recognize it. You see the way certain foreign car brands are romanced. Advertisers suggest that you can drive with the skill of a racecar driver, you can have flowing hair and you will be something special because you drive their brand of vehicle. Notice that none of the presentation has anything to do with the features of the car itself, rather they all have to do with the image that's created around the proposed benefits of owning and driving that particular car. People truly want to achieve these feelings so they buy that particular car. Conceptual presentation is all around us. I've chosen to use this type of expertise to help people to achieve their needs, wants and desires. When a consumer can truly benefit as a result of the goods and services presented, they have been done a great service by the sales professional that served them.

Wright

What do you mean by creating an atmosphere to buy?

Schilling

It's a whole other part to conceptual value-added selling. As a salesperson, it is my responsibility to make this a worthwhile transaction for both sides. With that, I don't ever want to sell anything to anyone, however, at the same time I always want them to buy a tremendous amount from me. That may sound like the same thing, a product goes from one side to another side, but in reality, it's quite different. When you create an atmosphere in which the purchase of a product or opportunity presented is the best and most logical choice for the customer to truly satisfy their needs, wants and desires it now becomes their decision. It is their will and wants to buy, not mine. It is truly my responsibility as a sales professional to create that atmosphere where my offering becomes their perfect choice. If someone doesn't respond to what is being offered, it's not his or her fault, it's the presenters (salesman's) fault. They haven't created a great enough atmosphere or enough reasons why what is being offering is such a wonderful choice for the customer.

Wright

I relate this to my employees that the paradox is since buying is an internal driver everyone loves to buy things. If you don't think so just go and sit on a bench in a mall. The problem is that people don't want to be sold.

Schilling

Exactly. It's human nature and in fact something covered during my presentation on selling.

Wright

Is that right?

Schilling

People love to buy and hate to be sold. When they're sold they will look for every expectation that has been committed to them, and if the purchase ever fails to fill any of those expectations they'll come back at the salesperson or organization. When they make the decision to buy, it is now their decision, there's no cognitive dissidence. People are customarily pleased with their decisions and in fact, because a salesperson helped guide them to that decision, that salesperson builds rapport and a relationship grows. The salesperson has ultimately satisfied everything that they've committed to or that they ask the customer to commit to regarding the purchase. That in turn causes the customer to refer the salesperson and their goods or services. The quality created in this transaction is how to really grow significant sales opportunities.

Wright

You talk about being proud to be a salesman. Why are you so proud to be part of a profession that is sometimes looked upon less than favorably?

Schilling

Because when products and services are presented properly, the presenter can be a true sales-professional. I'm very proud to be a professional sales person. Unfortunately, everybody at one time or another throughout his or her lifetime has come across a sales manipulator. A manipulator is someone who "techniques" prospects, getting them to do something that they truly didn't want to do. To me, that person is not a sales-professional. They are more of a trickster or hustler. Sales-professionals are proud of the time, effort and everything that they've put in to gain the knowledge and the confidence to be able to present opportunities to people with quality. Many sales-professionals believe deeply in their products and services, and are very proud to present their offerings the right way to truly benefit the consumer. Those who educate, communicate and don't manipulate are the true sales-professionals.

Wright

What makes you enjoy speaking from the platform so much when there are so many people that are naturally scared to death of speaking?

Schilling

It something you have to love because you get to see the flash in peoples eyes when something that you're are talking about hits home, You can see in an instant how something that you've said has already, or is going to make a difference in their lives. It's just such a wonderfully rewarding experience to be there, be able to talk the masses, connect with them and help them grow as others have done before me. Having that opportunity to share information gathered over the years, things learned from many of the great speakers and trainers and people that I've studied, being able to translate those messages in a way that the people in the audience can really benefit from that is tremendously gratifying. It's so rewarding to have people come up to you afterward and say, "Thank you, you've really made an impact on me today."

There are many people that are afraid to get up in front of a group of people. Please let me encourage them to change their mindset and understand the tremendous good that they can do. So many people have such amazing talents that they don't recognize or put forth. With a little work, anyone could get up in front of people and provide that encouragement, that inspiration, that bit of knowledge, that would really impact somebody's life. When you understand the good that can be accomplished from the front of the room, the little bit of nervousness, or whatever in front of a group goes away really easily. It's just a blast— talking, presenting and having total fun up on the platform.

Wright

How did you get started selling in the first place?

Schilling

It's a funny story. In 1962, our family headed cross-country by train going to the Toastmasters International convention. It was kind of a long train trip from Milwaukee, WI to Los Angeles, CA. About the middle of the second day, looking for something to keep me occupied, I started wandering up and down the isles screaming "tickets, tickets, who needs tickets," and people would respond saying, "I do, I do." I took a pad of paper and scribbled a few lines on the piece of paper and handed it to them. In return, they would hand me some money—not bad selling them tickets to a train they were already on! I went up and down the isles like that for a while and by the time we arrived in LA; I had over fifty dollars in coins in my pocket. In 1962, $50 was pretty good, especially when you understand I was only four at the time. Some people say they choose their profession—I'm pretty sure this profession chose me.

Wright

What is it about training others that excites you so much?

Schilling

I have been very blessed to have some amazing people take me under their wing and invest in me to share their knowledge, share their expertise and help me expand my capabilities. Because it is only right to model their efforts, it's part of the give back, the obligation and responsibilities that I feel for those who have done it for me previously. When you go and help train others, it's exciting, because I relate back to the impact that others training and sharing their information had on me. We all have a responsibility to share our blessings and hope to have similar impacts with others. It was relayed to me that we all are infinitely capable of doing so many more things than we actually do today. It's extremely rewarding to be able to offer that assistance to others in a way that it was offered to me.

Wright

You start your days with proclamations and acclamations; can you give us a couple and explain why you use them?

Schilling

The one that I rally around that is the most exciting to me is—"I am attracting into my life everything that I need to cause over one hundred million dollars in charitable giving." It's pretty hard to start your day poorly when you start it with that mindset. It's such a great focus to be able to go and say something like that repeatedly. What's really interesting is when I say that proclamation to others—"I 'm attracting into my life right now everything that I need to cause over one hundred million dollars in charitable giving," they go "Wow, that's awesome, how can I help?" You might think they'd look at you and go "Where are you coming from on this?" There's no predetermined expectation, it just becomes a goal that you can visualize, it becomes something that you can say, "What is going to happen today that would help lead toward that situation."

Another affirmation I start my days with comes from The Masters Circle program. It is "Today is a great day and I have the opportunity to show up the best me ever. I'm an irresistible magnet that with the absolute power to attract into my life everything that I desire. My life is a huge success! I am committed to constant and never-ending personal improvement, and I take massive action steps to create the future, as I want it. I will do whatever it takes to become the winner I know I can be." Again, when you start your day that way, it puts you on track to face the issues of the day. We all have setbacks, and need to handle them gracefully. Those are real easy to identify, but sometimes when we don't get our mindset right to start the day, we don't see the little things that are really going to be huge and beneficial just down the line. Again, we all have the ability to determine whether the glass is half empty or half full. I choose to have it be half full, flowing over and going crazy. Those are the kinds of thoughts learned from "The Masters" that need to be shared with others.

Wright

You have a training platform called *STEPS: Success Through Education Performance System,* why did you develop the system?

Schilling

STEPS is very exciting. It has nearly one-thousand courses in the library currently and will grow by approximately 500 courses per quarter. Including the various courses and the programs I have produced in my training programs, it is a collection of some of the best and the most learned trainers and teachers across the professional, personal, academic and technical areas.

The reasons we worked to develop STEPS came about while working with Fortune 500 companies that may have thousands of employees. They will typically train the top fifty, the top eighty, and the top one hundred people within the organization. While that's wonderful, I often wondered about the rest of the people throughout the organization and how we could get them the identical training in an efficient manner. Another consideration has always been the effectiveness of the people that were personally trained in implementing the information we shared down the road. It became apparent that spreading the reach of our training would be valuable along with insuring those that did get the training implemented it appropriately. The fact that short term memory is only 37 seconds and even if you write things down, the question then becomes how much of what you were able to relate did they internalize. Spaced repetition really becomes the way to insure success.

STEPS is a delivery platform available 24/7/365 over the Internet that's allows subscribers to relive the course material anytime the person wants to review the information we covered. They cannot only relive the courses we did together, but they can also review the nearly thousand other courses that are available on professional, personal, academic and technical issues. They can view Les Brown, Jack Canfield, Barbara DeAngelis and many more of the greatest trainers and educators through their programs designed to better anyone's station in life. Currently there are a thousand different courses on the platform and we are committed to add five hundred more courses every quarter. Consistent and continued education is one of the huge keys to anyone's success. You have to be constantly striving to learn more and now we have a way to insure that even without being personally in front of everybody, there is a system available to translate the messages in those educational opportunities. Making sure that we have success after the fact—in other words, aftercare is very important. I'm very excited about www.successthrougheducation.com.

Wright

You're a professional speaker; you're an author, trainer and streetwise sales consultant by trade, what's it like to wear these various hats?

Schilling

As you go throughout your life and your career, we're all exposed to many different experiences. As you gain that information, that knowledge, that expertise, you should be able to catalog it to be called on at a future date. Some people really enjoy doing one thing and doing one thing over and over and over again. It's fun doing a variety of compatible things that all tie together. Ultimately, that kind of makes everyday a fresh new and exciting experience. Speaking professionally is presenting one to many and it's extremely rewarding in a certain way. Training to a small group, whether it is twenty-five, fifty, or a hundred is rewarding in another way. When you pass along your thoughts through the written word, being an author is a whole different approach. Just the fact that I have been selling on the street for twenty-eight years, the challenge of figuring out how to present items that other people have difficulty presenting or can't figure out how to sell is invigorating. It's a blessing to have the opportunity to wear these various hats because it keeps me fresh, its keeps me excited, and as we discussed earlier, having a true passion for what you're doing is so important.

Wright

Can you fill us in on any of the projects you are involved with?

Schilling

Absolutely! A couple years ago my good friend Dr. Fabrizio Mancini, the President of Parker College of Chiropractic enlisted me in his vision of spreading the word of Worldwide Wellness through Chiropractic care. As a chiropractic patient, many potential opportunities on how to better present the wonders of chiropractic care came to mind. I began presenting and helping relate how amazing the "technology" of Chiropractic can be to those that don't understand it. The thought that God has made the perfect being and that the only thing that can heal the body is the body makes perfect sense. It also seemed that not nearly enough people understand the simple concept that a Chiropractor uses their knowledge and skill to align the spine to allow the natural internal communication process to work unimpeded throughout the nervous system.

When the nervous system communicates through the nerves throughout the body effortlessly, the body naturally, without drugs or outside influences will stay healthy and disease free. If interference is developed in the communication flow, the Chiropractor makes the adjustments necessary to remove the interference. With the interference gone, the body heals itself. Chiropractic care is holistic and stands the chance of reducing the self-inflicted pressures that have been created in the country's medical and insurance systems. Not getting sick in the first place, or recovering quickly would save our nation and its' people millions of dollars and more importantly, bring a significantly greater quality of life to millions of people. Communicating this message and value of Chiropractic care has been extremely rewarding especially when you see the massive life enhancing effects of treatment. This is a message that needs to be shared far and wide!

Wright

I asked you earlier in this interview, "What are the keys to success as you see them and you said the first thing was one has to have passion." Why do you have to have such passion in helping others?

Schilling

It goes back to when my dad speaking was speaking on behalf of The United Way years ago. His love for wanting to help grow employee participation and contributions for the United Way was inspiring. Back in those years, I didn't understand his dedication to the task. I was pretty young at the time. He worked a regular job all day and then he would go company-to-company and work to spread the benefits of The United Way, all the good that they supported and ask people to join in that cause. Not understanding it, it just seemed like extra hours of time and effort.

As I've grown through my sales and speaking career, I was truly blessed enough to finally get it, I figured it out. It wasn't about him—it was about the number of people that benefited from the support that the United Way provided. Just like it's not really about us. It's about our ability to serve others for the greater good. We all can do and share so much more. I was extremely fortunate that Jack Canfield and Mark Victor Hansen took me aside at a speaking event a couple years ago. They said Scott, you are far more capable and talented than what your using in your job, you need to do more, you have an obligation to contribute more. They asked straight out what I was doing to help humanity. It caused me to stop and think about it. What I thought at the time was a good amount wasn't even scratching the surface of "what could be."

Some people would say, "Hey, that's kind of a heavy thing for them to hit you with." I thank them for what they did! To me, that event along with a couple others became wake up calls to get after it and do more—much, much more! When you stop and think, there is something more that each and every one of us can do to help others far more than what we have been doing up until now. I looked back to my dad, recalled the years of service he gave and all of a sudden, it clicked. It has become a true passion to do what I can to help forward others. I've grown to learn and truly understand that if I help enough people, the rewards will be limitless for all involved. It comes back to an old Zig Ziglar concept I learned many years ago, "If you help enough other people get what they want, you'll truly get what you want." If more people would live by that old saying, the world, our country, cities, and our schools, everything would be so significantly better.

The only way to do that is to live it by example, and therefore, that's my task. My task is to help people, and I've grown accustomed to finishing my conversations with, "If there is ever anything that I can do to help you in any way please let me know." People say, "What does that mean?" I say, "I really don't know, because I don't know what you need." Sometimes people are skeptical of the statement, but again, the fact of the matter is I'm responsible for what I put out into world. I'm working to put out my desire to help others. It's amazing how wonderful life can be when that environment of people helping people surrounds you. It's extremely rewarding, very exciting and you tend to recognize many of the successes through others, sometimes more than through yourself. It's an awesome way to approach the day.

Wright

Well, what an interesting conversation. I have learned a lot.

Schilling

Thank you for your time and the opportunity to share some thoughts with you.

Wright

I'll think about some of these things that you said and I'm sure our readers will get a great deal out of the chapter in this book. Today we have been talking to Scott Schilling, he has years of sales, marketing, speaking and training experience in several different industries. The same principles that he uses in maximizing business situations are easily translated into every selling situation and that's what he is all about and as we have heard from his very word today, helping people is what it is really all about. At least I can congratulate you on that Scott, thank you so much for being with me and giving me so much time today on *Conversations on Success*.

About The Author

Scott Schilling brings 28 years of experience in sales, marketing, speaking and training to business owners, corporations and entrepreneurs. Through his affiliations with Fortune 500 companies, innovative start-up companies and high paced individuals, Scott brings a wealth of knowledge and sales, marketing and implementation strategies to the podium. Scott has presented to thousands of attendees across a range of industries including the Chiropractic, Automotive, Transportation, Electronics, Appliance and Insurance organizations. Scott's goal is to maximize the potential and God given talents of the individuals and organizations he encounters.

Scott Schilling

Schilling Sales & Marketing, Inc.

4020 N. MacArthur Boulevard, Suite 122-183

Irving, TX 75038

Phone: 972.255.6565   (877) 305-6565

Email: Scott@ScottSchilling.com

www.scottschilling.com

www.successthrougheducation.com

44

Chapter Four

STEPHEN KREMPL

THE INTERVIEW

David E. Wright (Wright)

Today we're talking to Stephen Krempl. He is an international speaker, trainer and human resources development veteran. Stephen has worked for Fortune 500 companies such as YUM! Brands, Inc., PepsiCo, and Motorola, and as a consultant for the largest training and educational institute in Asia. His assignments have provided him the opportunity to work with and train leaders in 25 countries. Stephen has authored three books: *Training Across Multiple Locations* (Berrett-Koehler Publishers, Inc.), *Business ER* (Xulon Press), and his newest book, *Leadership ER* (Cornerstone Leadership Institute). He is currently Vice President of YUM! University and Global Training, YUM! Brands, Inc., Louisville, Kentucky. YUM! Brands is the largest quick-service restaurant chain, operating 34,000 restaurants worldwide under five brand names: Kentucky Fried Chicken, Taco Bell, Pizza Hut, Long John Silvers and A&W.

Stephen speaks regularly at local and national association conferences, public seminars and company conventions around the world on topics such as organizational change, process improvement and solving complex business problems. His unique and engaging presentation style has evolved from his many experiences participating in stage and video production and presenting to diverse audiences across many cultures in Europe, Australia, Asia, and the Middle East. He is also an inventor. Drawing on his facilitation experience, he has developed a new presentation methodology that has led to the invention of new software and hardware which allows one person to easily run a multimedia presentation, thereby increasing interest, retention and recall of the information presented. Stephen appears in the 2000 edition of *Who's Who International* and is a member of the American Society for Training and Development (ASTD), the National Speakers Association (NSA), and the Asian Regional Training and Development Organization (ARTDO). Stephen, welcome to *Conversations on Success*.

Stephen Krempl (Krempl)
Thank you very much.

Wright
Stephen, how do you define success?

Krempl
That's the most interesting question you could ever ask anybody. I guess it means many things to many people. But I generally categorize success two ways: professional and personal. Under professional success would be things like education, career, and business relationships. On the personal side are things like health and fitness, personal investments, family, relationships (which could include friends), spiritual pursuits, hobbies, etc. The true measure of success, I believe, is being able to balance the two. Now that may sound a little esoteric to some, but how many times have you known people who worked themselves into the ground, excluding what I would call personal success, and felt a little empty at the end of it all?

Wright
So do you think a person can achieve success personally and yet not professionally or vice versa? Or do you believe that what happens in one area affects the other?

Krempl
The answer to me is pretty obvious – having one without the other is like having the right hand without the left hand. No one can say they've had a bad day at work and then say it doesn't affect them

when they go home, or conversely, say that something bad happened at home but that it doesn't carry over to the office. I know some people who can compartmentalize the two and shut out one from the other, but to do that for a long period of time is pretty hard to do...in fact, it's almost impossible. I actually talked about this in one of my books, *Leadership ER*. The book is about a middle manager in an organization who experiences a health crisis and how that situation is a metaphor for a crisis he's experiencing at work. The main character, Mike, is having problems in his department and he's having problems personally, from a health standpoint, and both are affecting each other.

Wright

What would you say is the greatest obstacle to success?

Krempl

The greatest obstacle to success? I would say the biggest obstacle is probably being in denial about your problems, both personally and professionally. And that is a silent killer – for both situations. If you don't acknowledge the problem, then you can't diagnose it and try to solve it. When people are in denial, it often turns into a major crisis. I like to say, "Don't wait for a major crisis to discover what is truly important."

Wright

So what happens when we're in denial personally?

Krempl

You come up with all these great questions. What happens when we're in denial personally? Well, let me give you an example. I remember a time a couple of years ago when I was busy traveling internationally, and I just had projects up to my eyeballs. You know how that goes. And because of those professional distractions, I wasn't paying attention to the signals my body was giving me that something was quite wrong. I said, "Nah, it's a small thing. It'll be okay." Twelve months later, I'm on the operating table having a 2½-inch growth removed that was, thank goodness, not malignant. But it sure scared the heck out of me. So don't get so busy that you don't pay attention to yourself and the signs that are usually there.

Wright

What happens when we're in denial professionally?

Krempl

There are a couple of different things. First, you may have unrealistic expectations about your own capabilities within the organization. You may think you're the best and that everybody should be responding to you in a particular way, and if there's a problem, it must be someone else's fault. Or maybe you expect things with the team you manage to go perfectly, and you may not want to deal head-on with the interpersonal or structural issues within your team that will almost always come back to haunt you. Or it could be as simple as not paying attention—not paying attention to details, not giving enough attention to the competition, or if you go a little higher up, not paying attention to changes in the industry. People can be in denial about a lot of different things. Sometimes, to please others, we try to meet the target no matter what. So we paint the picture rosier than it is, and we don't tell the real story. Or we burn the candle on both ends as opposed to working effectively. So there's really a whole range of different things that could go on.

Wright

What can leaders do to overcome these challenges?

Krempl

There are several different things leaders can do. First, they should look for opportunities to prevent problems before they happen, as opposed to waiting for problems to occur and then trying to be the hero and solve them. Many leaders do this because it's more "heroic" that way. But if you can put your energies into proactively addressing issues as opposed to solving them later when they've become full-blown problems, that would be a lot better. There are many simple questions leaders can ask that will help them proactively address potential problems. For example: 1) "What problems or potential problems could I be in denial about?" 2) "What are the symptoms or early warning signs of an impending crisis in my department, team or organization?" 3) "What tools or tests can I use to diagnose the problem?" 4) "Whom can I seek expert advice and help from?" 5) "What strategy can I develop to address the problem (either proactively or reactively)?"

Once leaders answer these questions, they just need to take action. Taking action is probably the easiest thing to talk about, but the hardest thing to do. The really interesting thing is that you can use these same questions on the personal side (for example, change the business words to "health"), and it actually has the same impact. For example, "What are the symptoms or early warning signs of an impending crisis in my health?" You know, many people don't even recognize the symptoms they're suffering from.

Wright

What warning signs should one be looking for?

Krempl

On the personal side or business side? Well, let's try at the office. There are lots of different warning signs, if you're looking for them. For instance, you walk around and talk to people, and they say they don't know what the main priority of the organization or department is. That's a big warning sign right there. Something is not being communicated. Or maybe they know what the priorities are, but even worse, they don't care. Another clue could be hearing people speculate about what was discussed at a high-level meeting about an important issue because no one took the time to debrief them. Another warning sign is when your people are saying things like, "I told management, but they're not really open to feedback" or "I told them our process is broken and about these problems that need to be fixed, but nobody seems to want to do anything about it." When people start saying things like that, then that could be dangerous. If employees think no one is going to fix the problem, they loose trust in the organization and won't bring up future problems and issues. Those are some warning signs that leaders should be looking for.

Wright

So how can leaders diagnose their problems?

Krempl

Diagnosis is probably the least difficult thing to do because there are so many tools out there. There are 360-degree instruments where you get feedback from your boss, your peers, and your subordinates. You've got communication surveys, culture surveys, business metrics, balance scorecards, quality metrics, cycle-time measures, customer feedback forms, etc. The issues are, first, are you using any tools to predict and diagnose problems? And second, are you incorporating them into your daily workflow so that the information is used and acted upon? The key question for many people is how do we do that exact same thing – get reliable information – on the personal side of our lives? It's funny, I ask people, "You go to the office, you use all these great tools...do you use any of that in your personal life?" The answer I get is, "Well, that's different." No, it's not different. We can, and should, use tools to measure and diagnose things in our personal lives. We can keep watch of our weight, get annual or biannual physicals, and keep track of our results each time we're on the exercise machine. You've got your financial data – bank, brokerage and insurance statements, bills, all your financial numbers. Do you have short- and long-term plans for your finances? And if you're not inclined to do it yourself or you don't have the time, just like in your organization, you go to an outside consultant to get help – in this case, a financial planner. The same things we should do in our organizations are actually the same things we should do in our personal lives, but many people don't necessarily see the link.

Wright

What are some of the key elements that should be included in a prescriptive strategy for addressing problems?

Krempl

I think the key elements are pretty self-evident. One is just listening. There are a couple of key questions I learned from one of my leaders. Just go around and ask your team these questions, especially when you take over a new role or a new job: 1) "What's working that we should keep doing?" 2) "What's not working that we should get rid of?" 3) "What one thing should I be focusing on that will make the biggest impact?"

Then just listen. Then do your analysis and say, "Okay, I've listened to you, and here is what where're going to do...." Take action and then make sure you follow up – that's vital. If you do this, I think a couple of things happen. One is, you increase your credibility because you asked people for input before you took action. That builds trust in you as a leader, which in turn cycles back to your credibility, and it does a spiral up. If you don't listen to your people, then it's a quick spiral down.

Wright

You do a great deal of work internationally. How do people in other countries and cultures define success, and what challenges do they face in achieving success?

Krempl

The definition of success is very common, especially if we're talking about the financial definition of success. If you go to Asia, they always talk about "The Six C's" – that is, Career, Car, Cash, Card (which is credit card), Condo and Club. So if you achieve five or six C's, then you're a successful guy. But then, in many cultures, success often means family. Whether you go to Latin cultures or Asian cultures, relationships and family (even the extended family) are a big thing. If the family doesn't stick together, the matriarch or patriarch sees it as personally being very unsuccessful. It's harder nowadays as the new generation comes up, but it's still a very big thing. Even in business, relationships are key. The tendency in many Latin, Asian and European cultures is to focus on establishing a friendship before talking about business. People want to get to know you, the person, first before they do business with you. So if they don't like you, they may not want to do business with you, even if you have the superior product, a better process, or the best quality. Many times you end up with a situation where business associates are actually best friends. This is an interesting observation: In America, we tend to be transactional first and then think about relationships. This doesn't mean we don't have good friends who do business with us, but we tend to start transactional first. We usually start with, "Here's my product. I have a great product, and I have a great process, and I'm going to deliver the best customer service." It's not, "Let's get to know each other first before I introduce my product."

Wright

Some would call that "relationship selling" wouldn't they?

Krempl

Yes, you can call it "relationship selling," and many organizations teach that method of selling. My observation is that in many other cultures, it is "the" way you are expected to do business and it doesn't necessarily have to be taught.

Wright

Is that the way it's done in the Asian cultures?

Krempl

Yes, a lot in Asia, and even in the Latin countries it's the same. I remember one time sitting in Indonesia on a sales call. I was going in with a big potential contract to be won. I went in on a Tuesday, and I swear I wasn't doing anything. I was just sitting around the office, talking about everything under the sun – you know, politics to the economy. The next day I was in their office attending a meeting. Again, there was nothing mentioned about our products. The big deal was where we were going to eat lunch and dinner. Right at the end of the trip, on Friday, about half an hour before I'm leaving for the airport – this is four days now, right – the general manager turns and says, "You know that contract you sent us? It's okay." Now, if I had brought that contract up on Tuesday, I guarantee you I would have been on a plane on Wednesday out of their country.

Wright

As you travel around the world, do you think the American people are trying to make inroads into other cultures – personal inroads? The reason I ask the question, I read an article the other night about a family whose child was born without the ability to speak. The child could communicate very well through sign language and other methods, but the family never learned sign language, which was astonishing to me. The first thing I would want to be able to do is communicate with my child. I have a friend who's from Vietnam; her family is quite old, and they speak in Vietnamese, but only when they're together. Everything else is in English. They have that much respect for our culture. When Americans go to other countries, do they at least try to learn the language and communicate with the people?

Krempl

I would say that it's a mixed bag. I've seen expatriates who go and immerse themselves in the culture, and I've seen others who just want to remain in the "American club," be around more Americans, and stay in their comfort zones. But those who are willing to say, "Look, I'm going to a foreign country (or I'm living in this place), if I open myself up just a little bit and learn what the locals do, I may come out of the experience a lot richer." I'm not saying one is wrong or right, but it seems to me it would be a waste to go somewhere and not experience what that place is and what it has to offer. Through my experience with many multinational companies, I've seen them both – you will get those who want to learn the country, people and culture, and others who will just treat it as a three-year assignment.

Wright

What would your advice be to leaders?

Krempl

Leaders are astute people – otherwise they wouldn't be where they are. The smartest and the best leaders are the ones who: first, realize they will never be able to predict a crisis; and second, are farsighted enough to prepare so that one doesn't happen. As we all know, no one can predict or know what is coming around the corner, personally or professionally. But if we keep our ears to the ground and actively look for and pay attention to the signals that preclude most impending disasters, then we may have a chance to prevent a crisis from happening...or at least minimize its impact. But if you wait for it to happen, it'll happen right in front of you and slam straight into your face. I think that if you know what to look out for, you watch the indicators, you keep ahead of the curve – then you might be a little better prepared than those who think they've got everything figured out.

Wright

Well, Stephen, I really appreciate you spending this much time with me and answering all these questions I've thrown at you. I've learned a lot here today. It's obvious that you've got a lot to share, and I really appreciate the time you've taken with us today.

Krempl

Thank you. I've enjoyed it as well.

Wright

Today we've been talking to Stephen Krempl. He is an international speaker, trainer, and human resource development veteran. He is also an author, he speaks regularly, and he is an inventor. And as we have found out today, he knows a lot about being a leader and how to be successful both in our professional and personal lives. Thank you so much, Stephen, for being with us today on *Conversations on Success*.

About The Author

Stephen Krempl is an international speaker, trainer and a Human Resource Development veteran working for Fortune 500 companies such as YUM Brands Inc, PepsiCo and Motorola, and as a consultant in the largest training and educational institute in Asia. He is based in the USA and speaks regularly at conventions, public seminars and company conventions around the world on topics like organizational change and process improvement to solve business problems. His assignments have provided him the opportunity to work with and train leaders in 25 countries.

Stephen has co-authored three books: *Training Across Multiple Locations*, (2001, Barrett-Koehler Publishers, Inc.), *Business ER* (2003, Xulon Press), *Leadership ER* (CornerStone Leadership Institute).

Stephen appears in the 2000 Edition of *Who's Who International* and is also a member of the American Society for Training and Development (ASTD), the National Speakers Association (NSA) and the Asian Regional Training and Development Organizations (ARTDO).

Stephen Krempl

Phone: 502.419.3484

Email: skrempl@bellsouth.net

Chapter Five

ED KUGLER

THE INTERVIEW

David E. Wright (Wright)

Today we are talking with Ed Kugler. Ed is a successful Fortune 50 executive and former Marine sniper who's never stopped learning from his life experiences. He climbed the corporate ladder after two years in the Viet Nam War and without a college degree he rose to be world wide vice president for Compaq Computer. He is the author of *Dead Center, A Marine Sniper's Two Year Odyssey in the Viet Nam War,* as well as three other books with three more on the way, including his first novel which is a romance set in the sixties between a Marine and a protester. Ed is President and OEO, which means the Only Executive Officer, so named by his wife of thirty-six years, of his own company. He is a popular speaker focused on helping people and organizations make real change that matters. Ed, welcome to *Conversations on Success*!

Ed Kugler (Kugler)

I'm glad to be here with you today.

Wright

You have a most unique background. Could you tell us a little bit about it?

Kugler

I sure can. I have been blessed, I guess you'd say with a lot of unique experiences. It all started when I joined the Marine Corps at 17 years old two weeks out of high school. I saw my first combat a few months out of boot camp in Santo Domingo where I was wounded for the first time. I then volunteered to go to Viet Nam where I volunteered to be a Marine sniper. I ended up serving two consecutive years as a sniper. I was there from March '66 to March '68. My last duty station in the Marines was conducting military funerals. When I got out I worked as a mechanic, drove truck, dispatched, opened a couple of small businesses, eventually became General Manager of a trucking company all before going corporate I guess. I left trucking to join Frito Lay where I was promoted five times in my first six years and I stayed with them for thirteen years. I then transferred to Pepsi Cola for three more and left them for Compaq Computer. I was lucky, I think, with these three; it's kind of the triple-crown of glamour companies. Without a college degree it was hard, but well worth it. So it's been a very unique experience, a wild ride at times but I never quit learning, and still read a book every week to keep me moving forward.

Wright

That doesn't fit very well with the guys in these corporations that advertise college degree necessary.

Kugler

No, it doesn't and it's not something I recommend these days. I once figured it out as best I could. It probably took me 10 years longer to get to the VP level than if I had a degree, but what I discovered was most people tend to get their degree and then quit learning. I learned in Vietnam to never quit learning and to out work people.

Wright

Right.

Kugler

Many people get their degree and that's it, they've arrived. That's almost the standard today. So I had to find a different way to get to where I wanted to be.

Wright

How has your background influenced the success you've experienced?

Kugler

Well, in the early days the influence was a little bit negative, probably. But once I got through that period, which was probably four or five years after Vietnam, it's impacted me very positively. In Viet Nam one of the things you learned quickly, was well, I guess the first was to survive, and second, to be responsible for you and your fellow team members. Somewhere near the end of those four or five years I realized, with the help of my wife, that I would have to use my past to build a better tomorrow. For me, the things I had been through were valuable only if I applied them to making tomorrow better than today. And I've found that's unique for a Viet Nam Vet, or at least that's what we usually hear anyway. Another thing from the Marines and Vietnam was discipline. The ability to survive and the ability to do whatever needs to be done. I realized about five years after coming home that some of the things we had to do and did very well, some incredible things, were very, very unique. If I could do that, I could do anything. I decided I would use what I had been through to draw upon to make me better today. So that's probably how it has spring boarded me to where I am today.

Wright

Were you able to apply the things you learned right away or did you have problems along the way?

Kugler

I had problems. I struggled a lot in those first two or three years. One of the big problems is the same thing I see with our kids in Iraq today. I struggled when I came home with perspective, with what to do after I had done my thing in Vietnam. I can best explain by sharing what I saw last year when the Marines were involved in the initial assault on Baghdad. I saw an interview done by Rick Leventhal on *Fox,* I think, with some Marines one night. It was following some tank battle they were reporting on. And he was interviewing these kids from a Marine outfit that called themselves the Saints and the Sinners. They were a Reserve outfit from both Salt Lake City and Las Vegas. So he is talking with this young kid who was telling him about knocking out the Iraqi tanks one after another in this battle he had just finished. He was the driver of this very sophisticated tank, I'm sure. And then Leventhal says to him, "Well, what did you do before the war?" And the kid says "Oh, I worked at Wal-Mart." And therein lays the problem. You are young, with tremendous responsibility and independence and a serious adrenaline high and what do you do when you come home? Work at Wal-Mart? I don't think so. I was a sniper team leader at 19 years old. I'm a Sergeant, with a four-man team doing all kinds of things for our Colonel. We went out for him and lived in one valley for six months. We grew our hair long, beards, and got pretty funky. I was authorized to call air strikes and artillery, it was wild. What do you do after that when you come home? Looking back with the benefit of years of hindsight and a little maturity I see the problem as power. The power we had, for lack of a better term, was intoxicating. So when we come back to the world, as we called it and as these kids will probably call it, the big adjustment was coming down to earth after all the power, responsibility and adrenaline. You wake up one morning and have none at all. So I drank a lot. I need to clarify that I had a drinking problem before I went...l mean I don't blame it on Viet Nam. I started drinking when I was 14.

Wright

Goodness!

Kugler

Yes, it was goodness! That was back before it was fashionable like it is today. I was drinking pretty well when I went in the Marine Corps, and I was drinking a lot more when I came home. And I've had a lot of time to look back at that and it really had nothing to do with Viet Nam other than trying to recreate that experience by tripping out about it. I think it was the adrenaline thing. I had a serious drinking problem until I was 29. I was an alcoholic. I finally overcame it and quit that year. So it did have an impact on my return to the world. It took me about five years and a really great wife to get me through that and a few other things.

Wright

You have a unique philosophy you call "nomore BS." Where did that come from and what can you tell us about it?

Kugler

Well, it actually originated in Viet Nam and then solidified and crystallized throughout my corporate life. It's a byproduct of bureaucracies. In Viet Nam we had one distinct experience I retell in my book, *Dead Center*. The quick story is that regular Marines carried M-14 rifles. Mr. McNamara, our illustrious former Secretary of Defense under President Johnson, not one of my favorite people, was trying to support the troops I guess. History shows he was big on public relations and he was pushing to bring out new gear to support the growing number of troops over there. So they introduced the new whiz bang M-16, which today has become, I think they call it the M-40 or something, but at the time it was rolled out in Viet Nam, it was untested and pushed out very early, before it was ready for prime time. This is written about and documented in history today.

I was attached as a sniper to a couple of companies of Marines going on a night operation. We got ambushed somewhere around midnight. It was in a low lying sand dune area, an area known as the "Street Without Joy," written about by Bernard Fall, who spent years there with the French. We fought all night, got overrun and it was a pretty ugly deal. The sad thing was that just prior to leaving on this operation, they handed out the M-16's and took the Marines M-14's. The Marine Corp didn't want the M-16 but it was forced down their throats. They took these Marines who normally carry M-14's and twice a year had to test out doing what they called field stripping. That means taking them apart blindfolded and putting them back together in 60 seconds.

The reason for that was so if your gun jammed in the night in a battle, you were so familiar with it you could fix it night or day. What they did was literally hours, and I mean four or five hours, before this operation, they took these Marines and they took their M-14's, gave them new M-16's, gave them two hours training and about an hour practice and sent them out to the bush and said go and do good. So we're overrun in an ambush, fight all night and finally last until morning. When the sun came up the next morning there was something like 35 dead Marines I had to help put in body bags and over half of these guys had their M-16's apart in their hands. The rifle had malfunctioned and they were trying to fix it.

Wright

Oh, My!

Kugler

The rifles had jammed. That experience changed something inside of me. It burned really deep just how bad the outcome can be from bureaucracies and from leadership so removed they don't know what's going on. It made me stand and fight against this mentality of just rolling stuff out, excuse me, but half assing everything. It has never left me and I see it getting worse and worse today. As I climbed the corporate ladder and got nearer to the top I saw the same thing, it didn't kill people outright it just killed careers and cost investors a fortune. It's very disappointing and quite frankly the reason I left Compaq and went on my own. The BS that goes on at the VP level was very disillusioning. It was all about taking care of yourself, your peers and your superiors, rarely about the business and never about people below you. I only lasted three years—three very difficult years—because I don't keep my mouth shut and that doesn't work at that level.

Wright

Right.

Kugler

Nearly every problem in business is a leadership problem. It's usually gets blamed on leadership at lower levels, as in the case of Lieutenant Calley in Vietnam and most recently the prison scandal in Iraq. It makes for very difficult times and it is more common than you might think. I am sure you see it in your business. The most common example of this today that nearly everyone experiences is they roll out a new computer system that comes too early and crashes everything. I have seen that countless times in small and especially large companies. People like to forecast heroism and that doesn't work. It takes weeks and months to fix. I'm consulting with a company now for that very reason. They rolled out a new computer system last August ...they're a retail company and did it just prior to their busy season in August when all the shipments start to flow into their stores, the CEO made the decision even though it was untested and you can imagine the results. He just took the word of the head of IT and his Chief Operating Officer and didn't listen to any of the "lesser" souls telling him to not do it. They rolled it out and brought the company to its knees. And it has just cost millions and millions of dollars and more time than the test would have taken to recover. It is the same problem I saw in Vietnam and it is BS. So that is where my philosophy of nomoreBS came from.

Wright

How has this nomoreBS philosophy played out in your life and what can it do for others?

Kugler

Well, I'll tell you. It has played out well. We need a nomoreBS philosophy in this country now more than ever. It's not easy. It's difficult, but what I can say is that in a personal or an organizational way, the "no more BS" philosophy says that I can't move forward unless I admit first where I am. I can't change anything I don't acknowledge. I have to decide up front what problem I am trying to solve. I spent years drinking and having a very patient wife who put up with that and everything else that came with it. But it wasn't until she put her foot down and let me know it was my drinking or her that I could change. Always remember people and organizations change for one of two reasons ... inspiration or desperation. I changed out of desperation.

Wright

Right.

Kugler

The whole "nomoreBS" philosophy, the way it plays out, is simply if you're going to change, you first have to look in the mirror and honestly admit where you are. You have to acknowledge it the way alcoholics do. They've got to look in there and say, "I am a drunk." And it's just as true for companies as it is for individuals. People and organizations that want to change do so from inspiration. Many, like me or Enron, change out of desperation. Probably the biggest challenge I have in my consulting is that senior leaders just love my "nomoreBS" philosophy until it gets pointed at them in headquarters. I had an experience with one company where the CEO said, "I have this operation out there in XYZ city and you need to come and fix it. I need some of that nomoreBS stuff." So I signed on and started fixing it, and as I did I found out that 50% of the problems were coming from corporate headquarters functions. I had major fights with the

CEO because he wanted me to confine my work to this location in XYZ. He, like many people, had a hard time looking in the mirror. When you can't look in the mirror you can't change. It's that simple. So the first step is really to come to grips with where you are and have the personal integrity to be honest with yourself. I couldn't overcome my drinking until my wife said a few years into our marriage "It's drinking or me. Choose." Once I did that it enabled me to begin to change. I haven't had a drink since I was 29 and it was a difficult transition at times, but...I would be somewhere so different than I am today without that change. So the first step in "nomoreBS" simply means that regardless of what you are trying to change, be open and honest, whether you're a company or a person, and look in the mirror and say "Here's where I am." That's the only way to begin the journey.

Wright

What is the success system that evolved from your journey and that you use and teach others today?

Kugler

It's really pretty simple. It has eight steps. I'm working to refine it down as I believe simplicity is the key to change. It is easy to understand and difficult to do. So to begin with the first step is as I said before—stop the BS. That means you look in the mirror and you go, "Here's the problem." If it's you, then say so. To stop drinking you say, "I'm a drunk..." To lose weight you say (and mean it), "I'm fat and it's killing me." To reduce your inventory you say, "Our buyers are out of control and not accountable." Then you go out and put a plan in place to do something about it. Only then are you empowered to really change anything. Step Two is that you have to make a decision that you really want this change. By that I mean you have to be able to do it and you have to commit to do it.

I'll give you an example. I coached a former sniper of mine who was raised in the Hell's Angels. By that I mean his mom and dad were active members his whole life. He joined the Marines and came to Viet Nam and became a sniper. He was a good one. He wanted to fight a war. He stayed 18 months with us and was wounded. He came home and rode with the Hell's Angels for 15, maybe 20 years afterward. This past February the Marine Corps had their first ever sniper reunion in Las Vegas and we came together for the first time since Nam, 30 some years ago. It was a great time and he and I were talking and it was impressive. He isn't an educated guy formally but he sure has wisdom to spare. He shared with me that he is on his fourth wife, but has been married to her for fifteen plus years. When he met her he knew he had to change. So he pulled away from the Hell's Angels, no easy task as he explained it. He told me he moved from Seattle to Texas, where he now lives. He has a horse ranch where they raise expensive horses to sell. I was intrigued so I took him aside and I said, "You know, how did you do that?" And one of the things—and this is my second principle on deciding to do it—he said, "Ed, I realized that I had to get a new group of friends." He said, "I knew if I was ever going to break away from this and put it behind me when I met my wife, I knew I had to really change. He said, "My wife was into horses. So I made a conscious decision to build a new life and just be with her and with her horses." He explained that it wasn't easy. He said, "It was hard after all those years. I was raised as a kid in the Hell's Angels. I used to run drugs for them. I used to do all kinds of bad stuff. The reason I'm in Texas is that I realized that just getting away from them wasn't enough. I needed to get a bunch of new friends and in Seattle that wouldn't be enough." So now he lives way out in the sticks on a horse ranch and he's doing great.

He validated my second principle and that is to decide to make a clean break with the past. A lot of people talk about change. I heard a great quote and use it often. *What we do everyday is what we believe ... all the rest is just talk.* That applies to everything we do. If you're going to change, you've got to change. That means that we're going to make a complete break with our past. So that's my second principle. My third principle is that the only way out is through. Period! That means that you have to think through what you want to do, what you want to change, and weigh the cost and decide if it's worth it to you. In the case of business change, you ask yourself if the cost, personal pain and aggravation of doing the change is something you are willing to do. Only then, once you've thought through the end to end pain of the change—like how much this is going to cost emotionally and/or financially, how people will react and how long it will go on, then and only then can you make a decision that you're going to do it. I tell CEO's that when you're thinking about a change, you have to think all the way through it every step of the way. After all the consideration you should only go ahead if you are willing to shoot your best person, if after all due diligence they stand in the way. Otherwise, you're just kidding yourself and wasting a great deal of money and time and focus in your business. From a personal point of view, that is the decision I had to make to successfully quit drinking. I had to break with the past, think through the pain and commit.

Wright

You also say you focus people on deciding what problem they're trying to solve. What do you mean by that?

Kugler

Well, you have to know what the problem is, admit it, and decide up front what the problem you're trying to solve is or you can't solve it. A personal example, again, is my drinking. If my wife focused not on my drinking but on the symptoms we wouldn't be where we are today. If she were trying to get me to quit going in a funk or quit driving erratically it wouldn't have worked. The drinking was the problem not my actions. From an organizational perspective I'll share this example. I was down in Mexico with a client where I spent three days, three frustrating days for both of us, because the client started out by saying to me, "I want you to help me fundamentally change the way I do logistics." He was the VP of one of the worlds largest cement company's. They're delivering cement and delivering it well by the way. I kept saying to him, "What does it mean to you to fundamentally change the way you do logistics?" Well, a day and a half later we're still having this conversation. He's having guys present all of this stuff, it was a full blown dog and pony show. When they were done I said, "I still don't get it. If I came up with a way to deliver cement with helicopters it would fundamentally change the way you do business, but I don't know that it would mean anything to your organization. So the bottom line, Mr. Client, what problem are you really trying to solve?" I had finally angered him enough and he slammed his fist down on the table of the conference room and he said, "If I don't take two dollars a ton out of our cost, I won't have a job." I said, "Well, that's the problem you're trying to solve. It's not about fundamentally changing the way you do logistics. It's about cost."

It's very important to focus on the root cause of what you say you are changing. It's kind of peeling back the onion and saying several times, "What problem are you really trying to solve?" That is my fourth principle. Deciding what problem you are trying to solve with this change.

My Fifth Principle is to define up front what success will look like when you're done. The two questions I always ask when consulting is first ,"*What problem are we trying to solve*" and second, "*What will success look like when we do?*" Say you come to me and are looking for a new job. We would first have to define what problem you're trying to solve. Is it working conditions, respect, money, what is it? If you just get a new job without knowing what the problem with this one is you haven't solved anything. We all know people everywhere who are unhappy about everything you know.

The Fifth Principle of defining what the success will look like is a key. It's defining your future clearly. It gives you the end zone so you know what you have to do and are happy when you get there.

The Sixth Principle is to answer *what will it take to make this happen?* It's about commitment. The operative question here is, "What will I do differently now that I want this change?" Whether you're trying to quit drinking or install a new computer system, it requires you to understand what it is going to take and make a commitment. It's about creativity. How might we make this happen? When I go into a business and they are under cost pressure it is easy to predict what they will do. They will cut people first. They don't think through what it really takes to reduce costs; they just take the easy way out. You can't drive change the easy way because there is no easy way. This principle is about leadership and leadership is in short supply these days.

Wright

That's for sure.

Kugler

The Seventh Principle is the power of relationships. In my personal journey I had the support of my wife. As the years went by, my children and then so many others were there for help, support and sometimes a good kick in the butt. Relationships are the glue that holds us all together and also the grease that makes things run smoothly. When people want to change and lose weight, if the family doesn't cooperate and support them by taking those tempting foods out of the house, they can't succeed. I couldn't have succeeded in Nam without all the great people around me and neither can you. Whatever we do in life we are going to need support. That's relationships and that's my Seventh Principle.

The Eighth and last Principle and key ingredient is *Action*. You have to do something. We can talk about it forever but until we take action and do something we can't change. You have to do something fundamentally different than what you have been doing. I have always been a *Mad Magazine* fan, and I now only pick it up about every couple of months just so I don't get in a rut. But Alfred E. Newman once said, "Just because everything is different doesn't mean anything changed." Or it's as people often say, the definition of insanity is doing the same thing over and over and expecting a different result. Either fits but remember ... to change you gotta change.

Wright

That's a good one.

Kugler

Well, how many times have we seen and heard organizations talk about how much they've changed and when you look at them they are the same? We live in a politically correct world and it is unfortunately full of BS. So those are my eight principles.

Wright

Before we go any further, let me clear up something for our readers. When you say you were a sniper, my mental image of that is a guy sitting up in the top of a tree taking single shots at the enemy. Is that what you're talking about?

Kugler

Well, yeah, but we didn't sit in trees, although it was single shot. We used Winchester Model 70 - 30-06, 5 shot, bolt action rifles. It was a match rifle specifically set up for Marine snipers. It was a very expensive rifle. We went out in teams of two to five Marines, for any where from a day to, like I said, in our case, I had a team that stayed out in the Co Bi Than Tan Valley for just one week shy of six months. They would bring us supplies, give us assignments and we'd go and do our thing. It was a very lonely occupation. I was in California at a business meeting this week, and it was so boring that I was thinking back when was the last time I was this bored? It was a time in Viet Nam waiting on a target. The longest I sat for one target was three days in a ten foot bush with one other sniper. I was in that business meeting down there this week thinking I would rather be sitting in the bush for three days than sitting in this place! So, that is what snipers did.

Wright

You say that people are at the center of all success. What do you mean by that?

Kugler

I mean that nothing gets done without people. Over in the war in Iraq and Afghanistan is a prime example. We've got all the whiz-bang technology, laser bombs and you name it. What I get a kick out of is how everybody talks about this fantastic technology, and it is good I am sure, but what they forget is that nothing happens without people in the end. In Afghanistan, everybody was amazed by pin point laser bombs like the ones that use binoculars for aiming at the target. Well the flyboys are fabulous and saved our butt many times, but those great new binoc's don't work without someone on the ground looking through them at the target.

Wright

Right.

Kugler

When you read what took place behind the scenes, the only reason those bombs were so accurate and so on target and we took out the Taliban so fast was because we had six special forces teams that went in there within weeks after the September 11th. They made it happen. They're the ones that had to live out in the mountains and be on site and in place when the planes came over at ten thousand feet to drop their bombs. So they can talk all they want to about what happened when we "took" Iraq, you see what is happening now. It's about the people, and it's about changing their hearts and that is a tough order. Whether it is in war, business or family, it's about the people. And people have to support other people, and that's forgotten many, many times in today's world. We live in a "me" society and it is killing us. The people and relationships in the end are all that matters, it's all we can take with us.

Wright

When you said people need to help a while ago, I can remember a few years back when I quit smoking. I think it was about 27 years ago. All of my friends, I mean you would think they would applaud and say, "Boy, way to go, David!" But they're the ones, "Aw, let's light up. One won't hurt you." Isn't that strange? Did you ever have any of your drinking buddies say, "Ah, man, let's have a few drinks. It won't hurt you."

Kugler

Oh, yeah. They say, "The thing is just have one." And boy, it doesn't work as you know from smoking. It doesn't work this way. If I had one beer today I would be drinking until I fell over and that took awhile.

Wright

Oh, yeah. I tried one and then three years later quit again, you know. It's terrible.

Kugler

Oh, yeah I do know what you mean. Whenever I try to lose weight I have people that say, "You don't look bad, why worry about it?" I inevitably fall back to my old habits. That is why getting real with yourself, looking in that mirror and being honest is so critical. That's also why having a support structure and people to support you is also so critical.

Wright

Right.

Kugler

So I've lost and gained, but ultimately it's no excuse. Our problems are our problems to solve.

Wright

Oh, I hear that!

Kugler

I continue to fight the good fight and learn from it. I'm walking four or five miles a day and starting to feel better. In spite of your good friends telling you to "come on and get something to eat and enjoy life," you have to stay the course and solve the problem. As the old saying goes, *"If it is to be, it is up to me..."*

Wright

So, that's exactly what you went through?

Kugler

Yes it is.

Wright

If you wrapped your success system up with a key ingredient, what would that be?

Kugler

It's really the Eighth Principle, the point of Action. It's about doing something and continuing to do it even when you don't feel like it. I make book marks out of three by five cards and I have my mission on it and what I'm trying to do. And the flip side of has what I'm trying to become. Over the years, I've got it boiled down to where I can get it on about a paragraph on either side. I read that every time I open the book. I have another one by my bed. I read it when I get up in the morning and go to bed at night. I use it all for focus. I use it to simply remind me that I have to do something every day to move forward. I have to take action. You take action everyday and sometimes you screw up, we all do. When we do, you just get up tomorrow morning and start all over again. Instead of going, "Well, you know, I didn't do it today so I'll just quit." You don't beat yourself up. That makes taking action the key ingredient. Taking action every single day that moves you closer to solving the problem you identified. I remind you again of that special quote I used earlier. *What you do everyday is what you believe, all the rest is just talk.* You know, a lot of us go to church on Sunday and feel good about that, but are we doing something everyday that's consistent with what we believe at church? Are we really becoming Christians? Or are we just talking about it on Sunday? That's my key ingredient.

Wright

Let me ask you finally one last question. All of this that we've been talking about and especially the last thing you said, what has it meant to you in your life?

Kugler

It has meant a great deal and specifically two things. My wife and my past are the two major things in my life. It's those relationships that have focused me to be able to achieve whatever I have in my life. We met shortly after Viet Nam. We were married about nine months later. At that time, I had a goal when I came home from Viet Nam, a very naïve goal, to become a mercenary. I had been there so long and was pretty hopped up and thought I'd come home, get out of the Corp, party awhile and head to Africa. I had met some British Marines who gave me the names of bars in Brussels, Belgium, that you could make contact for mercenary work. I don't know that I would have ever done that, but that was what I thought I wanted to do. And for whatever reason fate brings people together. I met and started dating my wife and began to change. I think that things happen to us for a reason. Whether we pick up on them or not is our problem. But something just told me that if I was ever going to be somebody and make something of my life, I needed to marry her. She was actually spoken for in a serious relationship with a guy going to MIT. Here I was a whacked out Vietnam Vet wearing cammo's and jungle boots, about anything but what she was looking for. Somehow I convinced her marrying me would be a wild ride but worth it.

We ended up getting married and that made all the difference in the world because she stuck with me. And she kept saying, "You just have to use this past you and your ability to get things done to your advantage." That support and direction has made all the difference. It has enabled me to use my past to help myself and now others to make a difference in their lives. So for starters that has made all the difference. It's been the difference between success and failure. It helped me to have the confidence to overcome my lack of formal education and never give up. It was learning to have the integrity to be yourself.

One time I'm counseling my middle daughter about her grades, she was a junior in high school, who did quite well. Unbeknownst to me, my mom gave her one of my high school report cards and she took the A's and B's and all that and added them up like they do today – 4.0 you know 3.0 – and she came to me and showed me the report card. And I thought, "Well, I'm in trouble." And she goes, "Dad, you do realize you graduated with a 1.9." But that was okay. My wife and I have always tried to be honest in our relationships. At least now when I speak to high schools, I tell them that there's hope for you kids, students with a D average. But all of this understanding of what I had been through and learning how to use it and the relationships with others, it has really changed my life for the better.

Wright

You and I have had some similar experiences. I failed math miserably in the eighth grade, and I generally was an honor roll student through high school and everything, but the only report card I ever kept was the eighth grade report card simply to show myself what could happen if you don't apply yourself. My daughter found it when she was 13 years old. I thought, "Man alive! What am I going to do?"

Kugler

They will find it like mine did, "You carried a 1.9 average!" But that gives us all hope.

Wright

What a great conversation! I really enjoyed it. I appreciate you spending so much time with me here this afternoon talking about success and the thoughts that go with it. Thank you so much for doing that for us.

Kugler

I appreciate the opportunity. I have been very lucky and very blessed in my life with unique experiences and lots of people along the way to help me learn from them. I enjoy life now, I really do, I enjoy the opportunity to work with you and share my experiences and learning with other people. I like to share and tell people to take what works for you and leave what doesn't it. There is no silver bullet. The only right answer is the one that works for you.

Wright

That's certainly right. Today we've been talking with Ed Kugler who is a successful Fortune 50 executive and former Marine sniper, who by his own admission has made it because he keeps on learning. He's the author of *Dead Center - A Marine Sniper's Two Year Odyssey in the Viet Nam War*, and the author of a new novel *The Well House – A Story of War, Peace, Love and Forever*. He now helps people all over the nation to be better and to be more successful and helps organizations to make real change that matters. Ed, thank you very much for being with us today, on *Conversations On Success*.

Kugler

Okay, thank you. It's my pleasure.

About The Author

Ed Kugler is one of America's leading change agents. A former Marine Sniper with two-tours in the Vietnam War, he worked for Pepsi and Frito Lay, and climbed the corporate ladder to become VP - Worldwide Logistics for Compaq Computer.

He is the Author of four books. Today he runs his own company from his home in Big Arm, Montana. He is married (36 years and counting—to the same woman) and has three children and two grandchildren.

Ed Kugler

PO Box 190

Big Arm, MT 59910-0190

Phone: 866.725.5506

Fax: 866.422.2895

Email: edkugler@nomorebs.com

www.nomorebs.com

www.edkugler.com

Chapter Six

PAUL MESHANKO

THE INTERVIEW

David E. Wright (Wright)

Today we are speaking with Paul Meshanko. Paul is an accomplished author, speaker and leadership coach who knows how to help people thrive, not just survive, in a climate of constant change. He knows that it is not what people think that determines their success or failure in life, but how they think. After twelve years in sales and new product development for a Fortune 50 company, Paul opened the Ohio office of Edge Learning Institute, a world-renowned leadership and staff development services provider. Paul uses familiar situations, concrete research and a broad knowledge of many topics to deliver exciting presentations that not only educate but inspire and entertain. Paul, welcome to *Conversations on Success!*

Paul Meshanko (Meshanko)

Thank you David!

Wright

You have spoken to audiences all over North America on the topics related to organizational and individual success. Is there a business challenge that seems to be the most common with your audiences?

Meshanko

It is almost cliché, but the answer is probably the same as it was twenty years ago. It is managing change. In fact, there was a *Harvard Business Review* article titled *Cracking the Code of Change[1]* that explored this challenge. The authors came to the conclusion, after much research, that as high as seventy percent of all organizational change initiatives, such as down-sizing, restructuring, mergers and acquisitions, changing company culture, and integrating new technology fail to meet the business objectives that are originally defined. This is a stunning testimonial of just how difficult change can be.

Wright

Yet, companies try to change anyway.

Meshanko

The global marketplace waits for nobody, and not changing simply isn't an option for most organizations. Unfortunately, with only a thirty percent success rate, a lot of companies end up struggling to execute those critical changes necessary to remain competitive and profitable.

Wright

So why do companies seem to struggle so much with change?

Meshanko

The difficulty stems from a fundamental misperception about what it takes for businesses, and individuals, to prosper in today's world. Many people think of Charles Darwin when they talk about survival in the business world. The term *"survival of the fittest"* is known to almost everybody, whether they have read Darwin or not, and this is where the misperception starts. When asked to describe what is meant by *"the fittest,"* most people think of attributes such as strength, intelligence, agility and speed, but that's not what Charles Darwin said. If you go back to his original work, *The Origin of Species,* published in 1859, he wrote that his observation was that it was neither the strongest, the fastest, nor the smartest of the species that survived. Rather, it was those species that proved to be the most adaptable to change, that in the end not only survived, but thrived in

---

[1] *Cracking the Code of Change*, Michael Beer & Nitin Nohria, May 1, 2000, Harvard Business Review. Reference #R00301.

their environments. I don't know about you, but I'll take thriving over surviving any day! And that requires that we focus on adaptability.

There is another misperception and it has to do with where the change process itself actually takes place. Organizations don't change. It's the people inside of organizations who change or, as is more often the case, don't change. The uncomfortable truth of the matter is that most individuals have not developed the necessary skills and tool kits for successfully managing changes in either their professional or personal lives. More regrettably, the majority of business leaders fail to adequately train their managers and employees on the change process. It takes more than having them read a book about mice looking for their cheese, and the consequences are long histories of both individual and organizational mediocrity.

Wright

That's a fascinating observation, and it raises another question. Just what is your definition of success and how can you measure it?

Meshanko

Everybody has their own definition of success and, proven or not, their own recipe for achieving it. There are, however, a few ingredients that should to be included in everybody's recipe. First, we should always start with a clear understanding of what's truly important to us. This includes both an up-to-date assessment of our core personal values and recognition of others, such as family and friends, who also have a stake in what we do. This kind of insight or awareness typically comes from personal reflection or, for some people, meditation and prayer. It doesn't take long, but it does require taking ourselves off of the hamster wheel of life long enough to give it the attention it deserves.

The second ingredient of success is developing the discipline to spend our time and our efforts in a manner consistent with those people and things we think are important. There's an old saying that goes, *"If you don't know where you're going, any road will get you there."* Knowing what's really important to you and then consistently allocating your time accordingly is critical. It's a simple strategy on the surface, but it's far from easy. Given the distractions that most of us face each day, it's easy to drift away from doing the things that really create value for us.

There's a third ingredient that is often overlooked, but is just as important. That's developing healthy self-esteem. When we feel unconditional warm regard and acceptance for ourselves, we gain confidence to better deal with life's inevitable challenges. We also find it easier to give ourselves permission to compete, not with others, but with our own best self. It's amazing to me just how many people go through their entire lives feeling poorly about themselves because they never quite stack up to the artificial images they see on television. Whether it's material wealth, athletic ability, physical appearance or professional success, focusing on these superficial indicators typically robs us of true enjoyment and satisfaction as we go through life.

You asked about measuring success and that's easy! There's only one sure way to measure whether or not you're on the right road—your road—to success. Simply look at the goals you're working on. If you're moving in the right direction, the goals that you're making progress on day by day, week by week and month by month will be in close alignment with your aspirations and core values. If they're not, it's time to rethink what you're doing.

Wright

What, in your opinion, prevents most people from achieving success?

Meshanko

A lack of undistracted personal reflection is the single biggest culprit. We live in a culture that increasingly devalues time for contemplation. The busier we are, the better. It's almost as if we wear exhaustion and being perpetually busy as a badge of honor! Some of us even have our kids' schedules booked for three months in advance. When we don't take time to evaluate what's really important to us, we fill the void with what we see on TV, the cover of a magazine or with what some self-proclaimed "expert" espouses. That's where trouble begins. We end up giving permission to complete strangers—advertisers, television and movie producers, and even religious zealots—to tell us what we should aspire to and how we should live our lives.

If you listen to all the images that are blasted at us from the media, images about the cars we should drive, the kind of houses we should live in, the kind of clothes we should wear and what we should do for entertainment, it becomes increasingly difficult for most people to have a candid conversation with themselves about what really is important. And while it may be convenient to let the media (or anyone else) dictate our values and priorities to us, we do so at our own peril. Everybody has an agenda. My advice is to build in at least 30 minutes every week to have a "conversation on success" with yourself. These are the most important conversations you'll ever have.

Wright

Is there a certain way of thinking that successful people just seem to be born with?

Meshanko

In some cases, yes. More often though, I find that it's something they've learned very early on, either from their parents or other mentors and role models. Either way, I think that there are three patterns of thinking that I see successful people continuously demonstrate. The first is a high level of personal awareness—these are people who know what's important to them and what they're willing to give to get it. Second, these people have an uncanny ability to stay focused on what they want to achieve and how they're going to get it. Rather than dwelling on obstacles and problems, they focus on opportunities and solutions. Perennial low achievers will moan that they weren't born that way and they just can't think like that. Baloney! Even if you weren't born that way, you can teach yourself to think that way. It's not always easy, but it can be done.

The third pattern that I see in "naturally successful" people is arguably the most important. It's the ability to maintain a positive attitude—even when things don't go well. In fact there's been a significant amount of research on this topic by a fellow named Daniel Goleman, a Harvard Ph.D., outlined in his books on emotional intelligence[2]. Part of his definition of what emotional intelligence includes is what I already alluded to—the ability to manage our emotions and stay positive, even during times of diversity. Again, even if you weren't born this way, it's a skill set and behavior pattern that you can learn.

Wright

So you're saying that even if you don't think this way naturally, or if you used to, but lost it somewhere along the way, you can you learn or develop these ways of thinking?

---

[2] *Emotional Intelligence: Why it Matters More than IQ*, Daniel Goleman, 1995, Bantam Books.

Meshanko

Absolutely! One of my favorite quotes is from a fellow named Albert E.N. Grey. He said, "The only difference between successful people and unsuccessful people is that successful people have developed a habit of doing things that unsuccessful people don't like to do." One of those things that most people don't like to do is be critical with themselves. The first step in changing how you think is to be willing to acknowledge what attitudes and behaviors typically get in your way and then start to figure out which ones might be more appropriate to give you better results. You don't change the way you think by rationalizing away our bad behaviors and making excuses for yourself.

Once you've identified the new attitudes and habits you want to develop, then you have to change your self talk. That means changing the actual words you use with yourself as you go through the day. It's like designing an advertising campaign for yourself. Rather than beating yourself up when you fall short or make mistakes, you begin to say, "Next time I'll do better." Rather than saying, "I can't do that," you start saying, "I haven't learned how yet, but I bet I can." If you fail to challenge your negative dialogue with yourself, there's very little chance that you'll ever be able to change our attitudes and habits.

Wright

You sound like a coach I used to have. He always told me what you just quoted, "Successful people do those things that other people don't want to do."

Meshanko

It's pretty funny when you stop to think about it. Most people know what those "things" are most of the time. They just can't seem to get themselves to do them!

Wright

He called me up one day all excited. I said, "What's wrong? "He said," I've updated my quote." I said, "Which quote?" He said, "I've got an addition for you. Successful people do those things that other people don't want to do, but the successful people don't want to do them either...but they do them anyway."

Meshanko

It's like knowledge without action. You've heard the phrase "knowledge is power." But it's really not. There are many knowledgeable people in the world who have very little power because they don't apply what they know. Successful people usually aren't any smarter than anyone else. They're just more inclined to take action.

Wright

One of your keynote topics that you speak on is titled, *Getting More Out of Your Day and Your Life*. How important is time management in achieving success and happiness?

Meshanko

The term "time management" is kind of a misnomer because none of us can actually manage time. What we can manage is the activities we choose to engage in with our time. That said, disciplined activity management skills are pretty important. We're all given the exact same number of hours every day and every week. Therefore, a big factor in how successful and happy we end up being is how efficiently we spend the time that is allotted to us. The happiest and most successful people I know avoid distractions and only spend their time doing the kinds of activities and tasks that are most closely aligned to their values and goals.

That's not to suggest that we should keep ourselves as busy as we possibly can. In fact, it's quite the opposite. We live in a workaholic society. But, like every addiction, workaholism extracts a tremendous price. In some cases it's our sense of well being and in some cases it's our families. In extreme cases it can even be our physical health. My personal philosophy it that we should spend as much time as we possibly can doing the things that will make us happy and create value for those who are important to us. Meaningful work is important to everyone, but what's meaningful to me may not be meaningful to someone else.

There's one other aspect of time management that I think is important to mention—the importance of play. Sometimes working through life's obstacles on the way to success requires a bit of extra creativity and thinking outside the box. Where does this creativity come from? Its best source is from play! The unconstrained joy of play causes our minds to become supercharged. Not only does it free us up to discover what's really important, but it also helps us tap into to our creative subconscious to figure out how to achieve our goals faster. The rest is just execution. It's doing what we know we need to do.

Wright

When you look back through your life, who were some people that you've tried to use as your own role models?

Meshanko

There have been many. Most recently, it's children—my own in particular—that I rely upon the most. When I watch my kids play, I am absolutely fascinated by their boundless joy, their inquisitiveness, their persistence and their never-ending willingness to make learning mistakes! As we get older, it's easy to lose these qualities. Being able to retain the attitudes and ambitions of youth—and then temper them with the knowledge, skills and wisdom of adulthood—is a balancing act that not too many people are able to achieve. But it's a great goal to strive for.

There's also an adult friend of mine who I've used as a role model throughout much of my life. His name is Dale. He was my sophomore-year dorm director at Ohio State University. Dale cut me absolutely no slack whatsoever when I stepped out of bounds. While I often resented his strictness, this promoted accountability. He also taught me to never get too comfortable with my current level of awareness. Every time I thought that I had something figured out, he would, in a very polite but firm way, point to some obvious holes in my thinking. While it ticked me off at the time, this gradually helped me recognize that no matter how much I thought I knew about something, there was always room to get a little bit wiser on the topic.

Wright

Paul, reviewing your web site, I noticed that you've already started working on your second book, a book about diversity and respectful behaviors in the workplace. I think it's tentatively titled, *Respect: Coloring Outside of the Lines.* How did you get interested in the topic of diversity and respect?

Meshanko

The biggest factor is that I'm in a mixed religion marriage. I was raised Catholic and my wife is Jewish. While I'll be the first to admit that working through differences in belief and opinion can be challenging, I can also say that doing so has been the single, most meaningful source of growth and learning for me in recent years. Looking outside our marriage, I have also become much more acutely aware of the subtle ways that many people unintentionally discriminate against, and ultimately disrespect, those who are different from them.

Another driving factor is my children. I have a three year old son and a 18-month old daughter for whom, like most parents, I would do anything. I have a fervent desire for my kids to grow up in a world where tolerance and respect for differences are more prevalent than what we see today. We currently live in a world—and a country—where many of the things that make people unique from one another are sources of suspicion and conflict. That makes it very difficult for any culture to really take advantage of its rich and contrasting ingredients. Increasing diversity in America, whether we're talking about ethnicity, age, religion or lifestyles, is a fact of life. We can either resist it and struggle endlessly or embrace it and thrive.

Wright

Do you think that there's a tie-in between business success and the way leaders and employees treat each other?

Meshanko

There are both organizational and personal benefits to fostering respectful work cultures. Organizations are able to achieve higher levels of productivity from their employees, raise morale, and subsequently retain more of their best employees when they have behavioral norms—cultures—anchored in respect. When they're able to attract and retain their best employees, the long-term benefit is that they can become learning organizations. This, in turn, fosters adaptability and resilience. It's pretty hard to intelligently process and adapt to business environment changes when your best employees don't feel valued and are shopping their resumes.

Wright

How about at the personal level? Is there a connection between personal success and how we treat and are treated by others?

Meshanko

Absolutely. When we work in an environment where respectful behaviors are the norm, a couple things happen. First, it reduces the inherent stress that comes from working with people who have different backgrounds, lifestyles, beliefs and opinions. Reduced stress tends to increase individual productivity and, just as importantly, creativity. When we become more productive and more creative, we gradually increase our value to the organizations for which we work. Not only does this enhance job security, it also leads to a more enjoyable work experience overall. How much is that worth these days?

There's also the advantage of increased support from others. As we pursue success, whatever that happens to be for us, we'll never be able to leverage all the assistance that's available to us from other people if we don't leave a trail of respectful behavior behind us. Whether it's emotional assistance, intellectual assistance, or in some cases maybe even financial assistance, people tend to extend themselves to those who treat them with respect, dignity and appreciation. The reputation that we create for ourself by our behavior and treatment of others travels very far and is extraordinarily long-lasting.

Wright

If asked, I'm sure most people would say that they're more respectful than their behaviors would actually indicate. Are there any suggestions you have for treating others with respect?

Meshanko

There are a couple things. First, we have to work through a natural bias that almost all people have to be "right" about things. Most of us wake up every morning with a belief about the way the world is, the way other people are and about the way we are ourselves. The number-one thing we try to do all day long is protect and validate that belief. We read the newspaper, watch television and interact with others, but are always on the lookout for evidence that supports what we already believe to be true. That's where the problem lies. If we're always trying to protect and defend what we already believe, it makes it very difficult for us to take in new information and improve the quality of our decisions and actions. It also makes it nearly impossible for us to interact in a truly respectful manner with others who may happen to see the world differently than we do. Controlling the need to be right isn't easy, but it's essential for treating other people with respect.

So how do you do it? We start by forcing ourselves to delineate between those parts of our "truth and reality" that are based on knowledge and those parts that are based on beliefs. We must learn to treat the two areas differently! Most people go through the day with their knowledge and beliefs in one big bucket and act as though they were the same thing, but they're not. Knowledge is fact-based information that can be supported by hard evidence or proof. Beliefs, by their very definition, are different. As strongly as they tend to be held, they can neither be proven nor disproven. This means that my beliefs are no more valid for someone else than theirs are for me. If we treat people adversarially or with disdain simply because they don't share the same beliefs that we do, we're acting both disrespectfully and ignorantly.

Our behaviors towards others ought to communicate that we offer the same deference and respect for their beliefs as we do our own. You don't have to share someone else's beliefs to respect them. Here's a suggestion: Ask yourself before every interaction with somebody else, "Will my acting in accordance with my beliefs hinder the ability of someone else to do the same?" If the answer is yes, then you may want to consider a different course of action. Allowing others to think and live as they choose is not only a prerequisite of respect, it's a source of wisdom. By making room for other people's "truths" to co-exist with our own, we expand our own awareness. Over time, we're then able to make smarter decisions and interact with others more productively.

Wright

Paul, I have a final question for you. I don't typically like to mix politics when I talk about success, but something came to mind when you quoted Charles Darwin way back at the beginning of our conversation. You said that the key to surviving and thriving was adaptability, which I do believe. And then you said companies don't change, people do. I remember when I opened up my first company in 1969, I wrote as its only mission statement—and I've never changed a word of it—*As the people grow so grows the organization.* Agreeing with you up front on those two topics, I watched a lot of the 2004 presidential debates and paid close attention to what was said. The top two candidates, one more than the other, were always talking about the economy and that "rushing sound" you hear as jobs leave the United States. I just don't know if that was pandering to fears or what, but I think that's the way it is and that's the way it's going to be. I don't think American workers are ever going to get those jobs back. It's almost like the old computer argument that computers were going to eliminate a lot of jobs. Well we both know that technology has actually created many more jobs than it's eliminated. So in your opinion, do you think that the shift in jobs to other countries is going to change or do you think that is just the way it is and we're going to have to adapt to it?

Meshanko

Shifting labor markets is a complex issue and certainly not my area of expertise, but I can offer an observation or two. To go back to your initial observation about the candidates, you alluded to the pandering to fear about jobs and how that seemed to permeate both candidates' campaign rhetoric. Unfortunately, fear is a powerful motivator and people can be horribly manipulated when they're afraid. Whether it was the fear of the loss of jobs, terrorism, global warming or the perils of same-sex marriage, I think both candidates were guilty of using scare tactics.

Take the issue of jobs, for instance. There are some U.S. jobs that are going to permanently move to other countries. That's not good or bad. It's just part of the reality of living and working in a global economy. Today we have workers in China or India who are willing and able to do some of the same jobs that U.S. workers do for a fraction of typical U.S. wages. If our companies are going to compete successfully, some of those jobs should go to countries where they can be done more cost-effectively. As consumers, this seems to be a choice we have already made. We can't expect to buy deluxe toaster ovens for $29.99 at Wal-Mart and then cry "foul" when we shift some of the jobs building them overseas. Companies are in business, in part, to make money. That's the way the economy runs.

Even so, you cannot ignore the sense of loss felt when someone does lose a job. I'm reminded of a classic book I read many years ago by psychologist William Bridges. It's called *Changes: Making Sense of Life's Transitions*[3] and is still in print today. He points out that many people spend so long grieving their losses or trying to get back to the way things used to be, that they end up handicapping their ability to move forward. His suggestion, which I think is sound advice, is to acknowledge the new reality and give yourself permission to grieve your loss. But then, sooner rather than later, you've got to pick yourself up by the boot straps and demonstrate that unique quality that all humans have; to be able to change course and move forward in a new direction. We have an infinite capacity to move into new directions.

---

[3] *Transitions: Making Sense of Life's Changes*, William Bridges, 1980, Perseus Publishing, LLC.

We just need to give ourselves permission to let go of the past and that need to be "right."

Wright

As I told you before when this interview started, I always learn from everyone I talk to. And I have certainly learned from you today.

Meshanko

Thank you.

Wright

It's very, very interesting, especially the part about change, which is very difficult for all of us. I want to thank you for spending this much time with me today and talking about this important topic.

Meshanko

It's been my pleasure.

Wright

Today we have been talking to Paul Meshanko who knows how to help people thrive, not just survive, in a constantly changing climate. And he knows it's not what people think that determines their success or failure in life, but how they think. Paul, thank you so much for being with us today on *Conversations on Success*.

Meshanko

My pleasure, David.

About The Author

Paul knows how to help people thrive, not just survive, in a climate of constant change. He knows that it's not what people think that determines their success or failure in life, but how they think.

After 12 years in sales and new product development for a Fortune 50 company, Paul founded the Ohio office of a world renowned corporate leadership and training organization, and then became a keynote speaker. Paul uses familiar situations, concrete research and a broad knowledge of many topics to deliver an exciting presentation that not only educates, but inspires and entertains.

Paul Meshanko

Edge Learning of Ohio

4807 Rockside Road, Suite 240

Cleveland, Ohio 44131

Phone: 216.674.1085

Toll Free: 888.892.0300

Email: paul@paulmeshanko.com

www.paulmeshanko.com

Chapter Seven

STACEY HANKE

THE INTERVIEW

David E. Wright (Wright)

Today we are talking to Stacey Hanke. When people want to know how to say the right thing with poise and credibility, they call Stacey. Her focus is on providing suggestions to enhancing communication skills through leadership, presentations, customer service, sales, and our personal lives. Her ideas and strategies are recognized by Fortune 500 companies for their winning results and immediate benefits. She'll show you how to build confidence, credibility, and stamina into your communication. As a coach, Stacey has provided personal feedback and instruction customized for over 4,000 individuals, both nationally and internationally. Whether you find Stacey delivering a keynote, coaching a CEO on the art of presenting or changing participants' communication behavior, you'll understand why clients keep coming back as a result of her practical strategies and concepts. Be aware, her energy, drive, and passion for communication are contagious. She'll lead you through an experience that allows you to captivate, engage, and connect with your listeners to get them to take action. She does this by showing you how to speak so people want to listen. And after all, isn't that what communication is all about? Stacey, welcome this morning! Thank you very much for being with us.

Stacey Hanke (Hanke)

It's my pleasure, David. Thank you for inviting me.

Wright

You're known as a speaker who takes the fear out of presenting and for your ability to change behaviors, not only in a presentation situation, but in any form of communication. You've coached thousands and shared your experiences on how to maximize communication while delivering a presentation, e-mail or voice mail message, facilitating meetings, sales calls and face-to-face situations. With the variety of industries and levels within an organization you've coached, are there any consistencies on what specifically most people struggle with when communicating?

Hanke

There are two elements of communication that consistently come up. Number one, we're unaware of what our non-verbal language communicates. We know that how we communicate has more of an impact on our listeners than what we say. Think about your own communication experiences. Whether you're involved in a sales call, facilitating a meeting, or delivering a presentation, you probably focus more on content than your non-verbal language. When there are inconsistent messages, our listeners will tend to believe what they see verses what they hear. Suddenly your non-verbal behaviors distract your listeners from understanding much less remembering your message.

To give you an idea of how unaware we are of our non-verbal language, several weeks ago I was coaching an Executive how to engage, interact and connect with his audience when he presents. When he communicated, his energy was overwhelming as he paced back and forth while fidgeting with his ring. He worked hard throughout the coaching session determined to channel the nervous energy and ensure that his non-verbal language was consistent with his message. With a look of determination in his eyes, he was ready to try his new delivery skills while presenting in front of the class. As he stood proudly in front of his peers, delivering his message with confidence and his arms comfortably relaxed at his sides, he suddenly found the side seams of his pants. Within minutes he unconsciously began grabbing the seams of his pants, pulling his pants legs up until they reached his knees. You can imagine the embarrassment he felt when he realized everyone had a view of his black socks and his white legs.

The second element of communication is learning how to deliver a concise message that "gets to the point." We tend to ramble and speak in run on sentences. We also clutter our language and jeopardize our credibility with nonwords such as; uh, um, and, so, but, ok, you know and like. We use these words to buy ourselves time to think about what we want to say. Nonwords will make it difficult for you to get to the point and to stay focused. Your listeners will focus on your nonwords and as a result, miss your message. When we use the "uh's" and "um's," we announce to our audience that we're unsure of what we want to say. Communicating a message is a lot easier and more effective when you can speak in short, clear, and concise sentences while giving yourself permission to pause. Incorporating pauses throughout your communication will captivate, engage and keep your listener's attention. It's what I call the "power of the pause." To have complete control over your thoughts is a skill many individuals strive for. How can you gain this control? By incorporating pauses in-between your sentences, key points, and transitions or when you loose your train of thought. The pause also gives you time to breathe which will help you relax. Think about when you exercise or participate in a sport. To get through the workout, we know we need to breathe. Communicating is like a workout that requires a lot of energy. You'd be surprised in the amount of individuals who realize they don't take time to breathe when they speak. No wonder they become nervous and experience anxiety. You determine what perception(s) your listener creates of you based on "how" you communicate your message. Avoid running the risks of giving your listeners the perception that you're unsure of yourself, the material and your purpose.

I believe we avoid incorporating pauses into our speech because we want to communicate too much information in a limited amount of time. We tend to live in an information overload society. We want to tell our listeners everything we know and then leave them scratching their heads saying, "Hum, what just happened here?" When we're told in advance that we have 30 minutes to present and find out minutes before we're scheduled to deliver our message that we only have five minutes, what do you think we do? You guessed it, we pick up our rate of speech, rush through the material, and somehow we deliver 30 minutes of information in a five minute time frame. If you're reading this right now, I bet you're grinning and thinking, "Yes, I've been there before." Next time you find yourself in this situation, take a step back. Take a look at who you're talking to and determine what must be communicated based on your objective, listeners and time frame.

Wright

When someone comes to you searching for constructive feedback on their communication skills, what steps do you take them through to make sure they see results?

Hanke

My clients receive a lot of constructive feedback through interactive coaching. The goal is to provide them with numerous opportunities to practice the skills and techniques I recommend. I realize every individual has different needs, strengths and areas of improvement. My focus is on changing behaviors. When an individual experiences the positive changes taking place in their behavior, they begin to increase their confidence, credibility and determination to reach their definition of a "successful communicator."

The secret to reaching this level of success is practice, practice and more practice. The first step to this process is a video taped exercise. During this exercise, participants are asked to introduce themselves like they normally would do it. I want to see an individual's skill level to help me identify what works and doesn't work for them. This exercise also allows individuals to see and hear for themselves what their listeners see and hear. This first video taped exercise is followed by a discussion around the twelve delivery skills that make or break an individuals success as a communicator. With numerous video taped exercises and coaching sessions, individuals have a clear understanding of their level of performance and what steps to take if they want to improve.

We then move to phase two. This is where I provide participants with a powerful organizational tool that assists them in designing clear and concise openings, closings, transitions and a message that gets to the point. A big component to designing this message is knowing who you're talking to. Participants use an audience analysis, to gather information about the needs, expectations and knowledge level of their listener(s). By the end of the workshop, each individual creates specific action steps customized around their needs, which they can immediately apply to every aspect of their life.

I'm always amazed, David, at the number of individuals who have never received positive feedback in regards to their communication. If you never receive specific feedback on your performance, you'll continue to walk blindly throughout life while everyone around you is creating perceptions about you whether good or bad.

Wright

You made an important point about knowing who you're talking to. That raises two questions actually. The first would be what specific questions do you recommend someone ask themselves before writing a presentation or any form of communication such as voice mail messages, sales calls, or face to face conversations? And secondly, what specific questions do you recommend someone ask in regards to who they're talking to?

Hanke

Most individuals will create their message too quickly without asking, "What's my purpose?" To guarantee you're designing a message specifically for a particular audience, consider the following "top five questions." Begin by asking yourself what is my goal. Is it to persuade, to inform, request my listeners to take action, to inspire or entertain? Second, what specific action do I want my listeners to take? Third, what specific behavior do I want my listeners to change? Fourth, what is the best form of communication to achieve my goal? Is it through a training session, a team meeting or presentation? And finally number five; what do I personally want to gain? You can see, David, when asking yourself these questions, you're able to identify what you want to discuss. Imagine if you have a lot of information you want to communicate in an e-mail message and you know that you're going to scare your reader away if you include everything. When you ask yourself these five questions, you'll easily identify what's critical to communicate at this time and what can be communicated at a later date. Now the second part of that question—this is a step many individuals skip. They assume they know their audience better than they really do and simply don't want to take the time to do their research. If they only knew that the more they know about who they're talking to, the easier it is to design, deliver their message and connect with their listener(s). I mentioned earlier the importance of an audience analysis. Let me share with you the top five questions to consider. First question, what are the listener's expectations? Second, how will the action I want my listener to take affect them? Third, what behaviors does my listener want to change as a result of my message? Fourth, why is this presentation happening now? And finally number five, what preconceived ideas do they have about my message? You'll notice that these five questions are all about your listeners, not about you.

Wright

During your coaching sessions and seminars, you discuss the importance of not only communicating with others but also connecting. Would you share with us a couple of the components you emphasize that make or break someone's success as a communicator?

Hanke

I referred earlier to the twelve delivery skills or behaviors that make or break our ability to communicate effectively. The only behavior that allows you to connect with your listeners is eye contact, which I refer to as eye connection. Eye connection conveys trust and believability and isn't that what communication is all about. Here's the trick. Only speak when you see your listener's eyes. Now I know this sounds too obvious, but think about how many times you've seen a speaker talk into their PowerPoint presentation. They talk to the floor, the ceiling, their notes, et cetera. As a listener, you begin to focus on where the speaker is looking and as a result, you miss their message. When you're talking to more than one individual, you want to have a series of one-on-one conversations. Stay connected by looking at one person at a time for a complete sentence or thought. You'll keep their attention, encourage participation, and most importantly you'll create trust. Once trust is created, you're more likely to get listeners to take action.

Wright

I hear a lot of individuals talk about how they struggle with creating audience interaction, motivation, and keeping their attention. We know that first impressions are created within 30 seconds and some I've heard lately even down to seven. Whether we're delivering a presentation, sending a voice or email message, or participating in a sales call, what can we do to instantly grab attention, keep it, and get someone to take action?

Hanke

There are several methods to create audience interaction, motivation, and attention. Most importantly, be yourself. Think about how we communicate with family, friends, or co-workers. We're our natural self. For whatever reason when we present, the behaviors we demonstrate that enhance our natural self are lost and we become someone that we're not. To make sure this does not happen to you, talk *with* your listeners not *to* them. No one enjoys being lectured to. You can forget about creating a trusting relationship with your listeners when you prevent your natural self from coming through.

Secondly, follow the rule of three. I spoke earlier about our temptation to communicate too much information in a short period of time. You may have heard about the rule of three, which states we remember in groupings of three. Which explains why we remember our social security and phone number. When you provide four, five, six key points or more, your listeners are so busy trying to remember each key point that they walk away with nothing. Keeping your key points to a maximum of three will also help you, as the speaker, remember what you want to communicate.

A third method is what I refer to as a S.P.A.R.K. S.P.A.R.K.s provide you with options to grab attention during your openings, closings, and throughout your message. Keep in mind, the moment you begin speaking, your listeners have multiple topics on their mind and your message may not be one of them. The quicker you can grab your listener's attention, the quicker you begin building a relationship and receiving the results you set out to achieve. Avoid falling into the category of presenters who go on and on during their opening remarks while the listener is wondering, "When are you going to get to the point." Instead S.P.A.R.K. their attention. Let me explain. S stands for stories. Everyone likes a good story as long as the point of your story relates to your topic. And be careful. A story that goes on and on suddenly loses its impact. P in S.P.A.R.K. stands for pictorials. It's no secret that pictures speak louder than words. I'll never forget a participant who was in my workshop several years ago. Her presentation was on marketing strategies. She stood in front of the class holding a photograph illustrating the congestion of people walking down the streets of Japan. Now the photograph gave you the impression of individuals walking towards you, right out of the photograph. Got the visual?

Wright

Yes.

Hanke

With confidence, she paused for several seconds and then went on to say, "Imagine the marketing potential here." Seven years later and

I still remember that visual. Let me tell you it was not what she said but how she presented her ideas on marketing strategies.

The A in S.P.A.R.K. stands for analogies. It's easier to explain a complex idea or concept if you can compare it to something your listeners can understand. Make sure you practice explaining your analogy to a friend or family member. Analogies can backfire if they're not used appropriately. The R stands for references and quotes. We use these methods frequently as evidence to support our point of view. Finally the K stands for "keep them laughing." Be careful. This doesn't mean telling jokes. I'll never forget sitting in an audience with a group of lawyers as the presenter opened his presentation with not one, but several lawyer jokes. By noon of this six-hour program, half of the audience members left because he had offended so many individuals with his "not-so-funny" jokes. Therefore the humor I'm referring to is your natural humor. You're guaranteed to create a trusting relationship quickly. Who doesn't like a good laugh? Incorporating questions throughout your message is also a powerful method to engage listeners. The key is to identify a question that is certain to elicit the emotion you want to evoke or begins the overall message that you want to convey.

Wright

You mentioned one way to grab the attention of your audience is with pictorials or visuals. We tend to fall into the pitfall of Power-Point overkill. What recommendations do you share with your clients when designing and interacting with visual aids?

Hanke

We've heard it before, David, less is more. How many times have you received handouts from the speaker that are identical to their PowerPoint slides? I would also bet that you've seen speakers use PowerPoint as their notes. Then to take it one step further to drive you crazy, they begin reading to you from their slides. No one enjoys being read to, yet as a speaker, we get too comfortable and rely on PowerPoint as our security blanket.

Wright

Right.

Hanke

You're the presentation, not your visuals. If you're clicking more than you're speaking, it's time to reevaluate how you're using visuals. There's nothing worse than watching a presenter create a path from their PowerPoint to the screen. Why do we make our work harder than we need to? In fact here's an example. Think about the variety of billboards you pass when you're driving on the interstate. There are billboards that will stand out in our mind and it's not because we need to pull to the side of the road, read the tiny print on the billboard, and then steer our vehicle back onto the interstate. Why are these visuals so memorable? Because they use pictures, colors, bold print, and fewer words. When designing visuals, ask yourself, "Will this visual support my message and is it memorable?"

The design of the visual has a tremendous impact on how we interact with it. First, provide an introduction prior to displaying a visual to grab your listeners' attention and create anticipation. Second, pause immediately after showing the visual to give you "thinking time" and time for the listener to see and understand the visual. Third, at all costs avoid talking to the screen, laptop, flipchart and your notes. These pieces will not speak back to you. When you talk away from your listeners, you'll disconnect and begin having a relationship with your PowerPoint. Suddenly your listeners are wondering, "Gosh, should I leave the two of them alone?"

Wright

Success as an effective communicator sounds like a skill that will not happen overnight, but rather occurs over time and takes practice. What first steps do you recommend individuals take to be an effective communicator?

Hanke

First you need to practice. Becoming an effective communicator is a process and unfortunately doesn't occur overnight. I recommend practicing these skills and techniques in your personal life because that's where you're comfortable! Since communication encompasses every aspect of our life, we have endless opportunities to practice these skills. Second, you need to find a coach. Your personal coach may be your significant other, family member, friend or co-worker. For example, when you're having dinner with your family, tell them that you're trying to eliminate nonwords. Ask them to point out to you every time you say a nonword and you're guaranteed to quickly increase your awareness. Listen to your voice mail messages before you hit the send button. You may be surprised at what you hear. Pro athletes, professional speakers, actors, and actresses consistently receive feedback from their coaches to help them improve. Why do we jeopardize our success by not having a coach to help ourselves excel? Again, I cannot emphasize enough the art of effective communication doesn't only apply to individuals who find themselves delivering presentations. That's not what we're talking about here today. But being able to communicate with credibility, confidence, and poise, applies to all of us no matter what our job responsibilities are.

Wright

Would you share with our readers how you have positively impacted someone's life through your coaching and feedback you've provided?

Hanke

I never allow myself to forget how fortunate I am to have created a career where I'm able to positively impact individuals lives on a daily basis. I've truly been blessed with the amazing and genuine people I've met throughout my career. Whether these individuals that I've coached realize it or not, they have positively impacted my life in some shape or form. You would think after working with thousands of individuals, it would be difficult to remember one person in particular, but last year in one of my workshops I met Jackie. I'll never forget watching Jackie walk into the classroom with expressions of fear, anger, and resistance. I walked over to greet her, and as I held out my hand to say hello, she turned away from me, and mumbled underneath her breath something that sounded like "hello." So I knew I needed to ignite this conversation to find out why she was here. After asking her several questions, which she responded with very short answers, she looks at me with a stone cold, look and said, "I don't know what you're going to tell me that I already do not know with my 25 years of professional experience." Well, all I could say to that was, "Wow! Today is going to be one of those days." The reality was that Jackie was absolutely terrified of public speaking. She was told that she had to attend this workshop and therefore determined to do whatever she could to make my life and her experience absolutely miserable. After coaching Jackie and providing her with constructive feedback, I saw the light go on in her eyes. Jackie turned out to be the star performer in the workshop. After coaching her on the skills and techniques, she found her comfort in front of the class.

The real impact happened at the end of the workshop, David. As she stood with confidence in front of her peers, sharing the next steps she had planned to immediately implement and thanked me for my work; tears began rolling down her face. At that moment the entire class rose to their feet and gave her a heartfelt standing ovation. After class, she waited until everyone left, and walked over to me. She pulled me close and said, "I will never forget what you've given me. Not just the ability to communicate more effectively, but the ability to get rid of my greatest fear and open so many doors of opportunity in my personal and professional life." I've had the fortune to reunite with Jackie at a conference a few weeks ago. As I was watching her walk towards me smiling larger than life, I felt that nervous energy and excitement inside of me. Without saying hello, she gave me a hug like only my mother knows how to give. She pulled away with her hand resting on my arm and said, "You have changed my life and have inspired me in so many ways." That has been the greatest impact so far.

Wright

We tend to hear this question a lot. How do you define success? Not so much as to how we define success, but what makes one person more successful than another?

Hanke

I believe a lot of individuals really struggle with this question. They're always traveling on this long road with no vision or direction in sight. When they hit a speed bump during their journey, without hesitation they sit down in the middle of the road because this is the easiest action to take. As they sit there, looking in front and behind them, they're looking for more speed bumps, almost as if they want additional reasons to avoid pushing through the obstacle. They create their own roadblocks, which give them endless excuses to stop instead of moving forward. When they finally stand up, instead of changing directions, they turn around, walk back to where they came from, and suddenly this behavior becomes their day-to-day routine. And then they wonder, "Why doesn't anything ever change in my life? Why am I always unlucky?" Someone who strives for success will take a moment to strategize the best approach for them to get through, under, over or around this challenge on their journey. They realize the purpose of a speed bump is to slow down, to check-in with their goals and expectations before moving any further. Their challenges are an opportunity to reevaluate the actions they're currently taking and to change their direction. I've learned a lot of my lifelong lessons from my father who believed in never giving up no matter how bad that storm may be or how high that obstacle appears.

After everything he's shared with me, I've identified three attributes to an individual's success. First attribute is someone who has balance in his or her life and doesn't take life too seriously. I believe once we stop having fun, David, success gets farther and farther out of our reach. We need to lighten up and enjoy the journey that we were given. Second, is someone who strives in taking risks. If we're able to look at the mistakes in our life and not only learn from them, but identify with these mistakes as a positive moment, we're going to be rewarded with success. If you're not making mistakes, ask yourself, are you really working hard enough and to your ability? Finally, someone who is constantly reinventing themselves and their business, staying current in making themselves more marketable, which requires the ability to quickly and relentlessly adapt to change. There's an anonymous quote that caught my eye, which summarizes these three attributes, "The difference between a successful person and others is not a lack of strength, not a lack of knowledge, but rather a lack of will."

Wright

Out of those three components you identified, I imagine people avoid or even fear taking risks. Why do you think people fear taking risks?

Hanke

I think we get too comfortable in life. We're afraid of failure or what others will think of us if we take action that is out of the ordinary or doesn't follow the crowd. Taking risks requires us to make changes. Most of us avoid change as much as possible not realizing when you do the same thing over and over; you're going to get the same results. If taking a risk was so easy and comfortable, then everyone would do it. Stop being the follower when it comes to your career and personal life. Now I know there are moments in your life as you're striving for success when it's beneficial to be the follower. It's critical to keep your eyes and ears open so that you can continuously learn from other's mistakes and successes. The difference is the individual who knows when to stop following and when to begin leading their own destinations.

Wright

So what gets in the way of someone being successful?

Hanke

We lose our focus of what we have the ability to do. Losing sight of who we are and the journey we want to take. Your uniqueness is in your style, your message, and your capabilities. That's who you are and no one can take that away from you. I believe this is truly a gift that was given to each and every one of us. A gift we cannot take for granted; yet so many of us do. Take five minutes today after you set this book down to reevaluate your purpose and who you are. This will allow you to put more of who you are in what you do. And when you can give and share your gift with others to help them grow, the gift will be returned to you time and time again.

Wright

In your work with individuals you're known for providing participants with practical tools they can use immediately both personally and professionally. What tool would you share with our readers to assist them in their success?

Hanke

In whatever area of success that you want to accomplish, know that you do not have to get there alone. I was fortunate early in my career to identify a coach who provided feedback in my personal and professional development. I chose carefully to find someone that I could trust and who was critical, yet supportive. Take some time to identify the characteristics of your ideal coach. Your coach will benefit you in many ways from helping you develop your skills to someone you can lean on. My family is my support and safety net that never weakens. Talking to them, even though we're miles apart, makes the challenge look possible to overcome. My father has said to me on a number of occasions, "Stacey, every day does not have to be a rock star day." Hearing what you already know from someone you admire is always more believable. When you're able to share even the small successes with those you love, you forget about the hard work, disappointments and long hours. Maybe it's because we need to slow down and take time to celebrate our successes. We tend to forget how fortunate we are with the abundance of freedom we have. Nothing is holding us back except for our public enemy, which is ourselves. We create our own destinies and our defeats. I have a sign hanging in my office that reads "No Excuses", because I truly believe that there are no excuses in life for achieving what we want to achieve.

Wright

What an interesting conversation! I really appreciate you taking all this time with me this morning. It's been rewarding for me. I took all kinds of notes. I'm going to use the S.P.A.R.K. theory the next time I make a speech.

Hanke

I'm glad to hear I've given you some valuable information that you can immediately use. It has been a pleasure talking with you, David. Thank you for the opportunity and your help through the process.

Wright

Well, you're more than welcome. Today we have been talking to Stacey Hanke. Stacey has worked in a variety of industries including medical, accounting, financial, law, manufacturing, recruiting, education, and the list goes on. With her wide range of professional experience and passion for her topics, she quickly connects with participants, persuading them to step outside their comfort zone and immediately apply the skills and techniques to maximize their communication. And I think we have found that out here in this conversation. Thank you so much, Stacey, for being with us today on *Conversations on Success*.

About The Author

Stacey's focus is on enhancing communication skills through leadership, presentations, customer service and our personal lives. As a coach, she has provided personal feedback and instruction customized for over 4,000 individuals worldwide.

Whether you find Stacey delivering a keynote, coaching a CEO on the art of presenting or changing participant's communication behavior, you'll understand why clients keep coming back as a result of her practical strategies and immediate results. Be aware; her energy, drive and passion for communication are contagious. She'll lead you through an experience that allows you to captivate, engage and connect with your listeners to get them to "take action."

Stacey Hanke

1341 West Fullerton Avenue

Suite #265

Chicago, IL 60614

Phone: 773.528.5378

Cell: 773.209.5970

Email: staceyhanke@ameritech.net

Chapter Eight

KEN KRISBY

THE INTERVIEW

David E. Wright (Wright)

Ken Krisby is the enthusiastic heart and soul of Success Solutions. Ken served in the United States Air Force during the Viet Nam conflict. He is an author and is also actively involved with breast cancer awareness and the fight for a cure. He brings over 30 years of experience to his sales training seminars, employee education classes, and industry specific talks. Ken is a people motivation expert who will improve any company's profit potential and individual's productivity. Helping people improve their skills is Ken's goal, and after hearing him speak, participants are reenergized and equipped with new tools to achieve successful results. Ken Krisby, welcome to *Conversations on Success!*

Ken Krisby (Krisby)

Thank you.

Wright

Success is the ultimate dream of a person. What dream started you on your road to success?

Krisby

Well, my dream started when I realized that there were other things I could do with my potential. Up until then, I hadn't realized there's more to life than I could see on the horizon. I figured the only way I could get there was just dive in and find out what it was all about. Amazingly enough, I found out that my dream was to be an educator.

In all my journeys, I've always been in sales and I've always been in management. I thought about these as teaching tools and I became focused on the idea that I'd like to be a teacher. Maybe years ago, I should have gone to school for education and become a teacher but, I realized by getting into sales, and getting into sales management, that's exactly what I'm doing. I'm teaching people. So the journey that I started on was taking my career skills in outside sales, adding the management experience, and realizing, "Wow! I can train people and coach people and serve people." So I opened my own business to facilitate and to train people how to be successful, how to make success happen, how to use the skills from their own occupation and take these to a higher level in pursuit of a goal. My new goal was educating people.

It took a light bulb for me to see this. You know, sometimes you look down the tunnel and you see a light coming at you. And you think it's a train coming at you. But, actually, it's the light of opportunity. The light of opportunity for me was that education, educating people, coaching, mentoring, and serving people is the way that I thought I should take my career, and I wanted to do that.

Wright

For those of us who manage people and lead and direct people, could you pass along some words of wisdom to our readers for motivating others to reach their success?

Krisby

Yes. To motivate others to obtain success, I have a very simple process. It's three words. The first word is **creativity**. Help people open their minds to creativity and stimulate this through projects and activities. Secondly, people need to understand the value of considering **diversification.** In other words, let go of the tunnel vision, drop the blinders. Take a chance and dive in with both feet. Try different things and take the creativity that you've applied in other processes and use it in new, diverse ways. However, none of that can happen without one word that circles those two words and it's **consistency**. Consistent application of the process is every day, every week, every month, every year. You don't need to change yourself, just allow creativity to open new doors, and when you find a successful tool that works for you, apply it consistently. And I try to tell people all the time... as long as they are brainstorming and focusing on results, they are creating diverse ideas that will end up giving them a focus that will put them on a successful path that can be consistently followed.

Wright

Tell us a couple of your success journeys. Everybody is motivated by success stories of others. Could you share some with us?

Krisby

A journey that's taken me to success?

Wright

Yes.

Krisby

Well, one of the stories might be when I got involved both professionally and personally. I was always focused on my health and always getting into wellness programs. I currently conduct a wellness program that's called *Wellness, Energy, and Success*. I started offering wellness and energy and success programs to the YMCA and to other health clubs. I'd offer it at a very reasonable rate. It helped people to get reenergized and understand that body energy is needed daily. It's like a nine volt battery. You've got to be charged up every day . If you have better health, you seem to develop a focus for success. So I went into health clubs, and YMCAs where I started teaching this. And by teaching this to folks, it led to some successful, professional networking because a lot of people that took my class, that paid the very reasonable fee, would come up to me afterwards and say, "Hi! I'm John Smith, Executive Vice President of ABC Corporation. I really enjoyed what you did for me today. Is there any opportunity for me to hook-up with you to do personal one-on-one training?" These arrangements then led into the professional business world when John Smith learned the other side of what I do for a living. He'd contract with me to provide his company employees with training. So my success journey in this story was a personal thing I started doing for my own personal wellness, taking it to the health club level, then turned it into networking, and turned it into a flow of business training opportunities. I maintain and got so many clients just from teaching my wellness program, which I began in 1980, that I still continue to teach this to this day

Wright

You know building relationships is a huge part of the process for successful outcomes. What are some of your techniques and what is your thought process for building those relationships?

Krisby

Building relationships has to focus on listening because the best relationships are built this way. So I get people to talk. It's hard to get people to open up sometimes, but the way you do it is to bring them to the center of the attention. Now, some people don't like to be the center of attention, but you do it with tact, grace and a delivery that makes them feel comfortable. Just like the little word *ask*. How do you ask for things? You ask for things either directly, abruptly, kindly, softly; but that little word *ask* is so dynamic. A-s-k, it stands for attitude, skill and knowledge. When you ask for something, it's making people understand that you need to hear from them. We're in the age of communication and sometimes we fail to communicate. The more I hear about you, the better we can build our relationship together.

There's four relationship traits that I see in people. They're either relaters, socializers, thinkers, or they're directors. And based on my experience and intuition, I can pick out what type they are and know how to relate to them. I'm a socializer major with a minor as a director.

Wright

Right.

Krisby

And you just ascertain the traits in people. So I try to identify their personality by using the "ask" tool and, with great listening skills, I can develop a relationship.

Wright

You had to have had situations in your life where the outcome wasn't as successful as you had planned. How do you deal with that kind of thing?

Krisby

Well first off, when the outcomes aren't what was planned, the first thing people usually do is they try to look for a scapegoat and they start pointing. But by pointing a finger at someone else, they need to remember that three fingers are pointing back towards them. They start doing what I cannot stand, excuse-itis and blame-itis. I think the biggest thing in overcoming the obstacles and pitfalls of your life is don't have any excuse-itis or blame-itis in your life. Attack it head on and admit your failure. A couple of situations in my life's journeys have taken me there.

How I overcame them was through positive reinforcement, knowing that it was wrong, and correcting the wrong by not letting it happen again. And I came upon a phrase that I use in seminars all the time now. I call it the RTR, and I keep reminding myself of RTR which stands for "right things right." Once you start doing the right things right, the failures, the obstacles, the pitfalls seem to lessen in your journey. I've been doing this for a long time over the course of the many years I've been in business since I got out of Viet Nam in '73. Everybody's had hiccups or pitfalls along the way. You overcome them like going over speed bumps. How do you go over a speed bump, fast or slow? People are always tell me they go over a speed bump fast. I tell them you are ripping the heck out of your vehicle's undercarriage. I tell them slow down, patience keeps you cool, and go over those speed bumps slow and easy. Everyone has them, a person who tells me they've never had failures in their life is not being truthful. It's what we do with the failures that matter, that allows us to overcome them.

Wright

How are your days, your weeks, and months focused for success?

Krisby

Wow! They're focused with success from staying healthy, getting up on time, having an energy level that drives me forward, just like I tell people. They say to me, "Ken, what are you on in the morning?"

My mother says, "You know, he was born excited." But it's all about life. I tell people, "Life, l-i-f-e, follow me, follow me. L-i-f-e, follow me, follow me." It's all about living life to its fullest. And why that's more divine in my life now is because of my dear wife's situation. She has breast cancer metastasized to her liver. But we fight that every day. I had to move my business from Columbus, Ohio, to Wexford, Pennsylvania, to be closer to her family because family support is needed. So we drive and we drive and we drive by staying consistent day to day, week to week, month to month, because the challenges of life are there every day. It's how you overcome them! And the way you need to do this is to get up, put a smile on your face, look at yourself in the mirror in the morning, and say, "Good morning, Ken." Three things: Who am I going to affect today? How much money do I want to make today? And who can I help today? Affect, money, and help. That's what I do every morning.

Wright

Can you tell us what motivates you the most?

Krisby

What motivates me the most is seeing people change their lifestyles after attending one of my seminars. Like I tell people when I'm doing a seminar, I just did one yesterday for a Design Group in Pittsburgh, I told them the most motivating thing one person can do for another is to listen. The thing that motivates me, I will tell you right now, if you walk out of this seminar with only one thing that changed your life, I've failed. You need to walk out of here with a half a dozen to a dozen things that I know will impact your life and add focus. We'll keep in contact. We'll measure the result because that is what is going to make it happen, because I am now part of your team. So what motivates me the most is seeing others change their lifestyles because they can, if they believe. And once they believe, and they change their lifestyles for the better, that's what makes me feel so rewarded.

Wright

Many people say opportunity has a small opening. Can you share some of the opportunities of which you were presented that turned into a huge success?

Krisby

Oh, absolutely. Once again, just seeing my calling. My calling was education. Now that I've seen that, hindsight is 20/20. If I could do it all over again, would I change things? I don't know. But the opportunity was there. I was in high end sales management and a director of sales for years. I was a training education director for a lot of companies in Ohio. After a sale was made, I heard, "Can you come in and teach my sales reps how to do it the way you did it? Can you come in and work with my sales team?"

I started seeing this light flashing at me, telling me, "Ken, you should get into training. This is what you need to do." So the opportunity was presented to me by the clients that I would sell to, while I was training sales reps for other employers. Those company owners, the CFOs, the CEOs, the COOs would come to me and say , "Mr. Krisby, Ken, can you come in and give me some of your time on how to do this so I can teach my people how to do it?"

The opportunity was thrown at me constantly, and I finally understood that I needed to get out and teach people. My business is Success Solutions and we do all sorts of training now. So, the opportunities were created by other companies telling me, "My gosh. Can you help me teach my people how to do this?" I thought that was pretty exciting.

Wright

What are some of your keys for successful business or family or home, for that matter?

Krisby

Well, you know, you've got to align these. I call it the alignment, but you've got to start with you. You've got to be self-motivated. You've got to be directed. You've got to have focus, number one. Number two, family. Family's got to be right there with you. You and family have to be aligned together. The third thing in that step is your business, and it's all circled by your spiritual belief and you can't lose that focus. It's very simple. Some people don't like to talk about the last one as much anymore in today's society, but you know, I can only do what I think is right in mine. Because back in Viet Nam when I was over there supporting troops with the KC135 air refueler, refueling B-52 bombers, refueling F-100s, it was the focus of taking care of you first, the person that was with you, remembering your family, doing the job that you had to do, and remember that there's somebody directing this whole thing above you. And you've got to stay focused, and I just stay focused. I tell people it's all about alignment. It's having time and task management alignment every day with my business life and with my personal life. You know, if the young men in sales or the young women in sales or the young woman that's an entrepreneur of her own business says, "Honey, I'll be home when I can get there. I'm too busy right now." That needs to change. Align first, business will be there.

Wright

If you see a situation that is in need of redirection for success, how do you tell those people that are involved that they need to change and refocus?

Krisby

Well, you talk to them about changing habits. It takes 21 days to change a habit, 21 consecutive days, but you also have to build what I call contingency plans against failure. A contingency plan can be diagramed on paper. Put the known problem in a circle and then brainstorm it with a group of people. You get a cross pollination of different people from your business, your personal life, community, and you look at the problem together with open mind and eyes. Then you draw arrows in from the left side listing possible causes for the problem. Then you go to the right side and you draw a straight line result for every incoming arrow, each one is a step to take to address each of the possible causes.

Wright

You have said that reaching out to others is your strength. What is your thought process on how to reach out to others for everyone's quest for success?

Krisby

How to reach out to others is to lead by example because then they will follow. Just like that old saying if you build it, they will come, in that great movie *Field of Dreams* with Kevin Costner. If you lead by example, they will follow. But while you're leading, you've got to maintain focus because you don't want to slip on a banana peel and do something that's out of line with what you told them that you do. So it comes back to that key word that circles everything in life, the "consistency" word. An example is how I tell everybody, playfully, when we have a meeting scheduled for 8 a.m..... please be on time. If you're 8 minutes early, you're on time. If you're on time, you're 8 minutes late.

Wright

You need to get them up and get them going.

Krisby

You've got to get moving. It's all a process. It's managing your time. My method is to use what I call time bytes. If you have three one-half hour time bytes in your life (early morning, lunch time, and late at night) to use to focus on specific items, you'll clear up your next day to be on time for everything.

Wright

Many cannot see the light at the end of the tunnel, as you referred to it. How can you assist them to turn the corner for a successful journey?

Krisby

The only way that they can turn the corner for a successful journey is to make the commitment to themselves. They have to have the strong belief that they want to change their lifestyle. And to make a successful journey happen, sometimes you have to belly up, let the rubber meet the road, and know / admit you have to *change your habits*. To see the light at the end of the tunnel, and make a successful journey, you have to commit to changing your habits! Once you change habits and you see results, guess what? That light at the end of the tunnel is not that hard to reach. You have to have energy to get there. You have to have the motivation and the drive to want to do it. You've got to stay totally focused, as I have been saying all along, about building the process and keeping it in alignment. You need to have support mechanisms in your life, from your spouse or significant others, whomever, you have to have support and buy-in from the significant others in your life when you're trying to change things. If you don't have buy-in from the significant others in your life, they may be the ones that are stopping you. So a lot of discussion should be happening when someone wants to reach that light at the end of the tunnel.

Wright

Well, what a great conversation. I've learned a lot about success here this morning. Thanks a lot. Before we leave this conversation, I do want to mention, my wife is an eight year cancer survivor.

Krisby

Bless you! Bless her!

Wright

And I want you to tell your wife that she is in my thoughts and prayers. And I understand, as I'm sure you do, that one person doesn't get cancer. The whole family and all the friends do as well.

Krisby

Absolutely!

Wright

So tell her I'm thinking about her and I wish you both the success and the cure that she so richly deserves.

Krisby

Right! That's why we moved here. I needed support because I need to support my family. It's something you've got to do to battle it. You've just got to be able to listen to them too. To listen to them, and apply the listening skills to anything in life are part of life's success path. Good listening.

Wright

Well, I know how hard it is, but this too shall pass.

Krisby

Yep!

Wright

Ken, I really appreciate you giving me this much time today, and this much information, and I hope that you do well. And I thank you for spending so much time with me on *Conversations on Success*.

About The Author

Ken Krisby served in the United States Air Force during the Vietnam Conflict, he is an Author and competitive weightlifter in the senior masters 50 and over division, he is also actively involved with Breast Cancer Awareness and the fight for a cure!

Ken is involved with three Chamber of Commerce Chapters in Western Pennsylvania, is President of his Homeowners Association, assists in youth baseball and is totally committed to helping people improve their skills and become re-energized for personal growth.

Ken Krisby, President

Success Solutions

Phone: 412.327.1518

Phone: 724.933.9386

Chapter Nine

JACK CANFIELD

THE INTERVIEW

David E. Wright (Wright)

Today we are talking to Jack Canfield. You probably know him as the founder and co-creator of the *New York Times* #1 best-selling *Chicken Soup for the Soul* book series, which currently has 35 titles and 53 million copies in print in over 32 languages. Jack's background includes a BA from Harvard, a Masters from the University of Massachusetts and an Honorary Doctorate from the University of Santa Monica. He has been a high school and university teacher, a workshop facilitator, a psychotherapist, and for the past twenty-five years, a leading authority in the area of self-esteem and personal development. Jack Canfield, welcome to *Conversations on Success!*

Jack Canfield (Canfield)

Thank you David. It's great to be with you.

Wright

I talked with Mark Victor Hansen a few days ago. He gave you full credit for coming up with the idea of the *Chicken Soup* series. Obviously it's made you an internationally known personality. Other than recognition, has the series changed you personally and if so, how?

Canfield

I would say that it has and I think in a couple of ways. Number one, I read stories all day long of people who've overcome what would feel like insurmountable obstacles. For example we just did a book *Chicken Soup for the Unsinkable Soul*. There's a story in there about a single mother with three daughters. She got a disease and she had to have both of her hands and both of her feet amputated. She got prosthetic devices and was able to learn how to use them so she could cook, drive the car, brush her daughters' hair, get a job, etc. I read that and I think, "God, what would I ever have to complain and whine and moan about?" So I think at one level it's just given me a great sense of gratitude and appreciation for everything I have, made me less irritable about the little things. I think the other thing that's happened for me personally is my sphere of influence has changed. By that I mean I got asked, for example, a couple of years ago to be the keynote speaker to the Women's Congressional Caucus and these are all the women in Congress, Senators, Governors, and Lieutenant Governors in America. I said, "What do you want me to talk about, what topic?" They said, "Whatever you think we need to know to be better legislators." And I thought, "Wow, they want me to tell them about what laws they should be making and what would make a better culture?" Well, that wouldn't have happened if our books hadn't come out and I hadn't become famous. I think I get to play with people at a higher level and have more influence in the world. That's important to me because my life purpose is inspiring and empowering people to live their highest vision so the world works for everybody and I get to do that on a much bigger level than when I was just a high school teacher back in Chicago.

Wright

I think one of the powerful components of that book series is that you can read a positive story in just a few minutes, come back and revisit it. I know my daughter who is 13 now has three of the books and she just reads them interchangeably. Sometimes I go in her bedroom and she'll be crying and reading one of them. Other times she'll be laughing so they really are chicken soup for the soul, aren't they?

Canfield

They really are. In fact we have four books in the *Teenage Soul* series now and a new one coming out at the end of this year. I was talking to one of my sons, I have a son who's 11 and he has 12 year old friend who's a girl and we have a new book called *Chicken Soup for the Teenage Soul and the Tough Stuff*. It's all about dealing with parents' divorces, teachers who don't understand you, boyfriends who drink and drive, and stuff like that and I asked her, "Why do you like this book?" because it's our most popular book among teens right now. And she said, "You know whenever I'm feeling down I read it and it makes me cry and I feel better. Some of the stories make me laugh and some of the stories make me feel more responsible for my life. But basically I just feel like I'm not alone." One of the people that I work with recently said that the books are like a support group between the covers of a book, to hear other peoples' experiences and realize you're not the only one going through something.

Wright

Jack, with our *Conversations on Success* publication we're trying to encourage people in our audience to be better, to live better and be more fulfilled by listening to the examples of our guests. Is there anything or anyone in your life that has made a difference for you and helped you to become a better person?

Canfield

Yes and we could do 10 shows just on that. I'm influenced by people all the time. If I were to go way back I'd have to say one of the key influences in my life was Jesse Jackson when he was still a minister in Chicago. I was teaching in an all black high school there and I went to Jesse Jackson's church with a friend one time. What happened for me was I saw somebody with a vision. This was before Martin Luther King was killed and Jesse was of the lieutenants in his organization. I just saw people trying to make the world work better for a certain segment of the population. I was inspired by that kind of visionary belief that it's possible to make change. Then later John F. Kennedy was a hero of mine. I was very much inspired by him. Later a therapist by the name of Robert Resnick that I had for two years. He taught me a little formula called $E + R = O$ that stands for Events + Response = Outcome. He said, "If you don't like your outcomes quit blaming the events and start changing your responses." One of his favorite phrases was, "If the grass on the other side of the fence looks greener, start watering your own lawn more." I think it helped me get off of any kind of self-pity I might have had because I had parents who were alcoholics and that whole number. It's very easy to blame them for your life not working. They weren't real successful or rich and I was surrounded by people who were and I felt like, "God, what if I'd had parents like they had? I could have been a lot better." He just got me off that whole notion and made me realize the hand you were dealt is the hand you've got to play and take responsibility for who you are and quit complaining and blaming others and get on with your life. That was a turning point for me. I'd say the last person that really affected me big time was a guy named W. Clement Stone who was a self-made multi-millionaire in Chicago. He taught me that success is not a four-letter word, it's nothing to be ashamed of and you ought to go for it. He said, "The best thing you can do for the poor is not be one of them." Be a model for what it is to live a successful life. So I learned from him the principles of success and that's what I've been teaching now for the last almost 30 years.

Wright

He was the entrepreneur in the insurance industry, wasn't he?

Canfield

He was. He had combined insurance and when I worked for him he was worth 600 million dollars and that was before the dot.com millionaires came along in Silicon Valley. He just knew more about success and he was a good friend of Napoleon Hill who wrote *Think and Grow Rich* and he was a fabulous mentor. I really learned a lot from him.

Wright

I miss some of the men that I listened to when I was a young salesman coming up and he was one of them. Napoleon Hill was another one and Dr. Peale, all of their writings made me who I am today. I'm glad that I got that opportunity.

Canfield

One speaker whose name you probably will remember, Charlie Tremendous Jones, says "Who we are is a result of the books we read and the people we hang out with." I think that's so true and that's why I tell people, "If you want to have high self-esteem hang out with people with high self-esteem. If you want to be more spiritual hang out with spiritual people." We're always telling our children, "Don't hang out with those kids." The reason we don't want them to is we know how influential people are with each other. I think we need to give ourselves the same advice. Who are we hanging out with? We can hang out with them in books, cassette tapes, CDs, radio shows like yours, and in person.

Wright

One of my favorites was a fellow named Bill Gove from Florida. I talked with him about three or four years ago and he's retired now. His mind is still as quick as it ever was. I thought he was one of the greatest speakers I had ever heard.

What do you think makes up a great mentor. In other words, are there characteristics that mentors seem to have in common?

Canfield

I think there are two obvious ones. One, I think they have to have the time to do it and two, the willingness to do it. And then three I think they need to be someone who is doing something you want to do. W. Clement Stone used to tell me, "If you want to be rich hang out with rich people. Watch what they do, eat what they eat, dress the way they dress. Try it on." It wasn't like give up your authentic self, but it was that they probably have habits that you don't have. Study them, study the people who are already like you. I always ask sales-people in an organization, "Who are the top two or three in your organization?" I tell them to start taking them out to lunch and din-ner and for a drink and finding out what they do. Ask them, "What's your secret?" Nine times out of ten they'll be willing to tell you. It goes back to what we said earlier about asking. I'll go into corpora-tions and I'll say, "Who are the top 10 people?" They'll all tell me and I'll say, "Did you ever ask them what they do different than you?" They go, "No." "Why not?" "Well they might not want to tell me." "How do you know? Did you ever ask them? All they can do is say no. You'll be no worse off than you are now." So I think with mentors you just look at people who seem to be living the life you want to live, achieving the results you want to achieve. And then what we tell them in our book is when you approach a mentor they're probably busy and successful and so they haven't got a lot of time. Just say, "Can I talk to you for 10 minutes every month?" If I know it's only going to be 10 minutes I'll probably say yes. The neat thing is if I like you I'll always give you more than 10 minutes, but that 10 minutes gets me in the door.

Wright

In the future are there any more Jack Canfield books authored singularly?

Canfield

Yes, I'm working on two books right now. One's called $E + R = O$ which is that little formula I told you about earlier. I just feel I want to get that out there because every time I give a speech when I talk about that the whole room gets so that you could hear a pin drop, it gets silent. You can tell that people are really getting value. Then I'm going to do a series of books on the principles of success. I've got about 150 of them that I've identified over the years. I have a book down the road I want to do that's called *No More Put-Downs* which is a book probably aimed mostly at parents, teacher and managers. There's a culture we have now of put-down humor whether it's *Married With Children* or *All in the Family,* there's that characteristic of macho put-down humor. There's research now that's showing how bad it is for kids' self-esteem, co-workers, athletes when the coaches do it so I want to get that message out there as well.

Wright

It's really not that funny, is it?

Canfield

No, we'll laugh it off because we don't want to look like we're a wimp but underneath we're hurt. The research now shows that you're better off breaking a child's bones than you are breaking their spirit. A bone will heal much more quickly than their emotional spirit will.

Wright

I remember recently reading a survey where people listed the top five people that had influenced them in their lives. I've tried it on a couple of groups at church and other places. In my case and also in the survey it's running that about three out of the top five are always teachers. I wonder if that's going to be the same in the next decade.

Canfield

I think probably because as children we're at our most formative years. We actually spend more time with our teachers than we do with our parents. Research shows that the average parent only inter-acts verbally with each of their children only about eight and a half minutes a day. Yet at school you're interacting with your teacher for anywhere from six to eight hours depending on how long your school days is, and coaches, chorus directors, and all that kind of thing. So I think that in almost everybody's life there's been that one teacher who loved you as a human being and not just a subject matter, some person they were supposed to fill full of History and English. And that person believed in you and inspired you. Les Brown is one of the great motivational speakers in the world. If it hadn't been for one teacher who said, "I think you can do more than be in a special ed. class; I think you're the one," he'd probably still be cutting grass in the median strip of the highways in Florida instead of being a $35,000 a talk speaker.

Wright

I had a conversation one time with Les when he was talking about this wonderful teacher that discovered that he was dyslexic. Everybody else called him dumb and this one lady just took him under her wing and had him tested. His entire life changed because of her interest in him.

Canfield

I'm on the board of advisors of the Dyslexic Awareness Resource Center here in Santa Barbara. The reason is I taught high school with a lot of kids who were called at-risk, kids who would end up in gangs and so forth. What we found over and over was that about 78% of all the kids in the juvenile detention centers in Chicago were kids who had learning disabilities, primarily dyslexia, but there were others as well. They were never diagnosed and they weren't doing well in school so they'd drop out. As soon as you drop out of school you become subject to the influence of gangs and other kinds of criminal and drug linked activities. If they had just diagnosed these kids earlier, and there are a lot of really good programs that can teach dyslexics to read and so forth, then we'd get rid of half of the juvenile crime in America.

Wright

My wife is a teacher and she brings home stories that are heartbreaking, about parents not being as concerned about their children as they used to be or at least not as helpful as they used to be. Did you find that to be a problem when you were teaching?

Canfield

It depends on what kind of district you're in. If it's a poor district the parents could be drugged out, on alcohol, not available basically. If you're in a really high rent district the parents not being available because they're both working, coming home tired, they're jet-setters, they're working late at the office because they're workaholics. Sometimes it just legitimately takes two paychecks to pay the rent anymore. I find that the majority of parents care but often they don't know what to do. They don't know how to discipline their children. They don't know how to help them with their homework. They're not passing on skills that they never got. Unfortunately the trend tends to be like a chain letter. The people with the least amount of skills tend to have the most number of children. The other thing is you get crack babies. In Los Angeles one out of every 10 babies born is a crack baby.

Wright

That's unbelievable.

Canfield

Yes and another statistic is 50% of kids by the time they're 12 years old have started experimenting with alcohol. I see a lot of that in the Bible belt. It's not the big city, urban designer drugs but you get a lot of alcoholism. Another thing you get, unfortunately, is a lot of let's call it familial violence – a lot of kids getting beat up and hit, parents who drink and then explode. And as we talked about earlier child abuse and sexual abuse. You see a lot of that.

Wright

Most people are fascinated by these TV shows about being a survivor. What has been the greatest comeback that you have made from adversity in your career or in your life.

Canfield

You know it's funny, I don't think I've had a lot of major failures and setbacks where I had to start over. My life's been kind of on an intentional curve. But I do have a lot of challenges. Mark and I are always setting goals that challenge us and we always say, "The purpose of setting a really big goal is not so that you can achieve it so much, but it's who you become in the process of achieving it." A friend of mine Jim Rose says, "You want to set goals big enough so that in the process of achieving them you become someone worth being." I think that to be a millionaire is nice but so what? People make the money, they lose it. People get the big houses, they burn down or Silicon Valley goes belly up and all of a sudden they don't have a big house anymore. But who you became in the process of learning how to do that can never be taken away from you. So what we do is we constantly put big challenges in front of us. Right now we have a book coming out in a month called *Chicken Soup for the Teacher's Soul.* You'll have to make sure to get a copy for your wife. I was a teacher and I was a teacher trainer for years. But in the last seven years, because of the success of the *Chicken Soup* books I haven't been in the education world that much. So I've got to go out and relearn how do I market to that world? I met with a Superintendent of Schools. I met with a guy named Jason Dorsey who's one of the number one consultants in the world in that area. I found out who has the best selling book in that area. I sat down with his wife for a day and talked about her marketing approaches. So I believe that if you face any kind of adversity, whether it's you lose your job, your husband dies, you get divorced, you're in an accident like Christopher Reeves and become paralyzed, or whatever, you simply do what you have to do. You find out who's already handled this and how did they do it. Then you find out either from their book or from their tape or by talking to them or interviewing them, and you get the support you need to get through it. Whether it's a counselor in your church or you go on a retreat or you read the Bible. You do something that gives you the support you need to get to the other end and you have to know what the end is that you want to have. Do you want to be remarried? Do you just want to have a job and be a single mom? What is it? If you reach out and ask for support I think people really like to help other people. They're not always available because sometimes they're going through it. But there's always someone with a helping hand. Often I think we let our pride get in the way. We let our stubbornness get in the way. We let our belief in how the world should be get in our way instead of dealing with how the world is. When we get that out of that way then we can start doing that which we need to do to get where we need to go.

Wright

If you could have a platform and tell our audience something that you feel that would help or encourage them, what would you say?

Canfield

I'd say number one, believe in yourself and believe in your dreams, and trust your feelings. I think too many people are trained like when they're little kids and they're mad at their daddy, they're told, "You're not mad at your Daddy." They go, "Gee, I thought I was." Or you say, "That's going to hurt." The doctor says, "No it's not." Then they give you the shot and it hurts. They say, "See that didn't hurt, did it?" You start not to trust yourself. Or you say to your mom, "Are you upset?" and the mom says, "No" when she really is. So you stop learning to trust your perception. I tell the story over and over there are hundreds of people I've met who've come from upper class families where they make big incomes and the dad's a doctor, and the kid wants to be a mechanic and work in an auto shop because that's what he loves. The family says, "That's beneath us. You can't do that." So the kid ends up being an anesthesiologist killing three people because he's not paying attention. What he really wants to do is tinker with cars. I tell people you've got to trust your own feelings, your own motivations, what turns you on, what you want to do, what makes you feel good, and quit worrying about what other people say, think, want for you. Decide what you want for yourself and then do what you need to do to go about getting it. It takes work. I always tell people that I read a book a week minimum and at the end of the year I've read 52 books. We're talking about professional books, books on self-help, finances, psychology, parenting, and so forth. At the end of 10 years you've read 520 books. That puts you in the top 1% of people knowing stuff in this country. But most people are spending their time watching TV. W. Clement Stone told me when I went to work for him, "I want you to cut out one hour a day of TV." I said, "OK, what do I do with it?" He said, "Read." He told me what kind of stuff to read. He said, "At the end of a year you'll have spent 365 hours reading. Divide that by a 40 hour work week and that's nine and half weeks of education every year." I thought, "Wow, that's two months." It's like going back to summer school. As a result of that I have close to 8,000 books in my library. The reason I'm on your show instead of someone else is that people like me and Jim Roane and Les Brown and you, read a lot. We listen to tapes and we go to those seminars. That's why we're the people with the information. I always say that your raise becomes effective when you do. You'll become more effective as you gain more skills, more insight, and more knowledge.

Wright

Jack, I have watched your career for over a decade and your accomplishments are just outstanding. But your humanitarian efforts are really what impress me. I think that you're doing great things, not only in California, but all over the country.

Canfield

It's true. In addition to all of the work we do we have all of our books. We pick one to three charities and we've given away over six million dollars in the last eight years, along with our publisher who matches every penny we give away. We've planted over a million trees in Yosemite National Park. We've bought hundreds of thousands of cataract operations in third world countries. We've contributed to the Red Cross, the Humane Society, and on it goes. It feels like a real blessing to be able to make that kind of a contribution in the world.

Wright

Today we have been talking to Jack Canfield, the founder and co-creator of the *Chicken Soup for the Soul* book series, which currently has 35 titles and I'll have to update this. It was 53 million. How many has it been now, Jack?

Canfield

We're almost up to 78 million. We have a book coming out in just a couple of weeks called *Chicken Soup for the Soul of America*. It's all stories that grew out of September 11th and it's a real healing book for our nation. I would encourage your listeners to get themselves a copy and share it with their families.

Wright

I will stand in line to get one of those. Thank you so much being with us on *Conversations on Success*.

About The Author

Jack Canfield is one of America's leading experts on developing self esteem and peak performance. A dynamic and entertaining speaker, as well as a highly sought-after trainer, he has a wonderful ability to inform and inspire audiences toward developing their own human potential and personal effectiveness.

Jack Canfield is most well-known for the *Chicken Soup for the Soul* series, which he co-authored with Mark Victor Hansen, and for his audio programs about building high self-esteem. Jack is the founder of Self-Esteem Seminars, located in Santa Barbara, California, which trains entrepreneurs, educators, corporate leaders and employees how to accelerate the achievement of their personal and professional goals. Jack is also the founder of The Foundation for Self Esteem, located in Culver City, California, which provides self-esteem resources and training to social workers, welfare recipients and human resource professionals.

Jack graduated from Harvard in 1966, received his M.E. degree at the university of Massachusetts in 1973, and an Honorary Doctorate from the University of Santa Monica. He has been a high school and university teacher, a workshop facilitator, a psychotherapist, and for the past 30 years, a leading authority in the area of self-esteem and personal development.

As a result of his work with prisoners, welfare recipients and inner-city youth, Jack was appointed by the state legislature to the California Task Force to Promote Self-Esteem and Personal and Social Responsibility. He also served on the board of trustees of the National Council for Self-Esteem.

Jack Canfield

P.O. Box 30880

Santa Barbara, CA 93130

Email: info4jack@jackcanfield.com

126

Chapter Ten

SANDRA LEE

THE INTERVIEW

David E. Wright (Wright)

Today we are talking with Sandra Lee. Sandra is an internationally published author, speaker, and coach. Her mission is simple: to help people see the good in themselves, inspire them to discover what they want to achieve in life, and guide them to take action. She is president of Success Talks, Inc., and author of *Set Yourself Free: How to Unlock the Greatness within You!* currently printed in five languages. Sandra, welcome to *Conversations on Success!*

Sandra Lee (Lee)

Thank you, David.

Wright

There's a lot written about success and our culture seems to celebrate it, but what is success and why is it important?

Lee

There have been many, many, many definitions of success. And I think success is simply knowing what you want, and having an action plan to get there, and then achieving that plan.

Wright

And it's important because....

Lee

I believe that our lives are meant to be lived moving forward. Our purpose is to learn and grow, and that can mean a lot of different things to a lot of different people. We are all given certain gifts, talents, and interests, and if we're not moving forward then we're really not living life the way that I think we were intended to live it. And so success is a way of measuring our growth, and if we're not feeling successful or we're not achieving any level of success, then we're really not growing and we're not really living our full potential.

Wright

It is then different for everyone? So if it is, when do you know how successful you are or even if you are successful?

Lee

Well, yes, it is different for everyone because what you, David, want to achieve out of life and what I want to achieve out of life can be totally different, but yet we can both be very successful. The method of achieving what we want is going to be different for each person, and if two people are working on the same goals, they may have different approaches. So even if you and I were working on the same goal, the way that you get there might be different than the way that I get there. And as to when you know you are successful, I think that can be different for everyone. I think that one of the pieces that we have to be careful of when we're talking about success is that we not compare ourselves to other people or think that there is only one way to look at success. Success can really be measured against our own personal desires, our personal potential, what it is we want to achieve. So for example, as I've been working on different projects during my life, some have turned out a bit differently than how I originally thought they would. So, although, maybe I didn't reach the exact desired intention of what I thought I was going to reach, I still have been able to say that I am successful.

Wright

Do you have a written definition of success or a verbal definition of success?

Lee

Well, I actually follow much of what Webster's dictionary says, and that is *the achievement of something desired, intended, or attempted*. And that's pretty simple. While I was thinking about the project and success and what is it and why is it important, I pondered my own definition. The dictionary definition is a good starting point. I interpret that to mean achieving or getting to or accomplishing something that we set out to accomplish or something that we set out to attain. I think the more basic the definition we have, the easier it will be for all of us to achieve success. I think sometimes we make success more complicated than it needs to be. There's a wonderful phrase that I learned years ago from my friend and mentor, Jack Canfield, that I use almost daily. It's simply, *"Success by the Yard is Hard, but by the Inch it's a Cinch."* So if we can keep it easy and break it down, we can feel that we're having many successes everyday, even though we might not look at every step as success. Moving forward is the key. Movement toward what we want keeps us excited and engaged in what it is we're working toward. Too often what I see happening is people have a bigger goal and they think that when they reach that goal, that's when the success comes. What they fail to do often is to celebrate the little mini successes that they have along the way to get there. Take writing a book for example. There are numerous steps, as you know, to having the actual printed book in your hand; and for the author, it is important to celebrate each step along the way. For me personally, that's what helps keep the momentum.

Wright

Do you think there's a common thread that runs through the lives of all successful people?

Lee

Yes, David, I believe there are common threads. And I think there are three that somewhat blend together. First, and perhaps most important, I believe that all successful people believe they can be successful. They have the belief that they have the ability to achieve whatever they desire, or the ability to learn what it is they need to learn if they don't have a particular skill yet. And they really believe that they can reach that goal or reach that level of success and that they are worthy of having what it is that they are working toward. I think often one of the reasons people get in the way of themselves of achieving the level of success is at some level they might not think they're really, really able to do it or that they are worthy of having what it is they want. So having a strong belief is important. And a part of that belief is actually seeing ourselves with the success that we are looking to create. We call this visualizing or affirming our success. My home is surrounded with dream boards and dream books and cards with pictures of what I want to create in my life. I believe this is what helps to keep me focused on what I want. And then, of course, the other piece of that is taking action on creating the success that you want. So the element of success is threefold—believing that you can be successful, seeing yourself as successful, and taking action on creating that success.

Wright

Can you be successful and still be miserable? Or does success require a kind of joy and satisfaction?

Lee

I think that because there are many different levels of success and definitions of what being successful is, I think yes, you can reach a certain level of success and still be miserable. For example, let's say a person set out to create a new consulting company. They're of course very excited about it. They work hard and diligently and let's say it turns into a multimillion dollar company. Most people would say, "Wow! That's really successful!" However, in the process perhaps health issues arose or there were family situations that are now not stable or healthy. So this person may have this "successful business," but are they still feeling whole and complete and is their life in balance? If it's not, as a result of that, they might actually be feeling rather miserable.

Another example is a person that sets a goal to run a marathon. They run the marathon but unfortunately they sprain their ankle in the process and now they're miserable. It may be a short term misery, or it might be long term. So as far as what or how much we achieve, this can be different for everybody. For me, personally, balance in my life is very important. I am generally aware of what else is going on in my life as I'm working toward what it is I want to achieve. It's important to me that I don't get to where I want to go and find out that I'm there all by myself, or that I'm there and I'm not healthy, or that I'm there and I'm not happy. So I wouldn't say that success requires a joy and a satisfaction, but for me personally, that would be important to have along the way.

Wright

Following up on that question, do you think you can be financially poor but still considered a success? And can you be financially rich and still considered a failure?

Lee

Yes, I think you could be. Success, of course, in our society a lot of times is equated with money or financial gain or having a nice home and nice cars and perhaps a boat or a summer house. All of those pieces, generally, equate with being successful. However, let's say a person decided they wanted to learn a second language. English is their first language. They decide they want to learn how to speak Spanish and they do. Now they've been successful at learning a second language. This doesn't mean that they're going to have any more money. They may have been "poor" when they started out and they may still be "poor" when they finish their Spanish course, but they've had a success in learning Spanish. Now with being financially rich, you could label yourself as a failure if you've reach that level of being rich and maybe failed at something else along the way. Or perhaps you've reached a level of financial wealth in a way that is not acceptable to you, your values, your family or to society. So I think that, yes, you could be poor and still be successful and be rich and feel like a failure.

Wright

It's like becoming rich selling drugs.

Lee

You're exactly right! Robbing a bank is another example. That could be a temporary gain of a lot of money, but how good are you really going to feel about yourself with that money?

Wright

So what happens if you set your measures and standards for success too low? Could you be cheating yourself out of full success and what that might look like?

Lee

I think, yes, you could. Yet we need to be careful that we don't compare ourselves to others and how others define success. I think that we all have the ability to achieve much more than what we do throughout our lives. I've noticed that I personally go through cycles of success. I may have several months where I'm achieving a lot more and then there might be a couple of months where I don't feel like I'm achieving quite as much. And I think that's a natural cycle of life, much like the ebb and flow of the ocean tide. I believe that generally people are able to achieve even more than what they set out to achieve; however, if what they want to achieve is what is important to them, then I think that's okay. So I would never want to see somebody doing something because somebody told them, "Oh, you could do so much more." And again, I think we can measure that against ourselves. Even some of the goals that I have set for myself, I know I could probably plus those and go a little bit higher, but then when I look at the other parts of my life that are important to me, I say, "Okay, this is good for what I want to achieve now, and I can look at this at another time and decide if I want to raise the bar."

Wright

Are we all equally capable of success or are some people born with a greater likelihood of success than others?

Lee

I believe that we're all born with the ability to be successful in our own way. And the reality is that we also have a circle of influence that plays a part on how successful we become or what level of success we achieve. Studies have shown that, generally, we're born with this ability. As an infant, and even as a young child, we don't know that we cannot be successful! I heard a story that is a good analogy of this. Dozens of frogs were racing to the top of a mountain. One by one, the frogs fell off of the mountain. It was too much for them. Finally, there was just one frog remaining, almost to the top. Those down below were screaming and yelling, "You'll never make it! You'll never make it! You can't do that. Frogs can't climb that high." The frog finally made it to the top and they couldn't believe it. And what they learned later, is that the frog was deaf. The frog couldn't hear all the people telling it that it couldn't be done. I know this is a very elementary example; however, I think it does a good job in making a point. We're born with the ability to be successful and as human beings we are susceptible to allowing ourselves to be influenced by other people. These other people may be people who don't want us to work on a certain goal or maybe they don't want us to be successful because then it threatens their level of success. I understand it to be that it's between the ages of two and nine when we're at our most influential with the conditioning and development of our brain. But it's unlikely that a five-year-old child would be setting goals for what they want to achieve as an adult! So when we get into adulthood we find ourselves ready to work on what it is we want to create in our lives; we've got all of this "stuff" that we've brought with us that holds us back. I call this "stuff" our limiting beliefs. Perhaps we tell ourselves, "I can't dance," or "I'm not very smart," or "I could never achieve THAT!" Often, as young children, we're conditioned to believe certain expectations or conditioned to believe that we're not able to achieve a certain level of success. I recently heard Liz Murray speak. Her story was made into a movie called *Homeless to Harvard*. Both of her parents were drug addicted and alcoholics, and she started supporting the family at age 10. She was homeless at age 17, and then went on to graduate from high school and get a scholarship to Harvard. One of the most fascinating pieces about her story, David, was that she said when she was growing up, she didn't know that the way that she was growing up was not normal—because it was her normal. We all have what we think is normal and what our little box in the world looks like. Sometimes we have to break out of that box and say, "Wow! There is more. I do want more. I deserve more."

Wright

Is there a price one has to pay for success?

Lee

I don't know that I would call it a price, although, we often hear a phrase that goes something like, "Boy, that was a big price to pay for that achievement." I look at it as more of a cost rather than a price. And it is not always dollars. It can cost time, energy, effort, or sacrifices made. We have to take time; we have to work at it; sometimes we have to learn a new skill; sometimes we have to do things that maybe aren't that comfortable for us. So sometimes the cost might be looked at as a little bit of discomfort, but I don't think a person has to sacrifice anything that they don't want to. I think in order to achieve success and to be successful, you can go slowly or you can go fast. And if you go slowly, maybe the cost is going to be a little bit less because you're not sacrificing quite as much. I'm going to use the marathon example again. If I decided that I wanted to run a marathon in the spring, and it's now winter, this would probably be a big cost for me; I'm not even a runner! I've never run a marathon, so I would have a lot of conditioning to do to get there. Now, other people that have run marathons in the past, their price tag probably isn't going to be quite as big because they're already in condition to run a marathon. They already know what they need to do to get there. Author Barbel Mohr in her book, *The Cosmic Ordering Service* says, "There is no reason to make more effort than you enjoy." If you believe in balance in your life, and I do, that says a lot.

Wright

If you knew there was one thing that people who are even more successful than you, are doing something that you are not doing, what do you think that would be?

Lee

I think for me it would probably be what I would call output. You know, just putting in more time toward my goals and what it is I want to achieve. But as I have said earlier, balance is very important to me in my own piece of mind and my inner harmony, so I sometimes go at a pace that might be a little bit slower than one of my counterparts or colleagues, and I'm okay with that. So that's an interesting question and often people say, "Well, yes, I have this, this, this, and this, but my neighbor over here, he has all that . . . plus a sports car! Why does he have that sports car? Or why has this person written one more book? Or why have they run one more marathon?" Generally, it's because they've taken more action on that one particular success. It's basically the age old formula, what you put in is what you get out.

Wright

How do you reach beyond the expectations of other people to find your own level of success?

Lee

Well, I think it's important to have a support group or somebody that will affirm what it is that you're working to achieve. They believe in what you're doing. They want you to be successful. Sometimes the reality is that our closest circle of influence might not be the people that are going to give us the most support or help us to reach beyond some of the limiting expectations that may be within us. I think it's important to find that circle that will help you to work a little bit harder, maybe take one more risk, maybe make that phone call that feels scary, or do something that's outside of your comfort zone. I think the important piece is to take at least one action step every day. Remember, *Success by the Yard is Hard, by the Inch it's a Cinch.* Even if you're taking just one step every day, it will help you to reach beyond where you currently are and help you to achieve your own level of success.

Wright

How does one deal with failures or roadblocks encountered on the way to success?

Lee

I think one of the best ways you can deal with them is to first of all know that they're most likely going to appear and have a plan of what you will do when they show up. I love the analogy taught to me by motivational speaker, Les Brown. He says, "When you fall down, if you look up, you can get up." And I think the bigger our successes or the more that we want to achieve, the more likely it is that we're going to encounter roadblocks and possibly even failures along the way. And I think that's okay. I think we have to give ourselves permission to say that it's okay, this happens. I believe it's just the flow of life. As soon as we set out to do something, if it's not roadblocks or failures, it might be our own internal fear that holds us back. If I say I'm going to move to the west coast, well, all of sudden up comes an array of considerations. "Oh my gosh, how am I going to get there? What am I going to do? I have to sell my place here. How am I going to?" But if we know that obstacles are a part of achieving success, it makes it much easier to handle and deal with them. And if we have an idea of what we might do and ask ourselves, "Okay, when we reach a road-block, maybe we can't knock that roadblock down right away at that time; however maybe there's something else that we can do to keep us moving forward in the interim." For example, let's say you're out to do something and your vehicle breaks down. Now you might be thinking, "Well, I can't get to that appointment because I don't have a car." You can ask yourself if there is another way that you can get to that appointment in time until your car gets fixed.

Wright

Right.

Lee

Then of course, if we think about it, and we allow our creativity to come in, we'll always come up with another way to deal with what's in our way.

Wright

Tell me, is it possible for a person to be highly successful in business and have a balanced healthy lifestyle, and in order for this to be true, would one's spouse and family have to buy into their goals as well?

Lee

David, it would be helpful if they did. I don't know that the family has to buy into it 100%, but it's certainly helpful if they do. If your family, whether that be spouse, children, significant other, are not excited about what it is that you are working on, a couple of things may happen. One, you may still get to that level of success but it might be one of those situations that I had alluded to earlier to the possibility of getting there and then looking back and seeing nobody there with you. This would probably be an empty feeling of celebration. And then it also helps if you're surrounded by people that are encouraging you and are excited about what you're doing. So I think for the people that are heavily involved with their families, it's important that there is involvement. People in my seminars often say to me, "I want to do 'this,' but my spouse doesn't support me in my dream." Or, "I want to do 'this,' but it's going to take too much time away from my children." If there is open communication and they understand why what you want to do is important to you, perhaps they will "come on board" and support you. If your children are old enough, this is a great opportunity to have them work on their goals and share what is important to them. This can actually become a family project; make it fun for everybody. And when everybody is having fun, then you're going to get that affirmation and you're going to get that buy in. When I do work with parents and teachers, I encourage them to create a Classroom Dream Board or a Family Dream Board. This can be a piece of newsprint or poster board. Everyone participates by writing or drawing or posting pictures of what they want to create. Then, I encourage a Victory Wall where kids in a classroom or family members can write what they've accomplished or what they feel good about. The people we spend our time with are our co-creators in life. The more we focus on the positive, the more we will see coming to fruition that what we set out to create. Excitement, enthusiasm and support will take all family members to a higher level of success.

Wright

Well, what a great conversation. I could talk to you all day about this. It's a fascinating subject, one that's interested me since, gosh, the early '70s. But as all good things must come to an end, I want you to know how much I really appreciate you taking this much of your time to answer all these questions. It's just been delightful for me and I've learned a lot.

Lee

I'm glad you have found the information helpful. We can always learn from each other. I've enjoyed my time, too.

Wright

Today we've been talking with Sandra Lee. She is an internationally published author, speaker, and coach. And as I stated in the beginning, her mission is to help people see the good in themselves, inspire them to discover what they want to achieve in life, and guide them to take action to realize their full potential. Sandra, thank you so much for being with us today on *Conversations on Success*.

Lee

Thank you, David.

Sandra Lee is an internationally published author, speaker, and coach. Her mission is to help people see the good in themselves, inspire them to discover what they want to achieve in life, and guide them to take action. Clients include American Greetings, Forest City Enterprises, Institute of Internal Auditors and a variety of Associations. Sandy's first book, *Set Yourself Free: How to Unlock the Greatness Within You!* is now printed in five languages.

Sandra Lee, President

Success Talks, Inc.

PO Box 33593

North Royalton, Ohio 44133-3593

Phone: 440-237-7866 or 800-759-0138

Fax: 440-237-7257

Email: sandra@yourcoachoncall.com

www.yourcoachoncall.com

Chapter Eleven

GREGG FRALEY

THE INTERVIEW

David E. Wright (Wright)

Gregg Fraley is a successful entrepreneur and is now a consultant to the Fortune 500. He conducts "Ideation" sessions for these companies, which are highly structured brainstorming sessions, to develop new product concepts. He speaks and writes on the subjects of Creativity and Innovation, and is a board member of the Creative Education Foundation. Gregg's speeches are about the foundations and building blocks of Innovation—personal creativity. Gregg, welcome to *Conversations on Success.*

Gregg Fraley (Fraley)

Thank you, David.

Wright

Gregg, in looking at your background I note that you've worked in several very different fields in your career, including television production, software, and innovation consulting – you've even done improvisational comedy. What value does such a broad based experience bring to your consulting and speaking customers?

Fraley

Actually, it's even more diverse than it appears... have been a cab driver, bartender, theater manager, and an associated press photographer. The diversity of experience allows me to combine ideas from multiple fields. What allows me to think out of the box so easily is the fact that I've seen the inside of so many different boxes—most problems have already been solved somewhere else, in some other domain, so broad-based knowledge is very helpful in creative problem solving. My experience base also gives me a sense of what people care about in their lives and careers. It gives me a base of life experiences to draw upon for speaking that allows me to make speeches relevant to almost any audience. In other words, I've got a lot of interesting stories to share.

Wright

What was your most interesting experience in the television industry?

Fraley

I was lucky enough to work with Warner Cable's pioneering QUBE two-way cable system in the early '80s. I worked on a program called "Cincinnati Alive" and was part of a team that won an Emmy. Another team I worked on won a cable ACE award for innovation. It's a beautiful thing to work on a high functioning creative team—and it's not an easy thing to create, that wonderful synergy. The first few months of "storming" on that production team was really awful, but we got through it and then wonderful things happened. On Cincinnati Alive, I was fortunate to work with some highly motivated people, who were smart enough to listen to everybody's thinking and create things that were really amazing and out of the box. We were fortunate to have a visionary leader who gave us the support and guidance we needed to succeed. I learned a lot about leadership and creativity in a very concentrated period. While at QUBE I developed the world's first graphics-only interactive game show. It was a case of being the person who took on the unwanted job – I volunteered to be trained in computer technology when nobody else on the production staff would (which led me to my next career). I was able to marry my new software skills with an old skill of classic TV production. The result was a groundbreaking show called *PolyGames*.

Wright

Speaking of software, you were a founder of a software company called Med-E-Systems. I understand you helped create a very innovative product there, tell us about that experience.

Fraley

Med-E-Systems developed the world's first wireless point-of-care prescription system for physicians. Incredible experience to be part of developing that product and go through the process of taking a company public. It was an entrepreneur's dream. My talents were useful in helping define the actual patented product, "Smart Scripts," but also in selling that product, raising capital, and positioning the company for an eventual IPO. Very exciting time and an incredible entrepreneurial learning experience, we went from nothing to a 30 million dollar company in just three years.

Wright

You talk about Creativity & Innovation? What's the difference?

Fraley

Creativity is a widely misunderstood thing. Most folks think of the arts when they think of creativity and that's only one aspect of it. A better definition of Creativity is simply "Novelty that's useful." When you look at it that way, it broadens how you see creativity—and yourself as a creative person. A better route to work can be creative, a great soup, an interesting garden, a new approach to a problem relationship, these are all creative acts and acts people do every day. Creativity is what underlies Innovation, so in a sense it's silly to list them like that... it's like saying, "I like music—and reggae." Still, it's what people understand and I say I'm about Creativity & Innovation because it speaks to the listening of the average person in my audience. The difference is creativity is about foundational attitudes and principles. Those things must be in place in order to be more innovative. Innovation is highly focused creativity.

Wright

Is it really possible to train somebody to be more creative?

Fraley

Yes, absolutely yes. Anybody can improve their productive creative capacity by practicing certain thinking principles and techniques, regardless of IQ, or creative style. There are highly specific creative tools and techniques for improving idea output that anyone can learn and use. The principles and techniques I use, talk about, and write about, include: deferral of judgment as a way of life and staying open to your own ideas and the ideas of others, just that alone will boost your creative productivity. Simple techniques like making lists of ideas without judging and then selecting later are very powerful in allowing creative ideas to emerge from your mind. You have to alternate imaginative thinking and critical thinking—that is, not doing them at the same time. I talk about tolerating ambiguous situations and thoughts, and becoming fluid at generating a large volume of ideas. Just writing ideas down—that simple thing, can have a huge impact on your creativity. And doing this all with a sense of humor helps free your mind up to be more generative.

I've personally experienced the results of creativity training. The training I received years ago was a key component in my taking my business career to the next level. And I'm not standing pat—I'm always looking for ways to boost my creativity and I find new ways all the time.

Wright

What is the importance of creative style?

Fraley

Understanding creative style opens the doors to valuing your own creativity and the creativity of others. We are all creative, but in different ways. There are a lot of myths about creativity—that it's only for a select few people, those with high IQ's, those with obvious artistic ability, or those "big idea" people who are known to "think out of the box." Certainly people with those gifts are creative, but the truth is we are all creative. Creativity is as human as love and tears, and something it would be hard for anyone to get through any given day without. Creative style is about *how* people are creative. Creative style is measurable by psychological assessments, and people break down into two basic camps: Adaptor or Innovator. Adaptive folks solve problems by seeking a "better" way. Innovators look for a "different" way. Both types of creativity are valuable. Both styles have folks with a wide range of talents and knowledge. It's unfortunate that society typically only recognizes out of the box thinkers (Innovators) as the truly creative ones, because adaptive creativity is exactly what's needed in our lives, and our businesses on a day to day basis.

Thinking inside the box can work wonders and its very low risk! Employees looking to make small improvements all the time are what creates smooth running profitable businesses. And employees who are thinking of "home run" ideas are the ones who help companies create their next generations of products and leapfrog process break-through's. We need both styles of creativity, and teams need both to be successful.

Wright

Why don't more managers embrace creativity?

Fraley

Because they don't understand it for one, and because it usually represents a "lack of control" for them. Managers spend their time looking for ways to perfect systems, not reinvent them, and reinvention ideas can be threatening. Brainstorming, a very straightforward and well known creative tool, is often thought to be ineffective. The reason it is considered a waste of time is it's rarely done well. Brainstorming or Ideation as it is sometimes called, is not a skill that is practiced often enough in most organizations. When it's done rarely it's difficult for people to get expansive and difficult for managers to accept that expanded thinking. Managers tend to get where they are in life because they've been highly successful, critical - analytical thinkers and when it comes time to think differently it's uncomfortable. Unless that manager knows how to work with that uncomfortable feeling and knows the opportunity that might be buried in that dis-comfort, they are going to do their best to avoid it. This is truly unfortunate because it means that a key asset, the creative brains of employees, are being stifled.

Wright

I notice you perform a service for large companies called "Ideation." How often are Ideation Sessions successful and what can make them more successful?

Fraley

Ideation is highly structured brainstorming. I've been doing these sessions for larger companies and they can work like magic in generating and developing promising ideas for products and services. I'm amazed that they are not used more often by more companies given their effectiveness. I have a theory about that. Many folks who have been involved in brainstorming sessions leave with a bad taste in their mouth because the sessions are often done without clear objectives and without enough research done ahead of time to make them more meaningful. Also, some brainstorming sessions generate thousands of ideas – and then nothing much is done with them. The ideas aren't "processed" and this has participants thinking they were a waste of time. Fortunately, this doesn't have to be, Ideation sessions done with more research done in advance, more focused objectives, and more tools and techniques foster idea quantity and quality. Finally, there should be specific and visible session follow up. The probability of success is high if sessions are prepared and executed carefully. Ideation is a powerful competitive tool that companies ignore at their peril.

Wright

Why do some companies fail at Innovation?

Fraley

Bluntly? Because their cultures don't support it. Everybody knows deep down that you must innovate to have continuous success, and yet putting a structure in place to create and sustain innovation is something that many companies find very difficult to do. In spite of a lot of lip service, most companies tend to evolve away from their innovative roots. Here's what happens: start-ups are usually a small group of Innovators ("different" thinkers) who invent something new, and they take the company to the first levels of success. As the company grows larger, the skill sets needed to run the company become gradually more adaptive, in other words, they need good detail people to run things. So they hire more of these detail people—adaptors (who think "better") and things go great and the company goes to the next level with better organization and better process. The bad news is that those original Innovators are starting to feel unwanted because nobody wants to listen to their big ideas anymore. And they are excluded from things. Many leave for greener pastures. Nobody cares because it removes a source of conflict. Then an emergency happens— the competition invents an entirely new product and yours is now obsolete. Now you need big ideas again. You look around and realize all the Innovators have left the company because they were made to feel unwanted. Large companies need to remember that big ideas are important to their future—even if they don't need them right now. They need to set up Innovation departments to hold onto their big thinkers, and they need to respect those who think differently, even very differently, if they want the kind of thinking diversity that keeps innovation alive all the time.

The other thing that occurs is that nobody keeps track of ideas. It's so simple and yet it's amazing how overlooked "Idea Management" is. Companies throw ideas away. It's interesting how often I'll lead a session and somebody will mention a really great idea and somebody will say, "Jim thought of that three years ago." Too bad nobody wrote it down or banged it into a centrally accessible database! Ideas die if they are not willfully kept alive. There are some amazing new web-based tools for idea management that help keep the idea factory in motion, and companies should make use of them.

Wright

I notice that you did Improvisation with Players Workshop of Second City. What's the relationship of Improvisation to business creativity?

Fraley

It's closer than you might think. Really, an improvisational actor has to be two things, a good listener, and a good "reactor" to situations in a scene. The same thing is true for a business person. A business person has to be a good listener—to customers, to team members, employees, and they need to react, like an improviser does, with authenticity, honesty, and creative ideas to solve problems. What it comes down to in a sense is training yourself to trust your own intuition. Your intuition is almost always right. Many of us have lost touch with what our intuition is saying to us because we are over-thinking and over-analyzing things and it can lead us into mistakes. In an "improv," if you think about what a player is saying and how you might react to it, its too late—the scene passes you by. You have to listen with your mind and your heart and respond with authenticity and that's what improvisational acting training helps you learn to do. In a sense that is not about thinking more, it's about drawing from the deepest knowledge base you have, your own intuition.

Wright

How does creativity relate to selling?

Fraley

Creativity is the most underutilized tool of all for selling. All good sales people are creative; they find novel ways to reach people, talk to people, present to people, and ultimately close deals with people. You can apply creative thinking and creative thinking tools to any sales challenge, but this rarely happens. It's unfortunate that most sales training is focused exclusively on either situation analysis or persuasion techniques. You need to know those things of course, but none of the sales books or sales trainers tell you what to do when the situation analysis says, as an example, "You need to get to the CEO." So, *how* do you get to the CEO? They leave it up to you to figure that out, and they give you few tools to help you get better answers, better options on *how to actually do it*. You are up the proverbial creek without a paddle. Creativity is the paddle! It's a real opportunity to improve sales force productivity that few organizations take advantage of.

Wright

Were you ever in sales?

Fraley

I still am! We're all sales people! But, yes, I was an account executive in the software industry for several years before I moved on to marketing and then ownership roles. I sold mainframe software systems, and then later on applications in manufacturing, health care and wireless infrastructure. Sales is challenging and I empathize with people facing the day to day challenge of it.

Wright

What's in your future?

Fraley

I've just finished a novel that illustrates the power of creative thinking and I'm looking around for a publisher. I've just started writing a second book on the role of creativity in selling. I was just published as an illustrator for the first time – a book called, *Moderating to the Max*, and I do a lot of drawing simply for the fun of it. I use some of my own drawing work in my keynotes – I use PowerPoint as a sort of canvas. I'll continue working with companies to develop new products and I'll continue to speak and write about my passion in life – creativity.

Wright

Well, what an interesting conversation. I appreciate all that you have shared with us today, as I am sure our readers will as well. Thank you for being with us today on *Conversations on Success*.

Fraley

Thank you, David.

About The Author

Gregg Fraley is a successful consultant to the Fortune 500. He conducts "Ideation" sessions for these companies, which are highly structured brainstorming sessions, to develop new product concepts. Gregg's speaking topic is Creativity & Innovation, and his career direction is to do more speaking and writing somewhat less consulting.

To clarify Gregg's interpretation of Creativity & Innovation: Creativity is usually interpreted as "arts" or "self-expression" and not typically as problem solving, or decision making. That's why the "& Innovation" is included in his tag line. Gregg's professional experience is geared to using creativity to do something useful in a business sense; developing new products and services, having more business ideas, and solving sticky business challenges. His keynote "The Creative Choice" is oriented to a general audience and is geared to personal creativity and problem solving. For a business audience the tenor of the speech changes to be more focused on product development and business challenges.

Gregg lives in Chicago with his best friend and wife, who luckily happen to be the same person.

Gregg Fraley

1205 East Madison Park

Chicago, IL 60615

773-536-9630

gregg@dsfraley.com

www.greggfraley.com

Chapter Twelve

SCOTT T. BURROWS

THE INTERVIEW

David E. Wright (Wright)

Today we're talking to Scott Burrows. Scott's a renowned Professional Motivational and Inspirational Speaker, International Business Owner, Wheelchair Athlete and now an Author.

In 1983, at the age of 18, he played one year of college football under legend head coach Bobby Bowden at Florida State University, and was also ranked number one in the State of Florida's light heavy weight Kick Boxing Division.

In 1984, at the age of 19, he was also involved in a horrific automobile accident that changed his life forever. Scott broke his neck, cervical six and seven vertebrates, was left paralyzed from the chest down, and diagnosed a quadriplegic. In the days that followed he was told that, due to the severity of his spinal cord injury, he would be confined to a wheel chair for the rest of his life and never walk again. Today, he is not only a survivor, but one of the few in the world that turned the impossibilities of every walking again into reality!

With his powerful presentations, Scott moves people into action by challenging them to go after their own challenges, face their fears, and take more meaningful risks in both their personal and professional lives by welcoming and embracing unexpected change and adversity. Scott, welcome to *Conversations on Success.*

Scott Burrows (Burrows)

Thank you. It's truly my pleasure to be part of this experience.

Wright

Tell us about your life prior to the automobile accident you were involved in on that fateful day of November 4th, 1984.

Burrows

Well, I was born in Northbrook, Illinois, just outside Chicago. I lived there until the age of three when dad moved the family to Lake Geneva, Wisconsin. When I turned eight, my parents wanted change so they decided to move the family to a small town in Florida called Stuart where they still reside today.

Growing up, sports were my thing. I started karate when I was eight, and by the time I reached 15, I'd earned my first-degree black belt in Pi Lum Kung Fu. When I was 17, I started fighting in the professional kickboxing association with a record of 4-0; and by the time I turned 18, I had earned the number one ranking in the light heavy weight kick boxing division in the state of Florida. My most memorable fight was the time I knocked out my opponent in 42 seconds in the first round. It was unbelievable! My last fight was filmed by ESPN. They said they were going to air two out of the six fights that night. Unfortunately, my fight never made it on air, but I looked at it this way: My time was going to come!

When I was five, dad introduced me to the game of golf, and over the years I competed and eventually made the high school golf team with some success! As a freshman in high school, I also tried out for the football team and I worked hard for the opportunity to play...and I did. I started and lettered at the tight end position, and in my senior year our team earned conference champs.

During this time, I was being recruited and offered football scholarships, but I turned them down because I wanted to play for Florida State University's head coach, Bobby Bowden. When no scholarship was offered in my direction, I decided to be a "walk-on." I was one of those guys willing to pay my own way to play. (Okay, Dad and Mom were willing to help out there!) To stay in shape for the upcoming season I tried out for the track team and participated in six events, broke two school records: one in the triple jump and the other in the 440

440 relay. I also took the 880-yard run to the state finals where I took 8th place and was voted MVP. What a ride!

When I joined FSU's football team it was an amazing experience. To be pushed at that level on a day-to-day basis by one of the finest coaching staffs in the country was a great privilege. I had the chance to rub elbows with some incredible athletes like Heisman Trophy candidate, Greg Allen - and a future Super Bowl Champion for the Washington Redskins, Martin Mayhew.

Going into my sophomore year, I decided that college football at this level was just over my head, so I decided to focus on my professional kickboxing career. I felt I could take it much further than football; it was just a gut feeling, but to this day, no regrets and I can honestly tell you I was having one of those mountain top experiences and my future looked bright. Times were great...I was dating my high school sweetheart...I had amazing friends, I was involved in a fraternity and I had a loving family, and it was also during this time that I experienced some dramatic changes in my life and I found myself surrounded by more fear, more doubt and more uncertainty than I ever imagined possible.

It was one of those sunny afternoons in Tallahassee, Florida and a bunch of us had planned a beach weekend. It was eight o'clock at night when we set up camp and built a small fire. Right after that, a friend of mine challenged me to a foot race. Now being the competitive guy that I am, I took off my tennis shoes, bent down into my running stance waiting to hear the word go, and when I did all I could feel was the cool night air blowing through my hair. With each step I could feel the sand pressing between my toes, and as I crossed that imaginary finish line, I could taste the salt in the cool night air. It was one of the best runs I've ever experienced.

When we got back to camp I was asked to ride with a friend everyone called *Beeper*, to go find more wood for the bonfire we hoped would last all night. I climbed into the passenger seat, closed the door, and off we went. Driving too fast, and not realizing that he had been drinking, he lost control of his car, hitting a mound of sand and sending the car hurling into the air. As it tumbled back to earth, end over end, my mind had no time to comprehend that in that one fateful moment on November 4th, 1984, my life would change forever...

Wright

So it was a one-car accident, no one else was involved except the car you were in.

151

Burrows

Yes, that's right.

Wright

How difficult was it to fight back emotionally, mentally and physically after your doctors told you you'd broken your neck, resulting in quadriplegia, and you'd be confined to a wheel chair for the rest of your life?

Burrows

It was one of the toughest days of my life. I kept thinking to myself – is what I'm being told absolutely true? If so, what would this mean? How would I learn to cope with total confinement? Would I ever be able to hug my parents, my brother and sister, my girlfriend, again?

Wright

I can't imagine. Oh my.

Burrows

The first time I came to, I was aware of doctors and nurses standing over me. I was numb from my shoulders all the way down to my toes. I remembered having this itch on the side of my face, and no matter how hard I tried to scratch it, I couldn't. Every time I tried to move my arms, they just laid there limp. It was so surreal...my brain was fully functional, but my arms would not obey the simple command to move.

Then I watched as my clothes were being cut off with a pair of scissors and as they were being removed I could see the blood and I started to wonder just how bad could it be? Almost immediately after that, I experienced the most unimaginable excruciating pain coming from both sides of my head, close to my temples. It felt like my head was just lodged into a vice grip and someone was tightening down on it slowly. What I didn't know was my doctors were screwing two metal bolts into my scull with steel screws, to stabilize my neck—a technique known today as spinal traction. I screamed...pleading for the pain to stop. My vision began to darken and I thought to myself, "This is it, I'm going to die". It was then that I prayed to God for a second chance in life.

The next time I opened my eyes, I realized my prayers were answered, thank goodness. I was in a room all alone when a doctor walked in and introduced himself as Dr. Stringer, who came in with good news and bad news. The good news was that Beeper had made it through just fine. The bad news is, "Scott, *you broke your neck and there is spinal cord damage, leaving you paralyzed from your chest down and diagnosed a quadriplegic."* Then over the weeks that followed, I was being told by my doctor that I'd be confined to a wheelchair for the rest of my life, and finally that I may be dependent on my friends and family to take care of my basic daily needs. It was the scariest experience in my life.

Wright

For most people there's a turning point after dealing with such adversity. Can you tell our readers if and when that happened to you?

Burrows

Sure. You know, we all deal with change in our lives and when we least expect it some new unexpected changes always seem to appear right around the corner. Just as I was settling into the changes of my new circumstances, some newer life threatening changes surfaced. Over the next 45 days, I watched my body weight plummet from that of a 185-pound thoroughbred to that of a 140-pound weakling. I came down with a severe case of pneumonia, then one evening, I lost my breath, my right lung collapsed, tubes were being inserted into my body, blood clots formed in both my legs, then I was diagnosed with the life threatening pulmonary embolism, which means a blood clot is lodged in the lung...the same pulmonary embolism that took NBC correspondent David Bloom's life while he was covering the war in Iraq in 2003.

And yet, it was during this time, as I was fighting for my life, I was trying to figure how in the world could I turn this around? And it was then that a friend of mine came to my thoughts. His name is Royal West, my coach and my karate instructor, when I was eight years old. I remembered him teaching us the one third's in life. He said, *"Just like anything difficult or anything challenging in life, one third of us will lose interest over a short period of time, one third of us will challenge ourselves to a point we no longer want to be challenged, and one third of us will work hard for opportunity, persevere and be resilient. And if you choose that, then maybe you'll earn yourself a black belt someday."*

It was at that moment that I realized being paralyzed or not, I'm still in control of the choices in my life. I could choose to live and embrace the change I was experiencing. Or I could choose to die. I could choose to believe that what I'm being told is absolutely true (that I'd never walk again and be confined to this wheelchair for the rest of my life), or I could choose to believe, if I gave it my best shot...if I was willing to fight the fight of my life...work hard for opportunity, that with a little luck and a lot of prayer, maybe, someday I could turn the impossibility of ever walking again into a reality. For me that was **THE defining moment** that made me realize I'm still in control of the choices in my life. I could choose to fight or I could choose to give in, it was 100% up to me.

Wright

Scott, how did you acquire such a positive mental attitude during one of the most trying, difficult and frustrating times of your life?

Burrows

You know, lying there on my back during the first 45 days, I realized that I had a choice: I could choose how I wanted to experience this experience. Through my years of sports, one of the biggest attributes continually pounded into our heads from our coaches was **attitude**. They taught us that our attitudes can make or break success.

With that in mind, I started to realize that if I could somehow tap into my inner strength, pray for God to help me do this, whether I ever walked again or not, at least having a positive mental attitude during the darkest times of my life it could give me the inner strength and courage to get up everyday and prepare myself for the fight of my life despite the ongoing stress, the frustrations, discouragements and disappointments, the overwhelming fears, uncertainty and doubts and especially the pain.

You know, I'll never forget one morning when my doctor came in and said, "Scott, we need to get pure oxygen into your weaken body and there's only two ways to do it." He said, "The first way is to hook you up to a machine that will breathe for you, which requires surgery, **OR** we can put a claustrophobic mask over your face with an oxygen line attached to it and you can breathe on your own." I'll never forget looking at him and saying, "That sounds like a *no brainer choice to me, surgery versus no surgery.*"

Then he said, "You know, I guess it would appear that way, but unfortunately there's a Big catch." He said, "You'd need to stay awake for the next 24 hours and monitor every single breath to make sure you're taking in as much pure oxygen as possible because your lungs are so weak from your paralysis." Then he said, "Are you up to it?" And it was then that I realized that my doctor was giving me an opportunity; an opportunity to step in and try to retake control of my paralysis and I realized if I didn't take this risk in my life, I'd be risking even more.

And so it began. I started breathing in and out...in and out...in and out...for the next 24-hours, and it was in the wee hours of the morning when my mind drifted off to a time I was 15 years old and I was invited to the high school prom. I was so excited that when I went home to tell my parents, my dad was so excited he handed me the keys to his work El Camino and said, "Have fun!" Now, I wasn't sure dad had the same vision on how I'd like to experience my prom, so I said, "Thanks but no thanks. I'm going to borrow our neighbor's new Cadillac to make an impression on my date," and I did!

We had a blast and I drove that Cadillac like I owned it. At the end of the evening I dropped off my date, headed home and took a turn I've taken so many times in the past, only this time it had started to rain. The Cadillac decided to hydroplane around that turn. I hit a small metal post sticking out of the ground and did $900 worth of damage to the passenger side of my neighbor's car. I couldn't believe it, just my luck!

I drove home, still not believing what had happened. I pulled into our driveway, parked the car, then went into my room trying to think of a great story to tell my dad so he might consider allowing me to use his car insurance to pay for those damages! Always thinking.

My sister Heidi was the first one to my room the next morning and said, "Dad wants to see you outside right now because he wants to know what happened to the Cadillac."

I went outside and told him the truth, kind of. I told him that on my way home last night after I dropped off my date, a dog had run out in front of me; I said, "I'd turned the wheel real fast and lost control of the car and hit a tree instead." "Aren't you proud of me dad for not taking out that dog?" I asked him. Well, he just stopped and gave me **that look**. You know the one...the one that says he knows I'm not telling the full truth; the look that says, "You're paying for those damages, Scott!" And it was then that dad starts telling me a story I'd heard before: Just how difficult life was when he was growing up in high school, not having access to a car, having to walk both ways, rain or shine and my dad lived up north, so I had the snow version on that story.

It was then, lying on my back, breathing in and out during those 24-hours that I think I realized what life lesson dad was trying to teach me back then. I think what he was trying to say was "Son, you need to be more accountable and responsible for the choices that you make in your life." And it was then that I decided it was time to dig deep, search within and try to tap into my inner strength to give me the strength, courage and positive mental attitude to help me get through this experience. I then decided to take accountability for being a passenger in my friend's car.

I stopped asking the WHY questions. Questions like: Why did this have to happen to me? Why quadriplegia? Why of all things, my life was heading in such a great direction?

Then I started asking myself a new set of questions, good question in my mind's eye. I started asking the **WHAT** questions. Questions like: What can I do today to better prepare myself mentally for the fight of my life? What do I need to do to let my team of therapists know that I want to be pushed especially during the days I don't want to be pushed?

And when I started doing these things (changing the way I was thinking), I started making more forward progress than I could have ever imagined! You know what's funny? Just a few years ago I was asking myself one of those WHAT questions: What in the world does a guy who hobbles on a cane gotta do to find a girl to fall in love with him, and wouldn't you know, just when I started asking myself that question, I met Mona, whom I asked to marry about a year later. She's incredible! Never met anyone like her before and she's such a strong willed person who gives back to so many. I'm very lucky and blessed to have such a special person in my life.

Wright

Tell me about the physical rehabilitation and what it must have been like to work with your team of doctors, nurses, therapist and how they responded when you moved your big right toe, for the first time just one eighth of an inch.

Burrows

My mom was visiting me when my doctor came in on his morning rounds. He'd grab my big right toe as usual and ask me to move it, but I never could. But on this particular morning I said, "Hey Doc, I was thinking last night, that maybe if you put some pillows underneath my feet so I could see my toe, maybe I'd have a better chance of moving it. I've always been more successful in my life with a visual queue."

So he did. He put some pillows under my feet and when he did, I focused like I've never focused before, then I pushed. I pushed hard. I gave it my all and my right toe moved one eighth of an inch. Now I realize that doesn't seem like a lot, but to a quadriplegic, that's like moving a mountain. And it was then that I started to dream again. I started to ask the question so many of us were asking back then: "What do you think Doc; do you think I'll ever walk again?" And we would get the normal answers, answers like, "It's really not uncommon for quadriplegics to move a muscle, a finger and maybe even a toe, but what's rare is for a quadriplegic to walk again."

Honestly, the news was always discouraging, but I never bought into it. I never believed them because I was convinced my doctor didn't know me and what I might be capable of doing. So I continued to focus on rehabilitation and some five months later, my therapist wheeled me up to a set of parallel bars. She had two guys lift me up and out of my wheelchair. After they'd stabilized my body, my stomach and legs, Leslie, my therapist said, "Try to take a step if you can." So I gave it my all and moved my right leg forward about three inches. I was blown away! But I knew right then, that the fight of my life was paying off and over time I convinced myself that if I never gave up, who knows how far I could take this.

Wright

We just lost Christopher Reeve recently and he had a lot of those stories to tell. It's devastating we know, but with the right mental adjustments do you think more people can handle that sort of paralysis and maybe come out on the other side like you did?

Burrows

That's a hard question to answer, but today, so many things are being done to help people who suffer spinal cord injuries, especially in the first few hours of the injury. Today, it's my understanding that people who suffer a spinal cord injury after the first few hours are injected with steroids that helps reduce swelling in the neck to prevent more damage to the spinal cord. In some cases it may actually limit the amount of paralysis that person would have suffered otherwise.

You know, two things happen when you break your neck and your spinal cord is injured: You will either sever the spinal cord, like I believe Christopher Reeve did, or you damage it; but either way the chances of your being in a wheelchair for the rest of your life is most likely inevitable. That's just how it is.

Now, when a person doesn't sever their spinal cord, then your brain might be able to communicate with some of your paralyzed muscles over time, which means some of your muscle may actually return to have some sort of function, which you can use. That's why today, most people don't realize it's not uncommon for quadriplegics to move muscles in their arms, maybe their legs and even a toe, but what's uncommon is for them to walk.

The hardest thing to do, through my experience, was to train other muscles that were coming back to do more than they were originally designed to do, to carry the weight for the other paralyzed muscles. That's what I had to do and it took me years and years to put it all together with my team and figure out a way to walk with paralysis. Look at Reeves, how many years of fighting did it take him to move his finger? To come out on the other side is an impossible question to answer, but if you give up despite the improbabilities you may be facing, you'll never know!

Today, I'm very blessed. It took teams of people, doctors, nurses, therapist, family members and close friends, friends like John Salvador, Brendan McCarthy, Hank Dobbs, Steve Muro, Todd Laycock, and Rick Justice, just to name a few. It took tons of self-determination, a positive mental attitude and the will to believe I could turn the impossibilities of walking again into a reality. Today I use a cane to get around, yet it's my goal to this day that if I keep pushing myself, keep training, keep fighting the paralysis that maybe I'll turn another dream into a reality and run again.

Wright

Once you achieve the impossible, tell me what life was like for you when you re-entered the world of society with such physical limitations and confinement.

Burrows

It was a reality check, but I had to learn to adapt and be more flexible to a changing body. I had to focus on my strengths and not dwell on my weaknesses. On a lighter note, once I learned how to drive again, I started getting comfortable with handicap parking! I became the designated driver to my friends, especially during the holidays...Oh the perks!

Wright

I've got a good friend that had two legs and one arm blown off in Nam and he's in a wheel chair, and does very well as a matter of fact. I asked him what the worst thing was about it, he said "Well when I re-entered the walking people, and they all patted me on top of the head. I hated that because they messed my hair up.

Burrows

I had the same experience so I kept my hair real short! Too funny!

Wright

What inspired you to go back to college, taking your first job with Northwestern Mutual Life Insurance Company as an agent? And why did you choose to leave that career five years later to start up your own international export company and speaking business?

Burrows

After college, a good friend of mine, Steve Muro, arranged an interview for me with Jim Erb, Sr., the General Agent for Northwestern Mutual Life Insurance Company in Tampa. He hired me as a *Special Agent* to sell life and disability insurance and financial products to the professional market place, and I did that for five years. At the end of my fifth year I qualified as a Provisional Member of the Million Dollar Round Table, know as MDRT. MDRT is an independent organization, unique only to the life insurance industry and it represents over 485 insurance companies. It's a 100% commission driven reward, which only 4-6% of my peers from around the world qualify for yearly.

The annual meeting for MDRT was in Dallas, Texas that year and it was amazing. Just to run with some of the best of the best producers in the world was something special for me. There were almost 8,000 people on the last day in this auditorium listening to the President, Lyle Blessman welcoming the guest speakers to the platform to inspire us all, speakers like Jason Hall and Pat Williams. As I sat watching in my seat I remembered telling myself that maybe someday Scott, you'll be recognized and be invited to speak on the platform and address some of the best of the best in the insurance industry, and it's a dream I still have today. I can honestly say I was having another one of those mountaintop experiences again in my life and I was so looking for the opportunity to qualify for MDRT the following year, but that all changed one day I was driving to an appointment when a 70-year-old man, driving his car, ran a stop sign. As I tried to avoid the collision, our cars collided.

Fortunately, he was fine, but I had injured my right elbow. My ulner nerve, which controls the strength in my right hand, was damaged, limiting my strength and making it difficult for me to grip my cane. After surgery, the strength in my right hand didn't come back and it was advised by my doctors that I reside in a wheelchair if I wanted to remain in outside sales. But I'd fought so hard and so long to come out of that chair, I made a difficult choice and informed my new General Agent, Joe Teague that I was going to move on.

Later that year my brother Mark and my dad, who are both consulting agronomists, (soil doctors) to golf courses around the world introduced me to some contacts they had in Singapore... guys who are golf course superintendents that wanted custom blended golf course fertilizers from the United States. They thought it could be a lucrative business opportunity for me because of my business background, so I went to the library, learned the export business, opened up a company called *Global Golf Group*, paired up with a top notch fertilizer company in Florida, called Harrell's Fertilizer, who produce some of the finest custom blended fertilizers in the state of Florida, and financed this new venture with everything I had.

Within the first year I had sales of over $1.5 million. I've had the opportunity to travel and promote the business throughout Southeast Asia, like Singapore, Malaysia, Taiwan, Indonesia and Hong Kong. One of Global Golf's premier clients is in Hong Kong, the Discovery Bay Golf Club, which is the premier golf course in Hong Kong today and it has one of the finest golf course superintendents in Asia, Lee Sellars.

You know, it was a few years ago that I also wanted to diversify and do something I've always had a passion for and that was Motivational Speaking. So many people I've met over the years told me that I'd be great at it because I have a unique inspirational story of overcoming adversity that could challenge people in so may ways. Today I've turned that dream into a reality and I'm traveling around the country speaking to so many different groups and business organizations, high schools and even colleges, sharing a story that's personal in nature, that's real close to my heart. I actually relive part of my accident experience with my audience. I roll out in a wheelchair, and then at the appropriate time, I say, "Don't let other people's beliefs determine what you believe you can or cannot do in your own life," then I get out of my wheelchair and walk with my golf club as a cane.

Now, you might be asking why a golf club? Because I'm also an 18-handicap golfer from the men's tees, believe it or not!

Wright

How has sports played a factor in both your personnel and professional life?

Burrows

It's played a HUGE part. Today, I play full contact wheelchair rugby, AKA **Murderball**, and I'm training to qualify to make the next Paralympic Quad Rugby Team that will compete in Beijing China in 2008. I also scuba dive, spearfish, parasail, ride wave runners, go lobster hunting, compete in wheelchair marathons and I've sky dived from 10,000 feet and freefell for over 40 seconds. Speaking of Murderball, a few years ago Directors Henry-Alex Rubin and Dana Adam Shapiro produced a film about quadriplegics who play full-contact rugby in Mad Max-style wheelchairs who've overcome unimaginable obstacles to compete in the Paralympic Games in Athens, Greece. A&E bought the rights and the World Premiere was held on January 21st, 2005 at the Sundance Film Festival in Park City Utah. What's fascinating to me is that my coach, Joe Soares, for the Tampa Generals Quad Rugby Team is the main character. If you're looking for an attitude adjustment "Murderball," the movie is beyond powerful and inspiring. It's a movie not to be missed!

Sports have always played a big part in my life because it's about competing with yourself or others. You use different approaches, tactics and strategies to help win and it's amazing how those tactics can actually run parallel to the tactics you can use in business. On a golf course you have peaks and valleys, sand traps and water, yet some of the best golfers in the world still find themselves in the woods from time to time. You can compete with yourself or you can compete with others. Scores are kept to monitor your progress. In business world we call them goals and to get there it takes hard work, sacrifice and concentration, as it does in golf. And it's within our sacrifices and within our setbacks that we have to keep swinging in life.

It's the power behind the swing that creates the momentum that we can use in both our personal and professional lives that can help us continue to move forward, especially during times of adversity. For me, it took years to adapt and be flexible to a changing body, to focus on my strengths and not dwell on my weaknesses. All of these things have allowed me over the years to get my golf handicap down to an 18 from the men's tees and put myself in a situation to compete and at times, beat able-bodied golfers, not to mention the success I've had in the business world!

Wright

It would be tough, knowing that I'm worse than that. And I'm not in a wheel chair or walking with a cane.

Burrows

Speaking of golf, for my honeymoon I took my beautiful wife Mona, my pride and joy, my inspiration, my rock, my true love, a women who means so much to me and it's my hope someday that will have a child together...anyway., I took her to a beautiful resort in the Caribbean that offered two sports that we love to do together, one which is scuba diving and the other is, of course, golf. And the day came when we decided to play a round of golf and we were paired up with a man named John. He was in his mid 50s, and on our way to the first hole he said, "Scott, go ahead and go first."

So I took out my golf club and hobbled over to the first hole, bent down and placed my tee firmly in the ground, placed my golf ball on it, took my stance, and it was then that I decided that this would be a great opportunity for me to make an impression on my new golfing buddy, John, and my new bride. I decided that if I could swing my club faster than ever before, then maybe my golf ball might go that much further. I took this monster swing. I swung my golf club so fast that my momentum took me off my feet and onto the ground. So there I was, lying there in the middle of the golf course looking like a beached whale, and to make matters worse—when I turned around, I noticed my golf ball was still standing firmly on my tee! I couldn't believe it. So much for first impressions.

Later that day when we'd finished our round, John tallied up the scores and I asked him how I did. "Not bad," he said. "I shot a 91." I congratulated him, but he just looked at me and said, "Thanks, but I'm the one who should be congratulating you because you beat me by two strokes."

I just love to compete! It's in my blood. Then he turned to me and said, "Scott, if you don't mind me asking, what happened to you and why do you walk with a cane?" So, I told him what I've already shared with you, but the short version, only he started laughing.

When I asked him why he was laughing, he said, "I'm not laughing at you Scott, I'm laughing with you. Do you know how difficult it's going to be for me to go home and tell my golfing buddies that a walking quadriplegic just beat me in a round of golf!"

Another sport I have a passion for is snow skiing, which I never did prior to my accident. A friend of mine, Brad Blessman, seven years after I was injured, challenged me to do something that would test me more physically, mentally and emotionally than the days I challenged myself to come out of my wheel chair. He wanted to teach me how to snow ski from 12,000 feet above sea level way up in the Rocky Mountains and he wanted to do it teaching me standing up, on my own two feet. The first day and a half, I fell down so much my hips turned black and blue and Advil became my best friend. Brad kept telling me, "If you want to be a successful snow skier Scott, then you need to lean forward while you're traveling downhill; be willing to allow gravity help to assist you down the mountain, be willing to break your fall line, you can do it."

But who in the world wants to travel downhill at a very fast speed knowing you might fall? Nobody! So what do we do? We resist and it's in the resisting that we turn black and blue! At the end of the second day, I gave in and stopped resisting and I found myself under Brad's coaching skiing in full control under my own weight for about 50 yards, and it was then, almost 12,000 feet above sea level when I lost it emotionally. The sensation returned to me...that lost sense of exhilaration...what I had lost on the beach moments before my accident. Skiing through the air was the closest thing to sprinting that I had ever known. The sensation of running had returned and yes, I found a new passion in my life. I also learned a new life lesson. Be willing to take a risk and break the fall line when it comes to our challenges! Be willing to fall down, fail, but treat it as a learning experience. It's within those experiences that unforeseen opportunities have a tendency to show themselves more often than not.

Wright

When you consider the choices that you've made over the years, has faith played an important role in your life?

Burrows

It's played a phenomenal role: I never blamed God for what happen to me. I truly believe that when things happen in life they happen for a reason and being a Christian it's reinforced my faith. These days, I'm just thankful each morning when I wake up and place my feet firmly on the ground that it's going to be a great day!

Wright

When you speak to businesses and organizations now around the country, do you ever hear back from the people?

Burrows

I get amazing testimonials! I'm blessed that I'm having the opportunity to touch so many people's lives. One thing I love to share with them are three strategies that I've been using over the last 20 years that have helped me improve my mental focus and turn my personal and professional setbacks into roaring comebacks and it's my hope it will do the same for them.

The first strategy has to do with having a positive attitude. It's what we choose to believe about our attitudes despite our circumstances that can play a significant role in our successes and failures. That's why the old saying is "If you think you can or cannot you're probably right." I believed that being optimistic and having a positive attitude, being mentally tough during my days of total physical paralysis whether I ever walked again or not would give me the inner strength and drive to keep pushing forward. And over the years I credit the belief in my attitude that has gotten me to where I am today. Are attitudes are like that of a foundation. Without a good one our foundations will certainly crumble.

The second strategy is risk taking. I've grown up believing my coaches that the most successful people in the world are those willing to take some degree of risk in their lives. They are the ones who will take a risk and open their hearts and minds to new opportunities, new experiences and new challenges knowing if they do they will be rewarded in some way, shape or form. With risk comes not only rewards, but also unforeseen setbacks and it's within our setbacks that we can find new opportunities that can add tremendous value to our personal and professional lives if we just open our eyes to see it.

The third strategy is putting together a plan. It's writing down our short and long-term goals and viewing them every other day. After you have a plan, it's about preparation and commitment. Once you can truly feel your ready to commit then it's about implementation. You have to want it badly, you have to be prepared for the obstacles and you need to be accountable in the process. It's never losing site of the common goal that can help us make the improbable a little more probable.

Wright

I understand you're planning on writing an autobiography in the near future that can help your audiences understand the details and experiences of your amazing life, of over coming adversity. Is that true?

Burrows

Yes, it sure is. That's my next Dream!

Wright

Realizing, as I'm sure you do after all you've been through that most people are handicapped some way or the other by their own devices, either through self fulfilling prophecy, they think they can't do things and I guess the audiences that you speak to, you challenge and motivate them. If you had to say any one thing to our readers today about how they can use what you have gone through to help them get through the struggles of their life. What would you say to them?

Burrows

Life is full of unforeseen circumstances; it has many challenges and our challenges are and always will be never ending despite our circumstances; yet we still have a choice in how we respond. We can choose to resist or we can choose to face them and try to conquer, and I've always believed that if we face them, a couple things are going to happen: We're either going to succeed or we're going to fail, but if you view failing as I do as an opportunity to learn from the experiences, then it really isn't failure after all. If anything, you'll learn something new about yourself, and who knows...you might even pick up a new skill that you never knew you had!

You know one of my biggest adversities I faced was dealing with fear. I found myself submerged in the fear of uncertainty, change and failure and it was then that I took my dad's advice. The first time I saw my dad, lying on my back, paralyzed from my chest down, he said, "Son, don't resist the change you're experiencing in your life and just let it happen; go with it and if you do, you'll come out on top, but it's going to take some time." And it was then that I decided to stop resisting my fears and when I did, I found myself being able to cope with them, not that they ever went away, but I found myself taking more control of my life! It's when we're willing to leave our know environment, which most people call their *comfort zones*. I like to call it a place of our self perceived limitations, because it's a place we're not challenging ourselves; it's a place we're not growing or trying anything new, and it's a place we're not changing. To stay there too long can be as paralyzing as physical paralysis was to me and to leave it requires courage, but the reward can be tremendous growth.

Wright

What a great conversation, Scott. I want to really thank you for taking this time today with me to answer all these questions and to tell our readers about the adversity and the winning attitudes of a walking quadriplegic. I've never heard of that term before, until you just used it.

Burrows

Thank you, I've enjoyed the experience.

Wright

Today we've been talking to Scott Burrows. He is an inspirational, motivational and adversity speaker. He's an international business owner, wheelchair athlete and author. As we have heard here, at the age of 19 he was in a horrific automobile accident and now he has come out of his wheel chair to talk to thousand of people in the business community and other organizations through out the country, to challenge them to be better and take more meaningful risks in both their personnel and professional lives. Scott, thank you so much for being with us today on *Conversations on Success*.

Burrows

It's been a real pleasure! And I'd just like to say it's my hope for the people reading this that I've challenged you out of life's corner, that you'll look for opportunities to grow and you'll search for the passion in your life. Because when you find your passion, you'll find your drive. And during times of adversity, it's also my hope that you'll take a risk and break the fall line in both your personal and professional lives; that you'll keep swinging and turn some of the impossibilities in your life into a reality.

About The Author

Scott Burrows is a Professional Speaker, International Business Owner, Wheelchair Athlete and Author. In 1984, at the age of 19, he was involved in a horrific automobile accident that changed his life forever.

Today, he's not only a survivor, but he's one of a few in the world that turned the impossibilities of ever walking again into a reality. In his powerful presentations he will move people into action by embracing change and welcoming new challenges.

If you would like to purchase additional copies of this book, *Conversations on Success*, then please visit Scott's secured website at www.scottburrows.com and go to the tab "Purchase Scott's Products" and place your order.

Also available on DVD, VHS Tape and CD Audio is a Live 45-Minute Presentation of Scott giving one of his most requested Programs, "You Gotta Keep Swinging - The Mindset of a Champion." It's a great Motivational Tool that you can watch or listen to when you're in need of an "Attitude Adjustment." It's also a priceless gift!

He's a once in a lifetime speaker and not to be missed!

Scott T. Burrows

Inspirational & Motivational Speaker

5105 Interbay Blvd.

Tampa, FL 33611

Phone: 813.477.0862

Fax: 813.837.2845

E-mail: scott@scottburrows.com

www.scottburrows.com

Chapter Thirteen

JEFF HANSLER, CSP

THE INTERVIEW

David E. Wright (Wright)
Today we're talking to Jeffrey Hansler, CSP. Jeffrey is the president of Oxford Company and author of *Sell Little Red Hen Sell*. He is an expert trainer, motivator, and educator with over a hundred articles published. A specialist in sales, negotiation, influence and persuasion, he focuses on the dynamics and interactions in business, while inspiring with his unique ability to translate organizational objectives into entertaining, absorbable and memorable programs. He is eager to serve those who are excited about their future and further contribute to their knowledge bank. Jeffrey, thanks for being with us today on *Conversations on Success*.

Jeffrey Hansler (Hansler)
Thank you very much. I appreciate it.

Wright
So what do you do for organizations?

Hansler

The most valuable resource for any organization is its people and people get things done by communication. I work in this area—an organization's communication systems. It's a specialty within organizational development. I ensure their executives, managers, supervisors, sales, purchasing staff and accounting all have effective communication skills. It is also important that the systems they have in place, enhance communication and help them build as much profit as possible as they grow.

Wright

So how do you do that?

Hansler

I do it a number of ways. Sometimes they invite me in for consulting, and I investigate their current situation to find ways to apply improvement. Other times they invite me in to conduct training sessions to improve aspects of their organizational communication systems: sales, negotiations, customer service, leadership, team communication, communication with suppliers, unions, and even communicating financial information throughout departments. I am also invited in to present keynote speeches where I am able to talk about the points that affect the most critical issues they are faced with at the time.

Wright

What type of organizations do you work with? Do you work with large and small companies?

Hansler

Yes, I work with large and small companies. More importantly, I work in a variety of industries. I am usually brought in when an organization is facing great change or would like to create great change. An outside pair of eyes that has seen what works and doesn't work is extremely valuable. Add to that someone who can create educational programs to develop the skills necessary within the organization and you have a winning combination. I've done a lot of work lately with associations. Associations that are trying to fill in the education gap for companies that either don't have the resources they need or they're simply looking to supply cutting edge education for companies within their industry as part of their growth plans.

Wright

So could you give our readers an example of some of the biggest and smallest projects that you've done.

Hansler

The largest project I did was for a health care organization, an HMO. The project took over a year and it involved the entire sales and marketing staff. I brought in two other associates of mine for various aspects of the project, and we exceeded their expectations by helping them streamline their operations to reduce costs, which in turn contributed over a million dollars to their net profits as a direct result of our efforts. Some of the smaller projects that I've worked on are short term consulting engagements with Presidents and CEO's. I help them develop their ideas, form a strategy behind them and then guide them through the process of communicating those ideas throughout their organization. Currently, I'm working on a project with an executive that is expanding their association.

Wright

So what can organizations do to best prepare their organizations for success?

Hansler

Organizations need to invest in and commit to continuous learning for their organization. It is the greatest investment they can make to increase the value of their most important asset, their people. Whether it's an association providing for its members or a company providing for its staff, employees or even for its executive board: new knowledge and the ability to process and apply that knowledge is what will prepare organizations for success.

Wright

So an organization like mine, a publishing company, a speaker's bureau, and a graphics company all put together, you could come in and help us reorganize, and beef up the profit on the bottom-line and help us better serve our clients at one time?

Hansler

Well, in your case, since your organization runs so well, I'm not sure that I could do that.

Wright

Obviously you haven't been to my organization.

Hansler

Someone coming in from the outside, even in my organization, will have a new perspective since they aren't tied to the processes that exist. So yes, I would come in to your organization and look at it in different ways. I'd look at your staff and find ways that they could implement your processes quicker and communicate to your customers more effectively: A little faster, a little better, a little more in depth in order to clarify what exactly they're doing and the value they bring into the organization.

Wright

So could you tell our readers, what is key to successful business communications?

Hansler

I always recommend full disclosure. Full disclosure requires that you talk about your successes, about current issues, and the possible pit falls that go on within an organization as well. I do a lot of work with sales groups, and telling a salesperson that they should have full disclosure with their clients terrifies them. And the reason is they think they'll never buy if they hear anything but a glowing report. Companies always get into difficulties when they hide information. Most importantly, because incorrect information sets up a chain of decisions based on something that is not true or information that is withheld. Additionally, today's world is becoming more and more transparent, and that's a word you will hear even more about in the coming years—"transparency," and it requires full disclosure. At the executive level, especially, in the accounting process, with shareholders and with new employees, even in government, full disclosure allows you to better partner with your clients, customers, and suppliers. You create trust with full disclosure. Understand that full disclosure is not just telling somebody, "here are all problems." That's not effective communication. All that creates is fear, even though you have a very valuable product or service. Full disclosure is part of keeping everyone informed about critical issues so they can make informed decisions. A company that operates in this manner will need to be flexible and responsive. They will need to have expert communication skills to develop strong partnerships. One of the things that I do for full disclosure is guide someone who brings me in and says, "O.K., run a training class and fix my people," to understanding that a training won't "fix" anyone. Training provides information that must be used properly in an environment that supports the changes. In many cases, it's not a skill issue at all; it's a system issue where any number of things could be going on. Even if it is a skill issue, with one day of training only a few of those in the program may be at that perfect spot, where they are able to utilize it. For the majority, it may be their first introduction to an idea that could be very valuable if it is re-enforced and that will require more than one day of "training." The best return on investment comes from educational opportunities that allow for and provide repetitive exposure to skills that will assist them in reaching their next objective.

Wright

What should an organization do when they want to create dramatic change?

Hansler

You did say dramatic change, didn't you? To create dramatic change, they should get rid of committees, not as a resource, just a committee's control of the final decision. I am seeing this a lot as I work with associations. They want dramatic change and a committee as a decision-making body is built on compromise. Dramatic change is much more likely to be brought about by an individual with decision-making authority and a clear vision of how to get there than by any committee. If you want change, it's better to have one person guiding that change. Committees have a tendency to dilute the message, to dilute the change. Dramatic change requires key individuals making key decisions based on the critical factors that add to profitability and growth for the organization.

Wright

So, what you're saying is you're not destroying the committees, the committees still functions as a information gathering operation, but the president, or whomever, is elected to make a final decision, that's the way it should go down?

Hansler

That's the way it should go down if you want dramatic change. The organizations need to pick its leaders well, because we've seen what a strong leader with ill intent can do to an organization. A strong leader with good intent also needs to understand where the organization needs to go and have the ability to communicate that clearly at all levels, including, financial, human resource, production, as well as the sales departments. Again, that's where I am invited in. To help these leaders and key executives communicate what they want, and assist those on the front line to communicate back to the key executives. This is all part of organizational communication and it ties right back into transparency and full disclosure.

Wright

What are the critical focuses a business needs for success?

Hansler

Most companies have invested in organizational development. They develop structure and they develop strategy. What they're lacking is developing the communications systems and skills of the organization. Things are moving in hyper-speed now. The front line people need to have the communication skills and the strength to be able to go back and persuade management that the strategy that was good six months ago is no longer valid, despite the prevailing thought that management built a structure they intended to last one or two years. Effective communication systems will help an organization maintain structure when necessary and change structure when necessary. An organization that learns to focus on organizational communication creates profits and growth and an environment where the very best people will stay, and that's a priceless result.

Wright

You spoke a moment ago of people at the top, saying come in and fix my people or come in and make them better, come in and change them. What is the thing that bothers you most about sales training?

Hansler

Whether it's sales training, internal communication, team leadership, or any other training program I provide, it is the same thing that I mentioned before. They look for the quick fix, for someone to get a Ph.D. in communication from a one-day program. It just doesn't happen that someone will change an entire lifetime of bad habits in communication in six hours. The same applies whether it is an initial investment or four times a year, it's not enough to create dramatic change. That's like going out and running four times a year and expecting to win a marathon, it just won't happen.

Wright

So have long-term continual training for everyone, at every level?

Hansler

Exactly. Adults learn through repetition and they learn through practice. It must be thought out practice that is structured and tied to their values at every level. While every situation is an opportunity for enhanced learning, not everyone takes advantage of that opportunity. When two managers are arguing of what position to take, not only are they arguing over the position to take, it also provides a dynamic that can be used for looking at how the organization communicates and how the organization makes decisions. Harvard case studies are built on the concept of working within the dynamics of the organization and providing suggested changes based on experience with similar situations. I assist companies in analyzing their communication process by guiding through their dialog, "How did this discussion go? How was this decision reached? Who are the people that were involved? What were some of their roles that they played? What are other driving forces?" I make people very aware of their contributions to their organizations, to supply a return to their profits as quickly and as immediately as possible.

Wright

What is the greatest value to an organization having a speaker?

Hansler

It's an opportunity to convey an idea, re-enforce an idea, to help the attendees understand at a new level where the organization is going and what is required to get there. It can be fun and entertaining and will relate some key points in a memorable manner. Now combine that with follow-up learning opportunities and you have a very powerful opportunity to communicate a commitment to change.

Wright

What behavior do managers need to exhibit to get the most out of their staff?

Hansler

They need to walk their talk. Every study that has been done clearly shows that it doesn't matter what is said or what reports are printed or what they have posted. What matters is what they DO. If they want something to change, then they have to change that behavior within themselves. The manager running around talking about time management and the value of time won't see results from staff unless the manager demonstrates better time management.

Wright

So what are the steps to achieve what you set out to accomplish?

Hansler

There are three steps toward attaining achievement or reaching accomplishment: decision-making, implementation, and review. The decision-making process determines what is going to be done and how it will be done. The implementation process is about putting the decisions into action and working to hit targeted milestones. The review process is the link between the implementation and the decision-making process; because once implementation is begun, a host of uncontrollable factors will affect the outcomes. New decisions will need to be made based on results and the uncontrollable factors and then these new decisions will need to be implemented.

Wright

So, you have spoken of the importance of a positive perspective. Why is that a better option?

Hansler

We have a tendency to be critical when we think of change. There is a tendency to view changing from something bad versus adjusting to "the best of the best." It is important to understand the importance of this fine line of distinction in our internal and external language. Our language is our connection to the world and others. The language we use affects us as much, if not more, internally as externally. The statement that something isn't good creates an internal thought process that we did something wrong and now we have to correct it and move on. It's more powerful to say, "What you were doing worked and now its time for a different action so we can achieve a new result!" This subtlety is called *agreement language or appreciative inquiry*. During the last twenty-five years, numerous studies have verified that positive communication and positive thoughts yield better results and make a better environment for people to work in. If internal dialog says, "I need to finish this report, *but* I want a cup of coffee," it creates stress and conflict versus "I need to finish this report, *and* I want a cup of coffee."

Wright

It's always been my experience that when I change in my company, I don't ever want to insult anybody by throwing away all of those great things that we have done in the past. Rather, add to them and congratulate the people, sometimes we were doing things without the right tools and when you get better tools obviously you can do a better job, but it seems to always be a negative effect, when I change drastically, without thanking everybody with the way we had done it before.

Hansler

That's exactly what we are talking about. It's not difficult. We just need to remind ourselves, especially when faced with challenges. Our habits depend on how we were raised and the type of environments we grew up in. When I began my career, I experienced some fast changing environments, and it was sad to see that organizations felt the necessity to make previous decisions wrong to justify the changes they wanted. By doing this, they created the notion that all previous decisions made and the people who implemented them were wrong. It's no surprise that when they did that, they had little support for the change and a great deal of conflict: It is not necessary to make something wrong to justify change, and it doesn't pay off.

Wright

My friends that do that always seem to think that they do that because they want to implement the change. If they say anything good about the old way, they feel that people will hold onto those ideas. I view the opposite. I believe this wouldn't be the issue if they were more effective in their communication skills. And that's why we feel organizational communication is an interval part of ongoing success.

Hansler

I'm glad you get it. More and more organizations are learning this truth and applying the principles needed to be extremely successful.

Wright

I'm interested, and I'm sure our readers will be, as to how you got into this business?

Hansler

It's actually pretty exciting from a business standpoint. I had an appointment to the United States Air Force Academy, until we all discovered I was colorblind. This fact and a later discovered fact that I didn't have the motored dexterity to be a good veterinarian was not information that I received well, until the owner of the veterinary hospital suggested this was a great discovery. He pointed out how I could make more money by being in the business of veterinarian medicine than by being a veterinarian. I think he just decided to sell me on a different perspective since my ideas of the future had just gone out the window. He was the one that got me into taking financial classes and focusing on business. In entering the workforce, through a series of comical errors, I was hired as a Southern California Sales Representative for Apple Computer, and this was before most everyone even knew what Apple was. If I had known it was a computer company, I would have avoided it like the plague; I hated computers. So at a very, very young age, I got to see what an organization faced with great opportunity and dynamic change was experiencing. The memories I have showed me how critical communication is and how it can make an enormous difference to the success or failure at any point of an organization. Apple made some strategic choices that went phenomenally well and they also made some grave errors. I was able to thrive in that environment and from there moved to a variety of different positions.

An international accounting and manufacturing software company eventually hired me to be their Vice President of Sales and Marketing for the U.S. operations. I eventually purchased the right to distribute their product in the United States, and ran it as the company owner. In selling, it put me in a position to explore some different markets and business opportunities, until a friend of mine dragged me back into the computer industry for a company that was supplying technical training. It was easy to see that outsourcing for training and education was growing. I began to study how training was delivered, how people learned, the best delivery methods, and how people would be learning in the future. In 1992, I launched the Oxford Company.

Wright

Well, I wasn't going to ask you, but it's driving me nuts, the title of your book, *Sell Little Red Hen Sell*, what is that all about?

Hansler

As a child, my favorite story was *The Little Red Hen*, if you remember in the story she went around and asked people to help her to bake bread, and nobody would help and when the bread was made, they came around to eat it and her words were, "You did not help make the bread, so therefore you cannot eat it." The moral to the story was if you don't do the work, you don't get the reward. So when I talk about the book in front of an audience, I ask them, "How many of you, by show of hands, have done the work and still not gotten the reward?" And almost everybody raises his or her hand. I use that graphic example to point out that The Little Red Hen didn't have a work ethic problem; she had a sales communication problem. In my book, The Little Red Hen is in a new environment, she's lost her nest egg and must re-create her fortunes. To accomplish this, we take her into the world of sales.

The book contains important lessons about persuasion, negotiations, and influence: sales skills if you will. The greatest compliments that I hear on the book are that it is layered and it applies to all aspects of life, which it is and it does. When you read the book a second time, and every time you read it again, you pick up clues to the dynamics of communication. You will pick up these dynamics when you are in dialogue with someone if you focus on your listening versus your talking. So, it's not a book so much about selling and convincing people, it's a book about what to listen for.

Wright

I'm going to go straight to amazon.com, then, I need that book.

Hansler

Great! I know you will enjoy it. Even though a small publisher has published it, it has sold over 50,000 copies this year alone and it's being published in nine different languages.

Wright

Well, well! I really appreciate you taking all of this time with me, Jeffrey. This has been a very interesting conversation and I've learned some valuable information that I plan on applying to my own company.

Hansler

Thank you very much, David, I really appreciate it.

Wright

Today we have been talking to Jeffrey Hansler, Certified Speaking Professional; he's a specialist in sales, negotiation, influence, and persuasion. He focuses on the dynamics and interactions of business while inspiring audiences with his unique ability to translate organizational objectives into entertaining absorbable and memorable programs. We have found out by listening to him today, that all of that is true, Jeff thank you so much for being with us today on *Conversations on* Success.

About The Author

Jeffrey Hansler, CSP, president of Oxford Company and author of Sell Little Red Hen! Sell! is an expert consultant, trainer, motivator and educator with over 100 articles published. He's a Certified Speaking Professional with the National Speakers Association and a member of the American Society of Training and Development. A specialist in sales, negotiation, influence, and persuasion, he focuses on the dynamics and interaction in business while inspiring audiences with his unique ability to translate organizational objectives into entertaining, absorbable and memorable programs. He believes the impact of great communication is as important in your personal life as it is in your career.

Jeffrey Hansler, CSP

Oxford Company

213 2nd Street

Huntington Beach, CA 92648

Phone: 714.960.7461

Fax: 714.960.5107

Email: jhansler@oxfordco.com

www.oxfordco.com

Chapter Fourteen

KEITH L. BROWN

THE INTERVIEW

David E. Wright (Wright)

Today we're talking to Keith L. Brown. He's the man who internationally acclaimed speaker Les Brown calls a powerful individual with a passion and energy whose SUPER-VISION is changing lives. Labeled special ed, at-risk and potential menace to society, Keith dedicated his live to overcoming those obstacles. Today he's a member of the National Speakers Association, and Whose Who in Professional Speaking. Keith, one of the most sought after professional speakers in the industry, creates an atmosphere of what he calls "fuber" a combination of fun and fiber. Mr. Brown's keynotes, workshops and seminars are guaranteed to make audiences laugh, learn, love and lead in every aspect of their lives. After leaving an event with the motivator of the millennium, individuals are empowered to uplift themselves and others. Mr. Brown is a consultant, leader and a teacher and most of all an amazing dynamic motivator. As a change agent he is committed to promoting professionalism and ensuring continual success, in short a catalyst, focused predominately on bringing people together and making a positive difference. Mr. Keith L. Brown is a legislative liaison and professional speechwriter. He has conducted a countless number of workshops and presentations to and for school systems, colleges, universities, state federal agencies, foundations, organizations and faith based institutions. Speaking engagements may be retained by logging on to www.keithlbrown.com. Keith, welcome to *Conversations on Success*.

Keith L. Brown (Brown)

Good afternoon, and I'm honored to be part of this great series of excellence with some of the most successful human beings on the planet.

Wright

Keith, you spoke a lot about "Supervision" and "SUPER-VISION," what's the difference?

Brown

Well, one of the saddest things in society today is many people are surviving in lives that do not represent their natural born greatness because they have relied on someone else's supervision of them rather than a SUPER-VISION for themselves. So in short, supervision is basically living your life or living one's life listening to the ideas and the total advice of others, just living under other people's ideas of what you should be and how far you should soar in life. Many people are going around in a workplace maze of despair on a daily basis under someone else's supervision. But a SUPER-VISION on the other hand is independent thinking. It's going above and beyond. If the status quo says, "Be good"; that would be supervision, but a SUPER-VISION says that we should be excellent. So a SUPER-VISION is a new mindset, thinking outside the box, going against what others see as your place in society. One should always have higher expectations for him/herself. For instance, if you want to go back to school in order to further your education, don't let age, people, or a lack of resources stop you. You may say, "I'll be (whatever age) when I finish if I go back." Well, how old will you be if you don't go back??? EXACTLY!!! Don't let the skeptics stop you from reaching an unfinished portion of your SUPER-VISION!!!

Moreover, there are financial aid resources designed especially for you. Go to a computer, your local board of education, Technical School or College and ask the questions you deserve to have answered. If you want career advancement, do the research and position yourself to be promoted. Those who possess a SUPER-VISION govern and monitor their progress, and it is usually promising because they do not settle for anything less than GREATNESS!!! Now let me make it clear that it is o.k. to have supervisors in life; we all need some type of supervision, but we don't need to totally depend on the ideas, ideologies and philosophies of others; we need to develop a SUPER-VISION for ourselves.

Wright

So why do you label some people as lemons?

Brown

There are some people who are very negative in society ,and I call these people lemon people because of their sour dispositions. I believe if you're seeking to grow, spiritually, economically, socially, culturally, or intellectually you should stay away from negative people. Now they can be in our environment but not of our environment. In other words, negative people in life will never get the picture, because they're in the wrong frame of mind. So we must take these negatives, place them in a symbolic dark room and hope they develop. We should get away from them in flash so we can become the empowered exposures we deserve to be. I've heard it said many times before that some people are so negative they can go into a dark room and develop. I really believe this.

I believe they are the dream killers; these are the ones who I once read about. They are called "tater" people. Some of them sit on the sidelines and they tell us what we should do in life, but they never give any assistance. They are the "commentators". Then we have others who do not like us to manifest our true gifts and talents; they want to control and micromanage our lives, and they are called the "dictators"; then there are others who say, "Wait, you don't have to go after your vision right now, just take your time and wait." These are the "hesitators." There are others who just like to gossip and they love negative communication and negative conversation; they are labeled the "agitators."

But I believe today you should never let anyone's negative opinion of you become your reality. Most important: NEVER LET ANYONE TELL YOU WHAT YOU CAN'T DO, ESPECIALLY IF THEY'VE NEVER DONE IT. They are labeled the "lemon people," because they are sour; they complain; they never exclaim. To complain means all they do is point fingers at others because of their negative situation and disposition. When you exclaim you realize we are all going to have situations; we're all going to have issues; we're all going to have problems, but we work with vim, vigor and vitality to overcome. So when you come in the company of the lemon people you had better be lemonade.

Wright

So what role does a family play in an individual's success or failure?

Brown

Family is very important. Family is very important to me. Early notions of success and failure are born in family settings. You have children who are looking up to adults, attempting to find an individual they can model themselves after. I believe family breeds thoughts and perception. I believe family either promotes high expectations or low expectations. I believe greatness starts in the family. For example, financial mismanagement either breeds generational mismanagement or a hunger by future generations, not to repeat the same process. I believe discipline is vital when it comes to an individual's success or failure.

Children who are not disciplined grow up spoiled, and with unrealistic ideas of living in a civilized society where a lack of discipline will not be tolerated. We see the reality of that on a daily basis. So family is very important and it doesn't have to be the traditional family unit we see. I grew up in a family where I was blessed to have two fathers, two mothers, brothers and sisters on each side and a partridge in a pear tree. I've had extended family members, aunts, uncles, grandparents, cousins, and so many individuals who nurtured my growth. Then there are those "lemon people" who are in our families, but we must understand "All relatives ain't family." I make no mistake when I say ain't. I must use that vernacular because there's nothing formal or standard about a family member constantly degrading another family member. So we get our earliest perceptions from our family members. We get our earliest notions of who we are, what we are and whose we are. They come out of family, so family is very important, but I would caution my reader not to dwell with the lemon people in your family.

Historically we often say things such as "Well, you know it runs in the family." That's a term, I think, we need to eradicate, because if it's negative and we allow it to run in the family, then our families of today will never be allowed to soar. So anything that's negative should not be allowed to run in the family. The positive should always be promoted because it's our nature to be positive beings of uplift, not generational curses. Issues will arise, but the basic fabric of the family should be one of love and support, not confusion and division. These characteristics only fuel generational misunderstanding and dysfunction. It may seem as if I am seeking a utopia. NO!!! I did not grow up in paradise. I had issues, pain, and suffering, but I also had an environment of love, discipline, healing and nurturing. In other words, I had the same experiences as you, just in a different family setting. Now I must provide that same nurturing for my son, nieces, nephews and cousins who are still developing ideas of what life is all about. In the final analysis, family should promote rather than demote the greatness which lies within each of us.

Wright

You have said that we should all quit our jobs, why would you give such advice, especially since there are so many unemployed?

Brown

I'm looking for each individual to quit his or her job. I'm one who loves acronyms and I believe today there are two meanings for jobs. One is Jumping Out of Bed, and the other is Just Over Broke. I believe we are dealing with a mindset, not so much financially broke as emotionally bankrupt. Do you feel valued? In order for you to feel valued, you must first say to yourself, "I DON'T HAVE A JOB. I DO NOT HAVE A JUST OVER BROKE. I DO NOT HAVE A JUST OVER BROKE MENTALITY. I'M NOT JUMPING OUT OF BED MONDAY THROUGH FRIDAY. I HAVE A CAREER, OR I'M A BUSINESS OWNER. I HAVE VALUE."

It starts with your mentality; if you believe you are a valued team member, you will come with a career conception; and those who have that career conception and perception are the ones who dwell in excellence at the career place. So that's what I mean when I say you should quit your job. In other words, everyone has a unique gift. I've met individuals who work in the career place and they were not making enough financially, but they tapped into their gifts, and hobbies to create multiple streams of income. When your nine to five income is not enough, don't let it ruin your total outcome. There is nothing wrong with providing a legal service that supplies you with extra income. That goes back to the supervision concept. Supervision will say just use your nine to five. Nine to five until you're sixty-five and then you can get some of that social insecurity.

Many people today retire, only to have to work again and re-tire(get burned out) all over again due to a lack of financial resources. If you choose to volunteer or mentor youth, that's fine. But it saddens me to see people have to work again once they've retired. I believe when you tap into your gift, the universe responds in your favor. My colleague and mentor Les Brown often says, "You don't have to be great to get started, but you need to get started in order to be great, and I believe this. So I believe each individual needs to examine him or herself and just release the job mentality. Start saying, "I have a career. I'm a business owner." It's self motivation and validation, getting rid of negative self talk. That's why I want everyone to quit their job and embrace a mentality of ownership and value.

Wright

Let me ask you a question, do faith and success have a genuine connection?

Brown

I believe faith is the most important asset one can have if he or she wants to not only be successful, but be great. We must have Faith in God, and as heirs to His throne, we must believe in ourselves, even when others are skeptical about our purpose. We were born to be great, so I believe faith plays a vital role in that. For example, if you believe you were created by an Omnipotent being, then your whole outlook on life will be one of greatness because as an heir to the throne here on earth and beyond, you will believe everything good on this earth should be able to link with you. So you must have faith.

Five years ago, I left the teaching profession but I did not leave students. I need to reiterate that I only left the classroom, but I work with students in schools on a daily basis all over the country. So I left one great school and classroom in order to pursue my purpose of empowering students, educators, parents, support staff, organizations, foundations, Faith Based Institutions, companies, state and federal agencies, and people in the universal classroom called LIFE!! I stepped out on faith, and I believe ever since then I've been walking in the FOG. For me the FOG stands for the "Favor of God." And I also believe when I stepped out on faith, I had to decrease my EGO because EGO stands for "Edging God Out." Quite often in today's society, we don't like to use the "G" word, but I understand within me who created me, and He created me to be great. So I must first acknowledge Him. He gives me the ability to motivate, stimulate and educate the masses. When I stepped out on faith many people said to me, "You're leaving your good job, what about the benefits?" My response was, "I don't know about the benefits, but I know about the Benefactor. I really don't know my total direction, but I know the Director." I realized when I stepped out on faith to promote the gift that was placed in me, I had to figuratively jump off the mountain and grow my wings on the way down.

I believe it was Mark Twain who said, "In life, when it comes to your vision, you must have faith, you must go out on a limb, you must take risks, you must go out on a limb because that's where all of the fruit is." Once I believed in that ability and natural birthright, I was able to get into the public speaking field, become an author, write my first book entitled *CHITLINS*, and that stands for "Creative Helpful Intuitive Thoughts Lifting Individuals Naturally Seeking.

I was able to soar on the legendary Showtime at the Apollo. I was blessed to work with the Les Browns and other industry greats in the National Speakers Association, do a keynote address at Bishop TD Jakes Megafest, and present workshops at the National Youth At-Risk Conference just to name a few. I am not saying this to impress you, only to impress upon you that your Faith will lead you into realms you never imagined!! Faith has allowed me to empower and be empowered by thousands of human beings who I never would have met had I had a lack of Faith. Memorize the saying, "Feed your Faith and your doubts will starve!!!"

Wright

How vital is networking in today's society?

Brown

As children we are taught, don't talk to strangers. But in order to be empowered as a young adult or an adult, then we must talk to strangers. So as we get older, this parental advice becomes invalid. I never meet a stranger and I caution the reader not to cover him or herself up in a shell, but to get out and network. For example, if you're a business owner, you need to make what I call cold calls. These are calls you make when you don't know the individuals or you don't know the business owners, but you're calling to make that individual know the only reason he or she was put on this earth is to support your vision. I believe you should make about five cold calls per day. That would give you about twenty-five per business week and that would equal one hundred per month. If you cannot get any business out of one hundred calls per month, then you're definitely in the wrong field.

I believe we should network everyday. I believe we should speak to everyone; most people on the earth don't realize in order to be successful, it must be born in mind that nearly fifty percent of the people who are going to help you reach your vision, you haven't even met them yet. So networking is a key. I'm talking about constantly networking, and exchanging business cards. If I'm an educator, I need to network with the administration if I have aspirations to be an administrator. I need to network with colleagues who have the same aspirations, as long as they are not "Lemon People." If I'm a student, I need to network with my teachers and my professors because their recommendations will be vital tools for my present and future growth. Quite often in life, we talk mostly to the individuals who cannot take us to the next level. There is nothing wrong with that, but we usually spend most of our time with individuals who do not want to exceed expectations.

So in order to network, we have to get out of what I call that click mentality. I say to all readers: IF YOU'RE THE SMARTEST ONE IN YOUR CLICK /YOU NEED A NEW CLICK. So you must network on a daily basis; you must become an outgoing person in America, in the twenty first century in order to maximize your greatness and empowerment. If you are just to shy or anti-social, invest in books, tapes, or courses that will assist you in networking. Or surround yourself with those who can assist you. Networking is the key. Open yourself up and be willing to show your gift and meet new people; be willing to explore new environments; be willing to step boldly into a SUPER-VISION and forget about the supervision of when you were little, when they said don't talk to strangers. That ideal is abolished once you move into the SUPER-VISION realm. Networking equals net worth in the twenty first century. Go out NOW and join networking organizations and professional affiliations. Not only will you feel fulfilled when you network, you will also create a support system of human beings who can enhance your purpose and peace of mind.

Wright

You're passionate about our youth, how do we inspire all of them so that no child sincerely gets left behind?

Brown

Well, I believe we need to have high expectations for all of our youth. We must have high expectations for every one of our youth regardless of race, creed or socio economic background. I always ask the following: What do you want to be? They usually respond like this: I want to be... I stop them in mid sentence and boldly exclaim: You are already a(chosen profession); you just have to go to school or get trained for it. So don't say I want to be; say I am(SUPER-VISION). I do a lot of work with youth, and I always tell our young people my story, the good, bad, and ugly. It's not popular to expose yourself to our youth, but they have a greater respect for you when you are "REAL."

Furthermore, I demand respect as their role model, not their FRIEND. Friend implies equal, and as adults, we are not their equals. Our standards have to be higher. Even when telling our faults, we shouldn't do it to gain popularity, we should do it to show we are human. In short, we don't want them to make the same mistakes we did. If they make some of the same mistakes, it could be fatal for them. The young people have a term called "CRUNK." That's one of their favorite terms today, and I love that term, but to me CRUNK is not what it stands for to them. To the youth of today, CRUNK means to be excited; it means to be energetic, and that's wonderful. I love those things, but to me CRUNK stands for Consciously Receiving, an Undertaking of New Knowledge. (Thanks Mr. JR Henderson/National Lighthouse Foundation). In other words, we must be able to give our young people the new knowledge they need; we must begin to tell our young people in order for them to be empowered, "THE WAY IN WHICH YOU DRESS IS THE WAY IN WHICH YOU WILL BE ADDRESSED." If you look like you're ready to make a hundred thousand dollars, someone might pay you that, but if you look like you are ready to go hold up a liquor store, or if you look like you're ready to make minimum wage when you are actually a maximum wage person, that's how people will treat you.

Many young people say my example is stereotyping, and that's wrong; yes it is wrong but we don't live in a utopia. So we must teach our young men and women that they must keep their heads up, they must keep their pants pulled up and then their purpose will go up. We must also begin to embrace some of their ideas as well. The young people are into hip hop. I love the hip hop culture. I don't like degrading lyrics, but I embrace the positive messages in many of the songs. We have to understand how to teach our youth how to differentiate between having character and being a character. We have to teach our young people that it's much better to have values than it is to have many valuables. In other words, what good is a Tommy Hilfiger if you're rolling down hill because you can't figure out your direction? What good is a fifty-dollar hat if we are going to wear it on a ten-cent head? So what good are two-hundred dollar Air Jordan's if you're mentally grounded? We must teach our young people that fashion is fine, the music is fine, all of that is fine, but your top priority is having character, your top priority is dressing for success, your top priority is academic excellence; these are your top priorities because many of our young people live in the "reel" instead of the "real" world. I tell them there is a big difference in the "reel," what you see on television and in movies versus the "real," what you're going to experience on a daily basis.

My mission with young people is to enhance their ability to make independent correct choices which will transform into life long learning, leadership and success. Robert Frost once said, "Two roads diverged in a wood, and I took the one less traveled and that has made all the difference." I want our young people to not just follow paths that have already been laid out, but to go and make their own paths and leave a trail.

Wright

Do you think educators are the scapegoats for the educational ills of our country?

Brown

Definitely!!! Being a universal educator myself, I fully believe that and I believe our educators are often ostracized by individuals who have not been back in a school since they left. We must realize that educators are the difference makers; we have Supreme Court justices, engineers, scientists, lawyers, and physicians, all because of educators. I realize there are some who have taught for twenty years, and there are some who have taught one year twenty times. I'm not talking about the latter, but I am talking about those who act as surrogate parents, those who have high expectations. Those who are often overworked and underpaid, that's who I'm talking about. It does take a village to raise a child; we have often heard that. Well the village must be comprised of more than just educators.

One of the programs I present is called the "PEP Rally" and that stands for Pupils, Educators and Parents. I rarely even go into a school and motivate and empower if I can't speak to the pupils, educators, and the parents because we are all one. The teachers are working hard. I would say ninety-five percent or more of our educators sincerely care, but they need more resources. I sincerely believe in the No Child Left Behind Act, but we must fund the No Child Left Behind Act properly. We must! If the funding is not there, then it becomes ornamental, so I believe in No Child Left Behind, but I believe a team effort of educators, administrators, support staff, parents, community leaders, and legislators (who vote on educational funding) must become genuine in America and not a sound bite!!!

I taught in the classroom for over five years; I have family members and a wife who nurture and educate in the classroom. I've been working for and with young people for the last two decades, so I understand exactly what teachers have to go through on a daily basis and they are professionals. One of the ills in America is "supervision" says educators and support staff should not be viewed as professionals, but a SUPER-VISION says they are professionals; they deserve to be valued and they don't deserve to be valued just by simply giving them a certain day out of the month or teachers appreciation week; they need to be valued everyday, just as the surgeon who is performing heart surgery is valued. The administrators, county office personnel, educators, para professionals, substitute teachers, those who are on the transportation staff, the custodial staff, the nutrition staff in the cafeteria, all of these individuals, all under one umbrella called education; they are molding the hearts, minds and character of our young people. I know this because when I was younger, I was labeled special ed, and at-risk, but it was a teacher who taught me that I was not special ed, but I was special, who taught me that I was not at-risk, but I needed to learn to take positive risks.

So we really have to examine our educational system today. Yes there are issues, but I believe most of our educators are simply doing the best they can do and they need more assistance, they need more funding, they need more resources and most importantly, the community and educators need to be linked, not in a ornamental sense of the word, but a genuine sense of the word, so all of our young people will move forward in the twenty first century. And to all educators: IT IS INNOVATIVE TO DIVERSIFY YOUR LESSON PLANS AND CONCEPTS. Because pop culture is a major factor in the lives of our youth, you may want to incorporate it into your classroom methodology.

For example, when I taught Shakespeare's Romeo and Juliet, I first asked the following: How many of you ever dated someone your parents did not approve of??? Many hands went up. I then said the following: Using correct grammar, write an 8-10 sentence paragraph comparing your situation with the synopsis of Romeo and Juliet. If there were students who did not fit the criteria, they created a scenario. The next day we figuratively moved to Verona and became members of the House of Capulet(Juliet) or the House of Montague(Romeo). I invited parents to participate in the "Electric Slide" extravaganza. This may sound unorthodox to most, but it was an innovative teaching re-enactment of Lord Capulet's party for Juliet.

After all of that, the students were eager to learn about oxymoron's, alliteration, similes, metaphors, and other figurative language. For those of you preparing your students for state and national mandated exams, use acronyms and other unique methods to motivate students to WANT to succeed, not just succeed BECAUSE IT IS MANDATORY!!! For instance, when I empower in Georgia, CRCT stands for Can't Regress Conquer Test!! In Florida, schools are the "Big Dog taking a bite out of the FCAT." In North Carolina, the EOG stands for Educating Our Geniuses. In South Carolina, the PALMETTO exam is Pupils Ascending Learning Making Educational Tasks Truly Outstanding. In California, the STAR exam can be Students Talents Arise Resourcefully/We are STARS! In Texas, the TAKS exam can be Testing All Kids Successfully! Nationally, for those who take the ITBS exam, their motto can be I Test Boldly and Successfully.

Those are just a few, but all states can adopt models which are repeated. After adopting the labels, I illustrate how incorporating creative teaching styles can result in higher test scores and more funding for school districts. When academics have relevance and value to students, they want to excel; my wife teaches third grade students who are thrilled to learn the capitals through a rap song, and they have turned their classroom into a community which includes lawyers, politicians, doctors, teachers, and business owners; they can't wait until lunch is over in order to get back to class(I am not exaggerating). I know countless other educators who incorporate creativity to enhance the entire learning process; the so called gifted 10% will succeed regardless, but the overwhelming majority will thirst for educators who can incorporate fresh ideas and perspectives on a daily basis.

So I choose to salute those in the education profession, and I boldly exclaim, Get CRUNK!!!(Consciously Receiving an Undertaking of New Knowledge).

Wright

What makes you the motivator of the millennium, and is there any responsibility that comes with that title?

Brown

I actually got that name from youth attending a "Life Skills Series" sponsored by the Sickle Cell Foundation of Georgia several years ago, so I really took that to heart. As the Motivator of the Millennium I can empower any crowd. That means I can be in the House of Representatives and I can empower our legislators. That also means I can go to a school and empower one thousand screaming young people. I can empower educators in a staff development workshop. I can go and empower an audience in any arena or genre. So there is a lot of responsibility that comes with being the Motivator of the Millennium. I often say, "IT'S NOT WHAT PEOPLE CALL YOU, IT'S WHAT YOU CHOOSE TO ANSWER TO." I choose to answer to the Motivator of the Millennium and that means I have to be versatile, creative, credible, and flexible. I have to have enthusiasm and I will tell all of the readers out there, when you catch on fire with enthusiasm people will come for miles to watch you burn. So that's why I'm the Motivator of the Millennium.

We don't see things as they are; we see things as we are. So I firmly believe I am the Motivator of the Millennium and that is not a statement of arrogance; it's a statement of confidence because on a daily basis, I must plant seeds of excellence in our young people and adults as well. Supervision says that you must look inside an apple to count the seeds, but as the Motivator of the Millennium who has a SUPER-VISION, I don't look inside of the apple and count the seeds, I look at the seed and I envision the many apples of greatness that will spring forth; as the Motivator of the Millennium, my SUPER-VISION must go beyond what common sense will allow.

Wright

You believe that language, communication, and diversity are powerful, how so?

Brown

I believe language is very important, because once you open your mouth, that's when people form an opinion of who you are, some of them valid, some of them not. I believe in today's society, when it comes to diversity, and language, there is a hidden curriculum. Let me speak to that for a moment. What I mean is, historically, some people of color, primarily African Americans, have been told by other African Americans that because they spoke correct English, they sounded proper, non black or white. I believe that is one of the most hideous things I've ever heard.

Bill Cosby recently caused a catharsis (a purging of emotions) because he challenged people in America, (primarily in the African American community) to take responsibility for themselves and their greatness, and one of those things comes from how you communicate. I think that it's senseless and it's a hidden curriculum because we never hear about it. When you are articulate, it is often assumed you can't be genuinely African American. But my question to everyone would be this: IF SPEAKING CORRECTLY MEANS I AM WHITE, WHAT IS THE CRITERIA FOR SPEAKING BLACK?

We must realize there is only one acceptable language on a universal standard and it is called Standard American English. So there's nothing wrong with slang or informal language in its proper place. But in order to be empowered, you must learn the value of Standard American English. For example, if I'm on the basketball court talking to some young people, I might go up to a young man and say, "Yo dog, I'm about to go to the crib and get my eat on." But if I am in an interview for College, an internship, Scholarship, or career, I will say, "Good afternoon, I'm about to go home and eat because I'm quite famished." It may get me ridiculed, but those who ridicule me or you for that matter often have no power in your quest for success.

Consider the following scenario: You have two surgeons who are about to perform heart surgery on you. The first one comes up to and says the following: Yo man, your heart be all messed up. The next one comes up to you and says the following: Excuse me sir we're going to have to perform surgery because there are complications with your heart. I think it's safe to say most people would choose the second surgeon, so language, is essential.

We must teach our children, our youth, and adults as well, that Standard American English is not racial in nature, its human in nature. So language is important and it goes back to networking; you must learn how to communicate; my grandmother used to say you must sound like somebody before individuals will treat you like somebody, so I believe we have to abolish this hidden curriculum that encourages individuals to have low expectations when it comes language. I believe language is one of the most powerful tools we can use and as a professional speaker; I embrace all types of language. I embrace the informal at times, but in order to be empowered on a universal scale, let me reiterate that American English is the law of the day.

Now if you're an athlete or entertainer, and your financial success is based on how many records or CD's you sell or how many touchdowns you score, or how many goals you score, if you play hockey, or tennis or whatever, then language might not be as essential, but most of these individuals have agents who know how to master the English Language when negotiating multi million dollar contracts. Furthermore, when the game or concert or video is over, these human beings, with extraordinary talents, are articulate as well. 99% of the American public will not be athletes, entertainers, or sportscasters, so in order to be fulfilled, let your SUPER-VISION include the ability to be bi-lingual, especially embracing Standard American English.

Wright

So, o.k. Motivator, motivate our readers so they can enhance their own lives, right now.

Brown

I really want to tell our readers that we must be diverse. We must promote diversity today; you know when I look at this great melting pot or symbolic salad bowl called America, I realize we(all ethnicities) didn't come over here on the same ship, but we are all in the same boat. So we must see the total person; we must see individuals for what they are, who they are, whose they are, and embrace them. I often hear people say things like, I don't see color. I just see you as a human being. I know they are attempting to be politically correct, but in doing so we often become emotionally incorrect. I believe that I should see color, and I should embrace and respect your total being.

David, you are a successful, sincere, intelligent, white male. I don't have the right to eradicate your racial heritage in the name of promoting diversity or tolerance. I need to be able to see you for who you are, and respect you for who you are; that's total diversity in America. I believe when we genuinely accept diversity, then we won't promote ornamental monthly celebrations only. I believe you should be proud every day of the year of your heritage, but you must respect everyone else's, heritage as well. You see, in America, that's what makes us all great; our differences make us great, so to the readers out there, I simply say, "IT IS NOT OUR MISSION TO SEE THROUGH EACH OTHER. IT IS OUR MISSION TO SEE EACH OTHER THROUGH!" If you are to be successful and great in the twenty first century you must stay away from negative people, stay away from negative communication, stay away from negative self talk, and stay away from negative environments.

In the twenty first century you must network, you must discover your own voice, you must discover your own SUPER-VISION, you must live your life with purpose, you must live your life on purpose and you must live your life in your purpose. You must have passion, you must have enthusiasm, and you must never give up. You know, most people say fake it until you make it. I say don't quit it until you get it. You must surround yourself with people who are eagles; I believe if you want to be an eagle you can no longer hang with chickens. So you must surround yourself with the visionaries. Dwell with those who want to be successful and have a keen desire to uplift all mankind.

In the final analysis, it's all about service. I believe every individual who reads this series is entitled to empowerment, financial, social, cultural, spiritual and intellectual. Just a footnote to our economy: There is an economic crunch here in America and many people are saying I don't have the money to invest in myself and my future and the future of my children; if you really want to be financially empowered then STOP SPENDING MONEY YOU DON'T HAVE/ BUYING THINGS YOU DON'T NEED/ TO IMPRESS PEOPLE WHO DON'T CARE ABOUT YOU!! Start asking if the items you purchase are assets or liabilities. A home is an asset; a vehicle is not. Don't allow your vehicle note to be more than your mortgage or rent. Clothes, jewelry, and other items are fine, but DO NOT LIVE ABOVE YOUR MEANS. Do not work simply to pay bills, and please teach your children and youth the value of saving money. Purchase items that will further your mental, physical, and financial stability. Books, motivational tapes, and Videos are all sources of life enhancement. So save and invest. Invest in our young people, invest in our children, invest in the community, invest in your Faith based institution. Invest in the gift that was placed in you. That's what it's all about today. Investing in your SUPER-VISION and not living under supervision.

Wright

Keith, I really appreciate this time that you spent with me, I know I asked you a lot of questions and taken up a lot of your time, but I want you to know that I really do appreciate you doing this for me.

Brown

Well, I appreciate you as well, and I would like to say you are worth it. This has been an experience for me today; it's what is called carpe diem(seize the day), and I was able to seize this day and this moment with you, my colleague and team member in a never ending odyssey to make the earth we live on a better place to be. I sincerely salute you for being a sincere vessel of uplift. Now, reader, the Conversation of Success is in you. Remember, if there is no enemy within, the enemy outside can do you no harm. Tell your story, leaving no pages unturned, for when the masses read it, they will rejoice. You deserve to be totally fulfilled! You are a CONVERSATION OF SUCCESS (Compassionate Outstanding Nurturing Vibrant Excellent Resourceful Sincere Aspiring Tenacious Inspiring Outspoken Noteworthy Owner Fabulous Super Unique Courageous Caring Empowered Success Story).

Wright

Today we have been talking to Keith L. Brown; Mr. Brown is a consultant, he's a leader, a teacher, and most of all an amazing dynamic motivator as we have found out this afternoon. As a change agent he is committed to promoting professionalism and ensuring continual success. In short, he is a catalyst, focused predominantly to bringing people together to make a positive difference. Thank you so much, Keith, for being with us on *Conversations on Success*.

Brown

Thank you, sir, and continue to be DAVID (Determined Ascending Vessel Inspiring Daily). Be empowered! To all of my readers, I leave you our Team cheer for a job well done...GOOD JOB! GOOD JOB!...GOOD JOB! GOOD JOB!...G-DOUBLE O D J-O-B GOOD JOB! GOOD JOB!!!

About The Author

Keith L. Brown is both motivational and inspirational. His focus is to assist others in developing a lifelong path, assembled with stepping stones, not stumbling blocks. His message increases self-esteem and leaves individuals empowered to uplift themselves and others.

Labeled special-ed, at-risk, and potential menace to society, Keith dedicated his life to overcoming those obstacles. Today he is a member of the National Speakers Association and Who's Who in Professional Speaking. Keith, one of the most sought after Professional Speakers in the industry, creates an atmosphere of what he calls "Fuber" (Fun and Fiber).

Mr. Brown's keynotes, workshops, and seminars are guaranteed to make audiences learn, laugh, love, and lead in every aspect of their lives.

Mr. Brown is a "consultant," a "leader," a "teacher," and most of all an amazing, dynamic "motivator." As a change agent, he is committed to promoting professionalism and ensuring continual success. In short, he is a catalyst focused predominantly on bringing people together to make a positive difference.

Mr. Keith L. Brown is a Legislative Liaison and Professional Speechwriter. He has conducted a countless number of workshops and presentations to and for school systems, colleges, universities, state/federal agencies, foundations, organizations and faith-based institutions.

Keith and his lovely wife Wakea, a bonafide educator, are the proud parents of one sensational son, Keon.

Keith L. Brown

20/20 Enterprises

115 Courtney's Lane

Fayetteville, GA 30215

Email: keithspeaks@keithlbrown.com

www.keithlbrown.com

Chapter Fifteen

DR. BILL BLATCHFORD

THE INTERVIEW

David E. Wright (Wright)

Today we're talking to Dr. Bill Blatchford. Bill is one of the strongest voices in history today for profitability with special emphasizes on increased case acceptance. He's a dentist advocate for net return, more time away, and increased enjoyment. He practiced for twenty years in Corvallis, Oregon, following the graduation from Loyola Dental School. He has helped thousands of doctors to achieve practice success. In his custom coaching program, Dr Blatchford works personally with doctor, spouse and team to achieve their dream practice. He and his wife Carolyn live in Sunriver, Oregon. They have two happily married daughters. He is delighted that one of them is entering the dental profession. Dr. Blatchford, welcome to *Conversations on Success*.

Wright

Dr. Blatchford, what is success to you? How do you define it and how do you measure it?

Dr. Bill Blatchford (Blatchford)

That's a great question, David. I think that success is defined by individuals. A story that I tell in seminars to define success is; There's a fisherman named Jose' down on the beaches of Baja, California. Everyday Jose' gets up, he goes fishing with his buddies, he catches his fish, he comes back, he sells the fish, he buys and has some beers with his buddies, he goes home, he plays with his kids, he has dinner with his family, he goes to bed and makes love to his wife. He gets up the next morning and repeats the whole thing all over again. Well this MBA from Harvard comes down and is all excited and says that he has some venture capitalist up in New York and they can raise some money and buy Jose' a whole fleet of boats. "Why, Jose' you can start exporting your fish to New York and, you and your wife can move up to New York, and you can just make all the money you've ever dreamed about." Now, Jose' is just not excited. Finally this MBA is real frustrated and he says, "Well, Jose', what would you do if you had all the money in the world?" "Well, I suppose I'd move down the Baja and buy a shack on the beach, and go fishing with my buddies." So the point is success is different for everybody.

One of the problems that I see among the clients that I work with is so often they're trying to define their success by other people's standards. I think that's one of the first keys for happiness and success, and I put happiness and success together because to me that's what it's about. They have to discover for themselves what it is that makes them happy. What it is that fulfills them. And not to impose other peoples' standards on their own life. What makes them happy and fulfilled is what makes them feel successful. To one person it's raising a wonderful family, and to someone else it's making millions of dollars. It depends on the individual. If we could sum it up, it's probably getting exactly what you want out of your short stay on this planet.

Wright

And you measure it by each client's personal needs?

Blatchford

I think that's one way to measure it. A lot of people look at my life and say, "Wow, that's really successful." Perhaps if they knew everything about it, it wouldn't match their measure of success. For example, we're heading off as I mentioned earlier, on this month long trip. We're going from Las Vegas, to London, to Switzerland, to

Scottsdale, Arizona, to Cabo San Lucas, to Orlando, to West Palm Beach, to the Florida Keys, and back to Chicago. They think "Wow, isn't that fun!" Yet, if most people tried that for about a month, they would probably say, "Hey this isn't so much fun." It just happens to be that I'm married to a wonderful lady and we enjoy traveling, so this is how we planned our life. For us, this is success. It's certainly not measured, in my opinion, by material things, although people look at that and say, "But you've got all those material things."

I've traveled and lectured in India, for example. I noticed that over there the dentists who I worked with, they closed their offices two hours in the middle of the day to go home and have dinner or lunch with their family. They have time for each other, and they have a lot more time for relationships. Yet, if you look at the material things they own, it's not even close to what we have here in the United States. I don't think success is always measured in material things. I know we're in a business environment, and I teach in a business environment where we measure our success by the bottom line and by the quarterly report, but there's a lot more to it than that.

Wright

Some people have said that there are common traits to successful people. Do you think that successful people have traits that are in common?

Blatchford

I've been in a unique situation for the last twenty years, David, I have worked primarily with dentists. Dentists are viewed by a lot of the public as relatively successful just by being in the profession. I work with the upper end of that profession and, yes, I think there are some very common traits that make people successful. I think that the first trait I see that makes people successful is a clear vision of where they are going with their life. What it is that's important to them and what they want to get out of it. Once they're clear on this vision, I think they start to make it happen. A book that I have quoted many times is Michael Gerber's book, *The E Myth*. E as in entrepreneur. One of the things that I see in dentists—though of course Michael Gerber was referring to all people in small business—is that about 75% of people go into business not to start a business, but because they enjoy the technical thing that the business does. In other words, in the case of the dentist if they like working on tiny white things in a dark wet space, and they do ok, they work 40 hours a week and they make a good income, then things are good. Yet, I see a lot of them not fulfilled, they're not happy, they're looking for a way out, they can't wait for Friday, that sort of existence.

They have found that about 15% of small business owners actually embraced the management. I really think that management is the next level you have to learn. Once you know where the business is going, you have to learn how to manage it. That's paying attention to the staffing issues, personnel, marketing, overhead costs, all of those types of concerns. We know that in a well-managed practice or business we can double the net income in less time. A question I very often ask is what is the difference between a practice that does 800 thousand-dollars with a national average overhead of 75%, giving a net of $200, or a practice doing $400 with an overhead of 50%. Of course that net is exactly the same and the other doctor works twice as hard. So management is the second level.

The third level that Gerber picked out is the leadership level. We find that we have doctors that are earning in the seven figure income and not working any harder, but they're working smarter. Part of that goes to that vision leadership; they know where they're going. They're clear and they surround themselves with a group of people that want the same thing.

If you are in business you have to have a good product. Your product has to be excellent. If you're in the service industry you have to provide excellent service. There are too many businesses that both of us are aware of out there, that do a mediocre job, they do just enough to get by and they're surrounded by staff members and everybody on the team is working as little as they can get by with. Sadly, we're reminded of that on a daily basis and when we run into someone that really goes out of the way to help a customer or a client or a patient, it's an exception.

I think the manager and the leader have to develop a marketing plan, as would any business. You can't be invisible; you've got to get the word out about what it is you do and why people would want to come see you.

The last area that is not emphasized enough is good communication skills. I've had a chance to work with about 1500 dentist over the last twenty-years and my observation is that doctors who have the communication skills to communicate, first off to communicate to the community what it is they do, who they are, and for whom do they do it, and then to communicate with the staff, and then to communicate with the patients, they are the ones that enjoy the success regardless of how you measure success.

I did say the technical skills, the product has to be on the shelf. I'll tell you, there are dentist out there, I'm sure in your field as well, who have a great product but can't communicate. As a result, they never enjoy the success that they feel they deserve.

Wright

So how important in this day and time, in the business community are clear goals?

Blatchford

Clear goals are important not only in the business community, but in every way. I think in a family and in a business, if you're taking a vacation, a physical fitness program, or almost any activity, goals are extremely critical. I don't know how to emphasize the importance of them. I go back to some training I received from Zig Ziegler thirty years ago and I still remember the statistic that only about five percent of people in this country have clear financial goals. We find that corresponds exactly with the 95% of the public that's totally dependent on the social security and the federal government for their retirement. It's so simple, it doesn't matter what your income level is, if you have clear goals it's easy to overcome that dependency.

It's clear in the rest of your life, but in business it is absolutely crucial that you have clear goals. Especially if you have a staff of people helping you. If they don't know where you are going there's a very small chance they're ever going to arrive at the destination that you have in mind.

I think goals have to be specific, they have to be measurable, they have to be committed in writing, and then they have to be communicated to those people around us that care about our success. If I have staff that doesn't share my goals, they can be my friend, *but* they can't be my staff. If the vision and the goals are clear, then every decision we make in business has a backboard. Is this action going to move me closer to my goal or not? And if it's not going to move me closer to my goal why am I doing it? So I like it extremely clear.

Wright

The readers of this book will be diverse. I'd like to ask you a question that would go across all industry lines, realizing that you specialize in dentistry. What do you think is the answer to assembling a great team? In other words, what are the characteristics of the individuals that would best make up a great team?

Blatchford

That is a great question and that's an issue that a lot of businesses never find the answer to. I think it's quite simple. I'm going to take it outside of dentistry for a moment, but there are two businesses here in the northwest that I have used as examples. The owner of one of those businesses has been a mentor to me. That is a man named Les Schwab. Les Schwab has the biggest tire store in the United States. He has 6000 employees working for him. He has 400 tire stores. I'm going to describe what happens when you drive your car in to a Les Schwab tire store. You pull on the lot and some young man in a clean white shirt literally runs to your car, cheerful, big smile, on his face, "How can I help you today sir?" And they're excited and enthusiastic about tires.

I asked this same question that you asked me to Les Schwab a few years ago. I said, "How do you train people to do this? How do you train this work ethic in people?" He looked at me and laughed. At that time he was eighty-six years old. He said, "You know, it's impossible. You cannot train this. You select them." I said, "How do you do that?" He said, "Well first, in our case, we hire farm kids from eastern Oregon and eastern Washington that aren't afraid to get their hands dirty. We hire people who see the opportunity in the job." You see, if you go to work for Les Schwab when you're eighteen years old, by the time you're fifty-five years old, you'll have well over a million dollars in your pension plan. It's a wonderful place. He's got about 400 stores, so he has 400 positions for managers and 400 positions for assistant managers, and he's looking for people that see the opportunity. I said, "How do you select these people?" He said, "Well, we interview them a couple of times, we hire them, and we put them on the floor and out in the shop, at the end of the week the boys make a decision." Now they have a bonus plan that's based on the results of that store. " If the boys decide that you have it, you get to stay. If at the end of the first week the boys take a vote and if they see that you're going to make a contribution to their livelihood and their success you get to stay and if not, you're out of there." The average new hired person there lasts five days.

Now, the other store is Nordstrom. I'm sure you're familiar with them. Founded here in Seattle, four generations ago, and they're known for customer service and quality. Our daughter graduated from the University of Arizona in fashion merchandising and got a job at Nordstrom. That was her goal; she wanted to work at Nordstrom, selling clothes. The average new hired person at Nordstrom lasts four days, and it's the same philosophy. Here is how we do things here at Nordstrom, here is how we do things here at Les Schwab's, here is how we do things in this dental office. If you share these values with me and you're willing to do it the same way I want to do it, stay, and if you don't its ok with me. You can be my friend, but you can't be my employee. I think rather than spending a lot of time trying to teach a duck to climb a tree or a chicken to swim, we put people in this situation by screening interviews and we see how they do. If they literally love what they do, it shows and if they don't they can't fake it. I think it's selection. I think it's the willingness on the part of the employer to say I made a mistake in hiring this person, this person is not who I'm looking for. Rather than trying to change this person, they need to move on. I feel it's a very simple problem and I've done that in my own business.

I have an absolutely incredible group of people. When I had a larger group it was the same way. I didn't have to worry about what they did because I know they would use their own best judgment. Their own best judgment might not be the same way I would do things, but I knew that their intent was to get the same results I wanted. I think that people try to micro manage employees. They try to teach them. They have these thick manuals on how to do every procedure. I think the government is the typical example of that; they've got a manual for everything, rules and policies. And as a result, no one can make a decision. I like to tell people what the vision of the organization is, what our goals are for the next ten years, what our goals are for the next twelve months, and tell them to use their own best judgment.

Wright

In the scheme of things, when you consider hiring practices and building staffs/teams, how important is accountability?

Blatchford

That's one of the keys. I think you give them the direction and you check on their progress to ensure they're moving in that direction. I think accountability is based on results. Like in our case, or in the case of a lot of business people, accountability in a sales position, for example. Sales people probably have the most freedom in most organizations. They talk about having great conversations with people; the bottom line is what are your sales? We measure that in business in this country in US dollars. There have to be some concrete goals and you have to hold people accountable. I have outside sales people in my organization. One of the things that I hold them accountable for, rather than how much they sell is how many calls did they make and how many people did they actually see face to face. I find that there's a formula to this. It's different for every salesmen, but if you make a certain number of cold calls, you will get a certain percentage of appointments and a certain number of appointments will lead to a certain number of sales. I hold my sales people accountable for how many calls they make. I believe the rest all falls into place. Now we do look at results of sales. I have consultants that call on doctors and I hold them accountable for the results the doctors get. If the doctor's having a personnel problem the first thing I do is call my consultant in that office and say, "What's going on, how do we get it solved, what's the problem?" I think that we don't do our employees a favor when we are not—and I hesitate to use the word— demanding. Let's just say that we're clear on what results we want and either you help me get these results or if it's a training issue, I need to train that person more, but if it's a work ethic issue, I can't help them. I feel my life is too short to try to convince somebody to have that work ethic issue.

Wright

So how important is differentiating yourself from your competition as well as from other business people?

Blatchford

Well let me talk about dentistry for a moment, I think that for years the public saw the dentist as the *generic* dentist. As an example, I think that when you read that article in *The Wall Street Journal*, you'll get a real clear idea on this. About 25 years ago I gave a talk to a local hospital. I told them pretty much what the future of medicine was going to become and at that time my projection was rather radical. The public was going to start viewing physicians as generic, a doctor is a doctor is a doctor, and once that happens the public is going to see you as a commodity. When it's a commodity like buying paper towels, I go to Wal-Mart. I go where I can get them for the least amount of money. The reason that was happening is the medical profession, at that time, was treating the patients as a number.

I made the prediction that in just a few very short years the HMOs would be the way of the future. Not that I agree with HMOs, but I said you're leading yourself right into that with your actions. So we started working with the dentist because the public viewed dentists the same way. We had to ask why would you come to my office when I don't even accept your insurance plan? Why would you come to my office, when my fees are higher then the other dentist in town? Why would you come here? Well, the answer is, it's the same reason people choose a nice restaurant, a nice hotel, or a more expensive retail shop. We go there because of perceived value. I think that we have to learn how to get that perceived value across to the potential customer or patient. It's critically important unless you want to become generic, and once you become generic the public is trained. They will go to the least expensive, generic dentist that they can find. Why do we have dentists? Why are my clients able to charge say $1500 for a crown or veneer when the average in the area may be $750? Why are my clients able to charge eight to ten thousand dollars for an upper and lower denture when the average may be $3000? And patients are paying it willingly. Of course, we always use the approach that no one needs it and you certainly can get one for a lot less money by any dentist here in the area. Why do they do that? I'd say it's that differentiation and the willingness and ability to communicate that.

Wright

When we're talking about perceived value, which is what would determine what you're talking about, that perceived value comes after marketing. So how do you not become an invisible dentist? How do you market professionally so that the people will communicate the value concept?

Blatchford

I think first off you have to remember, and this is where a lot dentist and a lot of professionals are missing the boat, a lot of our guiding principles and ethics were developed back in the '20s, '30s, '40s, '50s and even in the '60s. You have to take a look at retail. How many products were available at that time? I use athletic shoes as an example because Phil Knight, who started Nike, lives here part of the year in our resort. When he opened his business in the late '60s, athletic shoes consisted of about four models, high and low top converse, black and white. Now Nike alone makes over 200 separate pairs of athletic shoes.

I visited and spoke in New Zealand several times. When you go into clothing store and you want to buy a jacket, there are about three or four in your size and two of them are navy blue. You go into a men's store here and we have rack after rack after rack. You go into a sporting good store today, and I go back to when I was a kid, our local sporting good store was the corner island of the hardware store. Today we have these huge box stores with acres of sporting goods. I think the competition out there for discretionary dollars has changed.

So not only do professionals have to market by word of mouth, we have to advertise. Ted Turner said it best, "The key to success: get up early, work like hell and advertise." We have to do that. We have to advertise and we have to get out in the community and let people know what we do. We have to let people know why we're different. We have to let them know these features.

I recently noticed an article about a dental office that offers a different experience. First off, when the patient walks into the office, the first thing they notice is a fountain, the place smells good, and they're offered a cappuccino. I mean they're doing things that are not extremely costly, but they certainly make a difference. You walk in and you say, "Wow, this is a nice place. I like it here." You create some ambience that's a little different.

Wright

As you were talking I was thinking about my own industry. If you can imagine, I'm in the book publishing business. When I was growing up, you'd go into a book store and it was musty, it looked like a library. Now you've got Barnes and Noble and Borders. Now they put couches in the stores and it's become user friendly. My wife, who reads more books in a week than I do in a month, doesn't even want the books. She just wants a gift certificate from the book store. So it makes my wrapping easier and she loves me for it.

Blatchford

You're exactly right. Here in the little town of Bend, Oregon, it's a town that's grown from 20,000 to 55,000 in the last ten years. It is based around recreation. I would say it's similar to Gatlinburg, except the sport is different. We've got the Cascade Mountains and its high mountain desert; it's skiing in the winter and golf, white water rafting, fishing and hiking in the summer. We have both a *Borders* and *Barnes and Nobles* here. As you know, these are huge stores and this is exactly what's taking place, and those are discretionary dollars. My parents, who are eighty-six years old, are still going strong and still reading, but they never buy a book. They were both teachers earlier in their careers. They always go to the library. We've got a library here in our house that is huge, comparatively speaking. My wife and I both love books. We buy a lot of books. We're constantly giving books away just because we don't have room to store them. You see, that's what I'm talking about, that's discretionary spending that people do today that we didn't do a generation ago. That's what our competition out there is. That's exactly who we're competing with.

In marketing dentistry, what we've learned is people don't want root canals, gum treatment, crowns or veneers. We have to get across to them what they really want, and that is they want to look good, they want to feel good, and they want a certain amount of value for their money. We have to find out why they want to look good. How their perception of not looking good has affected their life. How their perception of having this fantastic smile is going to change their life. That's what we buy today. We don't buy the product; we don't buy the book. When I look at a book I don't look at them and say, it's just a novel, a non-fictional novel and it's thirty-five dollars or it's thirty dollars. I don't look at it that way. I look at it as how many hours of enjoyment I will get from this book? I think we have to sell all products based on that. That's a shift that a lot of business people don't understand. They think it's about teeth, or the car, the book, the fishing rod or the boat. I don't think that's what it is. I think it's the perception of how this will improve my life.

Look at the ads for boats. My wife and I happen to be boaters. The ads are not a picture of the boat, it's a picture of a family or a picture of a couple enjoying their time on the boat. The boat's in a beautiful setting and it creates this fantasy of all the good times we're going to have. It's a fantasy. I keep my boat at a dock in Seattle, which is a six or seven hour drive from here. Most of the boats at that dock are capable of going around the world. Most of them sit at the dock about 95% of the time. We spend about ten week's a year on our boat in the summertime and most of the winter it sits there. We know it's capable of going all the way to Alaska and back. We've been up almost to Alaska. It's the dream that people buy. I think that's true in almost any product.

Wright

I have had an interest in the dentistry and how it affects the life style now for a long time. I've seen people who make 15 thousand dollars a year go to 50 thousand dollars a year and within two years spend ten thousand on their mouth. What is ten thousand? The difference between fifteen and fifty is a whole lot more than ten.

Blatchford

Well, I think the value of a smile is something that is under estimated sometimes. A salesman, for example, what is it worth to feel good about yourself? We know that people spend an exorbitant amount on clothing, grooming products, so we know the public puts a high value on appearance. I'm sure in training sales people you see people who are perfect until they smile. It's so distracting. In fact one of the things that I have my dental clients do is have their own mouths restored to absolutely perfect condition. Not because they need it, but because they are an example to their patients. Adequate is not enough. It's just like clothing, I'm dressed right now in the clothes wore to work out in the athletic club this morning. I'm comfortable and I'm decent, but that's not the uniform I would wear if I were doing this interview in person. Appearance is important in our society. Very often when I'm role playing with somebody or talking to patients I would say, "David, you're a publisher, correct? And you probably work with the public quite a bit don't you? Have you ever considered the value of a nice smile in your career?" Well, they answer, "Yes, I really have." Then I reply that I'm concerned about that and you've probably thought that your appearance could probably even effect your income.

Wright

Absolutely, but not only for the obvious reason or cosmetic, but it does something to the self image and it's all about self image, every industry I've ever been in. It's all about what you think you are, not what you are.

Well what a great conversation. I wish we could talk all afternoon. Everything that you said strikes a cord in my goal setting plan. You're certainly right on about the things that we've been talking about. I really appreciate all this time you've spent with me today.

Blatchford

Thank you.

Wright

Today we've been talking to Dr. Bill Blatchford, who is one of the strongest voices in dentistry today. He is a dentist advocate for net return and more time away and increased enjoyment, as we have found here today in his talk. He is a graduate of Loyola Dental School; he's helped thousands of doctors achieve practice success. We really do appreciate all the time that you took for us today. Dr. Blatchford, thank you so much for being with us today on *Conversations on Success.*

Dr. Bill Blatchford is one of the strongest voices in dentistry today for profitability with special emphasis on increased case acceptance. He is a dentist's advocate for net return, more time away and increased enjoyment. He practiced for twenty years in Corvallis, OR., following graduation from Loyola Dental School. He has helped thousands of Doctors to achieve practice success. In his Custom Coaching Program, Dr. Blatchford works personally with Doctor, spouse and team to achieve their dream practice.

He and his wife, Carolyn, live in Sunriver, OR. They have two happily married daughters. He is delighted that one of them is entering the dental profession.

Dr. Bill Blatchford

Blatchford Solutions

PO Box 9070

Bend, Oregon 97701

Phone: 800.578.9155

www.blatchford.com

Chapter Sixteen

JOE CALLOWAY

THE INTERVIEW

David E. Wright (Wright)

Today we are talking to Joe Calloway. Joe is a restaurant owner, a business author, and a branding consultant whose client list reads like a Who's Who in business from newspapers in Sweden, Hotels in Great Britain, and computer companies in South Africa to the world brands like American Express and IBM. He's a guest lecturer with both the Graduate School of Business at the University of Tennessee and the Center for Professional Development at Belmont University. A recent issue of *Sales and Marketing Management Magazine* calls Joe "an expert on developing customer focused teams," and a National Customer Service Advisory Board called Joe "one of the most innovative and compelling people in the service industry." Joe's new book, *Becoming a Category of One*, has been released by John Wiley & Sons Publishing. He speaks frequently on the business competition and he has been inducted into the Speakers Hall of Fame. Joe is nationally known as a straight talking expert on how to compete and win in today's market place. Joe, welcome to *Conversations on Success*!

Joe Calloway (Calloway)

David, it's great to be with you.

Wright

Your book called *Becoming a Category of One,* what does it mean to be a category of one? That's a great title by the way.

Calloway

Thank you. Let me tell you where I came up with it. I was working with a group in South Africa, you mentioned South Africa in your introduction. It was an international sales convention of a company, and I had the group working on an exercise, which is something that really anybody can do when they're trying to generate new ideas for their business. Quite simply, what you do is think of a place where you are a customer. You absolutely loved this business. This could be a restaurant, your dry cleaners, where you get your car fixed, it doesn't matter, just some place where you love to do business. Step two is, 10 words or less, what is it that this business does that you find so powerful, so compelling? Step three is to think, "Well, okay, let me take what they do and apply it to my business even though we may be in totally different endeavors. What is it they are doing that we need to do more of? So I was doing that exercise and a woman, and this is interesting because here we are in South Africa and they were people from 40 different countries in the audience, but the woman whose story really, really got my attention was from of all places, west Texas. She said, "The business I'm thinking of is a little place called Walls Feed Store." I said, "Okay. What do they do at Walls Feed Store that's so powerful?" She said, "Well, my husband and I have a ranch with all kinds of animals – cats, cattle, dogs, horses, peacocks, llamas – it's like Noah's Ark. You name it, we've got it." She said, "As you might imagine in that part of Texas there's a lot of feed stores and you can buy feed from any of them. But Walls helps us take care of our animals. There's a difference." And it hit me. I thought, "You know, whatever this little feed store is doing, they have absolutely pulled off the ultimate in business because in the mind of that customer what they had done was taken themselves out of the very crowded category of feed stores and they had created a separate category and they were the only one in it." If you look back at what the woman said, it really gets to the heart of business. She said, "There's a lot of feed stores around here. You can buy feed from any of them, but Walls helps us take care of our animals. There is a difference." What that means is that store had been able to go from being seen as a commodity, meaning whatever you're selling, whatever service you're providing, I can get it anywhere, to creating a unique space in the mind of that customer that says, "Well, I can't get what these people do anywhere else." They do it in such a way that they separated themselves out. Sometimes when I talk about *Becoming a Category of One*, that's where I got the idea.

Sometimes people will quite naturally think, "Well, that sounds good, but you know, I don't know if you can really literally pull that off." And my response to that is, "Well, okay, I'm going to name a product category and you tell me the category one." All I have to do, David, is say motorcycles and the automatic answer is Harley David-son because Harley's done the same thing. They've created a mystique and a specialness around that machine that really goes be-yond product. A more recent example is I can say coffee shops and most people will say Starbucks. What Starbucks has done is a lesson for anybody in any kind of business because Starbucks has taken the simplest of commodities, the coffee bean—granted it's a great coffee bean; don't get me wrong, I'm not selling short the idea of product quality—and wrapped it with an experience that creates a category of one. You've got to have that. Starbucks starts with a really great product, but charging 2, 3, 4, 500% more than most other coffee shops isn't just the product. It's that they have surrounded this product with an experience that consists of big cushy chairs, internet connec-tions, the people behind the counter who, if you are a regular, start fixing your coffee the second you walk in the door because they know what you want and music that they play in the stores that you can actually buy and take home with you. They've taken a simple, simple product. So that's where the idea came from and that's what it's really all about.

Wright

If I were trying to become a *category of one* in whatever I was go-ing to do, is the first step more introspective than anything else?

Calloway

Well, I'll tell you something. The first step, David, is even more in-trospective than that. It's funny. When I was researching the book, the basis of the book being I was looking for the *category of one* com-panies and looking for the threads they all have in common. In other words, what is it that these extraordinary companies do that any of us can do? One thing kept coming up, and it was not something I was looking for. It really gets to the heart of the word that you just used, which is introspective. All of these extraordinary companies were able to point to a specific kind, or in some cases a series, of specific moments in time when they quite simply, yet quite powerfully, made a concrete decision to take their business to another level. Every company talks about getting better and going to the next level, but very, very few companies actually make the decision and the commitment to do it. And there's a difference. It's not just semantics. There's a subtle but incredibly powerful difference. What I have found is that very few companies, and I don't care whether it's a 10,000 or 50,000 employee company, or a two person company, very few businesses actually sit down (I'm talking about the people within the business) and have an eye to eye, gut level conversation around the topic of "How good do we want to be? How far do we want to take this? How much fun do we want to have? How much success do we want to create? How much service do we want to give?" There's just this unspoken assumption that, "Well, of course, we want to be a great company." But that's a dangerous assumption. It really takes getting it on the table and having a confronting conversation about who wants to go. The first chapter of the book ended up being titled, *We Just Decided to Go* because I came to the realization that the mandatory first step is making this decision to go, yet oddly enough, it's the step not taken in some of those companies.

Wright

So how important is innovation in sustaining success today?

Calloway

Well, innovation is almost a requirement. It's kind of inherent in the process of improving your business because there's an old saying, "Insanity is doing the same thing you've always done and yet expecting a different result." Well, if you're going to take your business to the next level, whatever that means to you, then almost by definition that means you're going to have to change. Even though I think virtually everybody out there agrees, intellectually, with the idea that you have to constantly change in order to stay competitive, on a gut level most people are still resistant to change. There's a statement that I use with people to provoke some thought around change, and it's this: Past success can be, and usually is, the enemy of future success. It's a really difficult and confrontive idea to deal with. It's confrontive for me. The idea is that whatever got you to the level of success where you are now, whatever has worked to get you to this point may in fact be the very thing that's keeping you from getting to the next level.

A lot of people say that Peter Drucker is the greatest business thinker of our times. He said something that really made me think. He said, "Success always makes obsolete the very behavior that created it." He also said that whenever you see a successful business that is successful over a long period of time, you have people within that business that are making courageous decisions. I think courage a lot of times comes down to innovation. Innovation by definition means you go first. A lot of times I'll talk with people that say, "Well, we're very innovative in our company because we benchmark our competition, and we look at what the best companies in our field are doing, and then we do that, too." Well, gang, that's not innovation. That's copying. If you do that it assures that I'm never going to be better than second place. I'm not saying that there's anything wrong with knowing what your competition's doing, I mean I want to know that too.

Innovation means you have to do those things that makes people look at you and say, "Well, wait a minute. You can't do that in this business. We've never done that! This is not the sort of thing that people in our business do." But those are the only ideas that are significant enough to ultimately have an impact competitively. It's to do those things that have never been done before. Quite literally, that is the definition of innovation.

Wright

There's a lot of talk, Joe, about brand these days. Obviously I know what branding is, but what does brand really mean?

Calloway

Well, you know it's interesting. I think the traditional definition of brand is one that includes things like your logo, the name of your company, the slogan that you use and your advertising. That's what is traditionally thought of as branding. It's taking an idea and slapping it on top of your company. My approach to brand is that you build your brand from the inside out. The definition of brand that I came up with that I think is incredibly useful for any business of any size is this: Your brand is your customers' perception of what it's like to do business with you. Another way of putting it is to say that your brand is your customers' experience of doing business with you. In other words, if I'm talking to one of your customers and she happens to mention that you know she did some business with you and I say, "Well, what's it like to do business with them?" Whatever she says next, that's your brand. If I want to know what your brand is, I won't even ask you; I'll ask your customers. And so that's why my belief is that everything, and I mean that literally, David, every single decision you make in your business should be looked at with the question of, "How does this decision affect the experience of my customers when they do business with me." Everything is about customer experience. It's not just about the product you sell. It's not just about the service that you provide. It's about everything that surrounds that product. That goes right back to what I was saying about Starbucks. The Starbucks brand is about much more than coffee. The Harley Davidson brand is about much more than a motorcycle. It's about what it is like to do business with you that ultimately becomes the differentiator between you and your competition.

Wright

Right. As you were talking about that it reminded me of something. I frequent a restaurant in my town where the food is not particularly all that good and certainly not as good as some others. I wondered, this has just been a few months ago, why do I keep going there? So after a little bit of introspection, I came up with the fact that I probably go there for the same reason that Norm went into Cheers; everybody knows my name.

Calloway

That's an interesting point that you bring up. James Beard, who was recognized as one of the great, possibly the greatest, chef of the 20th century, was interviewed once by a food magazine. He was asked, "Mr. Beard, what's your favorite restaurant?" His answer was, and you can apply this to any business of any kind anywhere, "My favorite restaurant is the one where they know me." Knowing your customer and creating an experience that becomes a relationship is as powerful a differentiator as there is in business today. It's huge.

Wright

What do you think is the biggest competitive issue that most businesses face today?

Calloway

It's exactly what we're talking about. It's the challenge of differentiating. Differentiating means demonstrating a difference between you and your competition. Differentiation is the answer to the question. I see a hundred different businesses that do what you do. They all do it well. They all do it for about the same price. So given that, why should I do business with you? David, that is the toughest question in business to answer. You ask just about any business what the difference is between them and their competition, and one thing you will often hear is, "It's our people." Well, okay that's probably true. But my follow-up question is "What does that mean? When you say it's your people, what is it that your people are literally willing or able to do that your competition is literally not willing or able to do?"

When you take it to that level, that's where a lot of businesses start hemming and hawing and stammering a little bit because they're a little hard pressed to come up with an answer. They say, "Well, we've got great people." I'm sure you do, but your competition says they've got great people. Tell me, specifically, what is it that you do that your competition doesn't do. If you say, "Well, we give great service," then does that mean if your competition can solve a given problem in three hours, you can solve it in 30 minutes? It kind of gets down to being able to quantify and go beyond a slogan in telling me why I should do business with you. I'll tell you what, though, the key is usually going to be in the people. It's very, very difficult to differentiate with a product any more. You know the nature of technology today is such that if you come out with a product that truly is different or better than your competitors', it's going to take them probably all of five minutes to catch up with that. So you have to find a way to differentiate somewhere in the relationship.

Wright

Going back to the example I gave about the restaurant where everybody knows my name. In my opinion, they actually have 100, if not more, customers inside the restaurant that are really working for them and not getting paid. Not only do they speak to me as I go in the door, but before I get to the back room where I generally sit, I have spoken to three or four lawyers or six or seven secretaries. It's like they are all waiting there for me and I'll disappoint them if I don't show up. It's infectious what these people are doing that work for this restaurant.

Calloway

What they've done is they've created a space in which business has become an act of friendship. I defy you to name any kind of business anywhere, and I'm even including in that high level business to business transactions, where making it an act of friendship is not appropriate. I want to give credit where credit is due. A friend of mine named Jim Cathcart, as far as I know, came up with that idea that business, when done correctly, is an act of friendship. I think that speaks volumes to the nature of what today's customer is looking for, regardless of the kind of business that they're involved with.

Wright

It seems like every company claims to exceed their customers' expectations. In your opinion, how many of them really do that?

Calloway

Virtually none; here's why. It's funny, David. We go through phases of slogans that become popular. I think the single most popular advertising slogan out there today is, "We exceed our customers' expectations." Businesses say that without really giving it much thought at all. My first question to anybody that says that is, "Well, do you have any clue how high your customers' expectations are?" The expectations of today's customer are infinitely higher than they've ever been in history.

I was doing business with a credit card company that I'm a big fan of. Not too long ago I called them up to track down the details about a particular charge that I had made. The young woman who pulled up my account was very friendly and very professional. She gave me the information I needed and she gave it to me quickly. At the end of the conversation they had built in a little customer survey. She said, "Mr. Calloway, do you mind if I ask you a question?" I said, "Of course not." She said, "Did I exceed your expectations today?" I said, "No, you didn't." And I could almost hear her jaw dropping on the other end of the phone line. She immediately said, "Oh my gosh, what did I do wrong?" I said, "You didn't do anything wrong. You were terrific. You met my expectations. You did exactly what I pay you for." What's funny to me is that there are businesses that will provide a good product and good service, and then they sit back and expect people to just fall over with delight because you did what they paid you to do.

If you give me a good product and good service and you're friendly and all that, that's fine. That's pretty much what I'm paying for. In all fairness I'll tell you something about that same credit card company, in a totally different situation. I had lost my credit cards. I called the two credit card companies that were involved. They both said, "We'll get you your replacement cards immediately." The first company sent me my replacement cards; it took about 10 days for it to get there, which was fine. The other company, who I made the call to within 30 minutes of the first one, had cards delivered to me by UPS at my office the next morning. Now that exceeded my expectations.

Wright

Right.

Calloway

I was not expecting that. I'll tell you the other thing that it did. It was a clear differentiator between them and their competitor. They paid for UPS to have those cards delivered to me the next morning. That made a big impression. So number one, it was a differentiator and number two, it did exceed my expectations. But if you're going to exceed my expectations, you've got to go way beyond doing a good job because that's what I'm paying you to do.

Wright

What do think are some ways that companies can achieve consistency of performance? I know there are a lot of people that will be reading this book will want to know what they can do. Can you help us out there some?

Calloway

Yes, the how to's, David, come down to basically three or four things. I think the frustration of a lot of people is that they hear the stories and they say, "You know that's all well and good, but how do you do it?" There's good news and there's bad news. The bad news is there is no template. There is no 10 steps that I, or anybody else, can hand a business and say, "Look, here's 10 steps. Do these things; it's easy." It's not easy. It's simple. The way to achieve category one status, the way to becoming extraordinary is simple, but it's not easy. Quite frankly, every extraordinary company of any size that I've seen, that I've done business with, that I've written about, that I've researched, they all have this in common. They figured it out on their own. Now, having said that, there are some basic truths. There are some things that run through all of these companies. I'll give you two or three of them. One is about knowing who we are. By knowing who we are, I don't mean what we sell. I mean who we are as people. How we want to do business with other folks. The way we want to treat each other, and the way we want to treat our customers. You know the really successful companies, when they hire a new employee, way before they start talking the job description, they spend a lot of time talking about, "Let me tell you what kind of people we are here." They talk about values. They talk about what's important. It really comes down to culture. The companies that had decided they are going to be a pleasure to work with, or that say, "We're going to be the best part of each customer's day," that's the sort of thing that they talk about all the time.

That brings me to the second point. Beyond who we are, I think it's about leadership. I'm not talking about management here. I'm talking about leadership, which I think is a different thing. Managing involves making the organization function properly. Leadership is this idea of constantly reminding everyone of who we are. Remember what's important. Remember how we treat people. Remember who we are.

A third element that flows from that is consistency. There are some companies that, if they were truthful in their advertising, they'd say, "Feel lucky? Well, come on in cause it depends on who you get." That's a brand killer. If it depends on who I get in your store, in your restaurant, in your consulting business, whatever it may be, then you've got a big problem. The really extraordinary companies that are the ones that are consistent in that it doesn't matter who you get on the phone, it doesn't matter what sales clerk or cash register you go to, it doesn't matter who you run into in the aisles of the store, you're going to get a consistency of performance that runs through the entire organization.

I guess the fourth element would get back to everything that we were saying about differentiation. That, ultimately, comes down to how we treat people. There was a service technician in our home a few months ago doing an inspection just to be sure everything's okay. The service technician knew that our little two-year-old daughter was upstairs taking a nap. He'd done the work outside. As he was coming back in the house, I saw him closing the sliding glass door. He did it in slow motion to be sure that he didn't make any noise. He turned around and saw me and whispered that he had finished the inspection. He said that everything was fine, and he'd let himself out the front door. And when he went out the front door, he did the same thing. He did it in slow motion to keep from waking up the baby. You may say to yourself, "Well, that's not that big a deal." No, that's everything because he understood that his business was not about just inspecting the air conditioning unit. His business was about taking care of our home, and that involved everything down to whispering when you know the baby's taking a nap. We try to make rocket science out of this stuff, and it basically comes down to the way you treat people. That's the essence of business.

Wright

What a great conversation, Joe. I always learn when I talk to you.

Calloway

It was a pleasure, David. I enjoy it every time.

Wright

I'm going to shamefully market this book. I didn't know you had a new book coming out, *Becoming a Category of One*.

Calloway

Actually, that one is already out. It's doing extremely well. We're just thrilled with the reception it's gotten and the reviews that it's gotten. It's available in book stores, Amazon.com and barnes&noble.com.

Wright

Great! I am heading to our local bookstore to pick it up. Today we've been talking to Joe Calloway, who is a business author and a branding consultant. He speaks all over the world – Great Britain, South Africa – and he talks a lot about branding, a lot about business and a lot about leadership. He is also a guest lecturer at the University of Tennessee, my alma mater, and the Center for Professional Development at Belmont University. Joe, thank you so much for being with us today. I really do appreciate this time you've taken with us.

Calloway

It was an absolute pleasure. Thank you.

About The Author

Joe is a restaurant owner, a business author, and a branding consultant whose client list reads like a Who's Who in business from newspapers in Sweden, Hotels in Great Britain, and computer companies in South Africa to the world brands like American Express and IBM. He's a guest lecturer with both the Graduate School of Business at the University of Tennessee and the Center for Professional Development at Belmont University. A recent issue of *Sales and Marketing Management Magazine* calls Joe "an expert on developing customer focused teams," and a National Customer Service Advisory Board called Joe "one of the most innovative and compelling people in the service industry." Joe's new book, *Becoming a Category of One*, has been released by John Wiley & Sons Publishing. He speaks frequently on the business competition and he has been inducted into the Speakers Hall of Fame. Joe is nationally known as a straight talking expert on how to compete and win in today's market place.

Joe Calloway

PO Box 158309

Nashville, Tennessee 37215

Phone: 615.383.2249

Fax: 615.383.4964

www.joecalloway.com

Chapter Seventeen

DAVID N. ROGERS

THE INTERVIEW

David E. Wright (Wright)

Today we are talking to David Rogers. You will find it hard to believe after reading about or meeting such a likeable and charismatic guy, but David was abandoned by his mother on the same day he was born. He was then adopted, and abandoned again as a young child. David spent much of his childhood on the street, and in foster homes, group homes, and even in military school. At 16 years of age, David was out on the street on his own. He found himself sleeping wherever he could find shelter and doing whatever it took to find work to survive. One day deciding that he actually deserved better, David began to look within to see what would be necessary to make that happen. As you read this book, you'll learn how what he found is possible for each of us. Now David owns and operates several successful small businesses, one of which was named as the number one automotive repair business in the United States, and two others in which he teaches other small businesses how to benefit from his award winning management and marketing concepts. David's advertising agency, Automated Marketing Group LLC, is the crown jewel of his interests. AMG, as he calls it, is very likely the most effective and affordable advertising a small business can engage in today! Auto Profit Masters

LLC is another of his interests. This business was designed specifically for the independently owned auto repair industry. Through APM, David has helped many family owned shops achieve lasting success and profitability. He is a member of the National Speaker's Association and speaks and trains for many companies and organizations, counsel's business owners and their families, and he hosts a weekly radio show in Denver, Colorado. David's views on success are exciting and truly make it attainable for everyone who really wants it! David, welcome to *Conversations on Success*!

David Rogers (Rogers)
Thank you, David. I am glad to be here.

Wright
Which is more important in your opinion, education or resourcefulness?

Rogers
Well, as you know I started out with nothing but what God gave me. Due to the lack of financial means, I had little hope of ever achieving what most would call a normal education. My business partner/mentor tells people I have a Ph.D. in the school of hard knocks! I'm a bit biased perhaps, but think about it for a minute. All the degrees in the world are of no use whatsoever unless you have the wherewithal and the motivation to get out of your chair and figure out how to find the specific information, the solution, the person, or the machine you need to get the job done. Then of course, you must research the situation and form a strategy, or find the right person or persons to form that strategy, especially if actually executing the task at hand requires an expert. So, you must be able to understand what, who, and how (in that order), before you can execute—that takes resourcefulness. Therefore, I think learning to be resourceful will benefit you much more than obtaining a piece of paper that says you should be smart enough to figure everything out! The only accurate measuring stick of resourcefulness is success. It is the necessary ingredient of true accomplishment around which all others are arranged.

Wright
This book is titled *Conversations on Success*. I'm talking to a lot of people about this subject, but something I enjoyed hearing you do in a

radio interview, was defining success. What is your definition of success?

Rogers

Well, my definition of success may be a bit unusual. I believe it's the fulfillment, the satisfaction, and the joy of finally discovering what you're truly meant to do. I am talking about more than your job. I am speaking of your entire life. To me, success means arriving or finding yourself at a point in life where your ultimate happiness is no longer found in just chasing material things. It includes finding satisfaction in seeking to become even more a part of the harmony of all things great and beautiful. It means being filled with a comfort and a satisfaction in helping others, and where for me the most rewarding feeling is the peace and happiness of knowing every day when I am on the right path, or what corrections I must make when I'm not. Happiness is sometimes very elusive to people who seem so successful when seen from a distance. I believe that my investment in life must have value to others, and that it is critical to multiply the energy and the momentum I feel by sharing the ideas and concepts that work in my business with others who are seeking similar opportunities and success. This creates a foundation for synergistic results. **Synergy is one of the most important principals to understand when developing a successful life!**

Wright

Do you think individuals with significant weaknesses ever succeed?

Rogers

If this wasn't true, I'd still be shoveling manure or washing dishes in a café (both of which I have done, as a matter of fact!). I believe that for many people those weaknesses are where the success begins. Maybe it's the motivation like Charles Atlas having sand kicked in his face, or maybe it's learning to overcome a physical handicap like Christopher Reeves. Maybe it's like me, a guy who used to get bad marks on his report cards for talking too much in class - that's now a paid speaker, trainer, and a radio show host. My parents always said, "If you could find someone to pay you to talk, you'd be a millionaire." That message was delivered in a sarcastic way, but I took their jibes and turned them into a fun and exciting career. I get to travel, see the world, and talk, talk, talk! I perform keynotes, as well as classes, seminars, and radio shows on various subjects including advertising, marketing, customer service, production management, performance, and many others. But, the thing I love most is talking with business owners. I help them take small family businesses from average or even struggling performance to a high level of success and publicity. I have learned to greatly respect and appreciate the opportunity to add true and lasting value to people's lives and businesses. I have learned a most important principle – a weakness can become a strength that results in happiness and satisfaction for me and those I associate with!

Wright

So how do you evaluate and make decisions about the risks that sometimes need to be taken in order to be successful?

Rogers

I've developed a test for making hard decisions that involves a risk or a conflict of interest of any kind. There are three questions I ask myself and if the answer to any of these is "no," then I pass up the opportunity and move on. The questions are, Number one: If there were no expectation of a reward, would this still be the right thing to do? Number two: Will this decision benefit all the people or the business entities involved? Number three: Am I willing to stick by my decision or at least the reasons for which I made it *publicly* and *permanently* even if it blows up and goes entirely wrong?

Wright

Those are tough questions.

Rogers

They are tough questions. But honestly if you really test it that way, life is much easier. Think about it. If you could spend all of your time focused on the true task at hand, and in constructing the outcome carefully without spending endless hours assessing and re-assessing the possible risks and "what might happen if...," you might find yourself making much more progress, and in much less time!

Wright

I can see how that would be the case! Spending too much time worrying will get you nowhere! I know you are a very spiritual and ethical man, I have to know though: Do you think there are things in life that are okay to sacrifice for success?

Rogers

Well, if you mean ice cream, or watching TV, or a vacation day or something, well sure! But if you mean my honesty, my scruples, or my healthy family life, surely you jest. Hopefully, you're not suggesting deeper more difficult to see things such as morals, faith, or ethics. A person's success is only a measure of their sum. Everything you give or take in order to get there either adds or detracts from the success itself. Hey, define success for yourself before you go running through life trying to capture it, otherwise you may find that you have a snake in your net instead of a butterfly.

I have known many people (including myself in my younger years) who climbed to significant levels of "success," only to find they climbed the wrong mountain. The safest, most satisfying way to true success and happiness is to be willing to sacrifice short-term, self-centered pleasures (or accomplishments) for long-term, long-lasting goals expressed in terms of service to others. I have found that this only brings true self-esteem and true success in everything I do—in my family, my businesses, and in others with which I work.

Wright

That makes a ton of sense to me. You know, we all have our ideas about who can lead, but since you have the track record, I want to ask you the "million dollar" question. What kind of leader does it take to be successful?

Rogers

Well, you may not like this answer. It's not an easy one. A great leader has to be direct yet kind. He has to be tough yet tender, ruthless but compassionate, and stingy yet generous. Most of all he has to know when to be which. He must be tuned in to his people and their families' needs as well as tuned in to their performance. I believe that a man without faith cannot lead people to great success long term. At the same time, a business leader must be willing to make the "hard decisions" and be able to separate from his emotional attachments to the people he cares for when their performance or behavior dictates disciplinary action or even termination. He does not have to be harsh, but the key is **consistency.** A leader can intimidate any man or any monkey into doing just about anything, but to lead them he must produce and live by an example that they wish, desire, and feel compelled from within to follow. He'd also have to be real to them and that means not hiding the fact that he is imperfect. We share our mistakes and weaknesses openly with each other in our businesses. Besides being good for stress relief (laughing at the boss without fear of retribution is always fun), it also gives us a chance to understand how to improve the business, ourselves, and obviously, our trust level. Through understanding and accepting my own weaknesses and then hiring, training, or working through the process of developing solutions for them, we all benefit and improvement is constant. When trust exists that no one in our businesses will be held back due to limitations of the leader, suddenly the lid is blown off! Now, there is nothing holding us back! Everything and everyone is then focused on "what's right, not who's right." Leadership is all about the performance of the team, not the elevation or status of the leader. In my companies, it's not about WHO is right, it is about WHAT is right!

Wright

I'm not going to ask you if you've ever had any failures.

Rogers

I promise I have.

Wright

I would like to ask, how have your failures helped you to prepare for success.

Rogers

Well, without failure, how would you know when you have succeeded?

Wright

That's an interesting observation!

Rogers

It's the simple process of comparison that unlocks the power to succeed. The painful and the bloody taste of failure is precisely what's driven me on and what strengthens my resolve to persist and to proceed in spite of, or perhaps even because of my failure...or maybe because of those who reveled in it. When I was a kid, I remember going through some of what I think of as normal phases and imagining becoming a doctor, a veterinarian, a singer…just some normal childhood thinking and fantasizing. I remember my mother asking me what I wanted to be when I grew up. "A veterinarian" I answered (as if I hadn't just decided twelve seconds ago.) She said "Did you know that 93% of the people that apply for vet school don't make it? You should pick something more realistic." She never gave me a single suggestion, or even attempted to encourage me. My adopting parents used to tell me that I would amount to nothing. I couldn't wait to prove them wrong. Things are very different now. I am the most stable and dependable member in our family. My siblings and parents often come to me for help or assistance. I enjoy providing for them. "Amount to nothing," huh?

Wright

I remember a math teacher in high school telling me that I would never be any good at math. I was on the honor roll and failing math, if you can believe that. So I just dropped it because I viewed her as a mentor. I thought she knew what she was talking about.

Rogers

That is very unfortunate.

Wright

When I was 37 years old, I was driving down the interstate after speaking to a group where I said, "Don't let other people tell you who you are, what you are or what you can do." That statement made such an impact on me I almost wrecked. I went directly to the University of Tennessee; registered in the Algebra I class, aced the final, and made an A in the course.

Rogers

I have found that the discouraging attitudes and comments of others can present large and sometimes difficult stumbling blocks to our success. But, there is something even more dangerous and formidable between a person and their dreams.

Wright

What is that?

Rogers

Whether we *believe them or not...* My life took a tremendous turn for the better and I started to experience consistent, little successes when I stopped listening to and believing those around me who said, "NO," those who didn't share my vision, or who intentionally tried to hold me back. Success is a choice!

Wright

Is it really possible, do you think, for the average person to achieve success?

Rogers

Well, that's a great question. Why think of yourself as average? I mean, what is average and who is labeling you as average? I believe everyone is unique and everyone has special gifts within them. I think a better question might be how do I find the part of me that is *bound to be successful?* Then you have something to work on. There's a part of every person that demands to be successful; that is driven to create and achieve. Each of us has a survival mechanism that I like to call a rational and logical inner referee. Once you unlock the winner that the referee is trying to hold back, to keep you from embarrassing yourself or from hurting yourself, then you can begin to find the joy of success. Look at it this way. If the guy who invented umbrellas stayed in out of the rain like his mother no doubt told him to, we'd all still be getting wet today, wouldn't we?

Wright

So what would your advice be to someone who is just starting out or who wants to start a successful business career path?

Rogers

The first thing I'm going to say, find a mentor who is still active and highly successful in your field or a similar field and for a relationship. It could be a consulting or a coaching situation, or it could be a partnership. The key is to find the proper experts and then as you grow, surround yourself with the best people for the job at hand, not with your brother-in-law who needs a job for the fifth time this year, or some other warm body. Then, learn as much as you can about the industry you are considering. Find a marketing expert who is successful and has a proven track record. If you are beginning a business then you must join the appropriate association, participate in as much industry training as possible, apply for BBB membership, and begin to work on building your credibility and identity.

Wright

I was raised in poverty and it was very difficult to overcome that mentally. But I had a happy childhood because I didn't know I was poor. But being abandoned and being adopted and abused, those are some pretty tough things to live through. How did you get through those first few years?

Rogers

It's similar to what you say. You say you didn't know you were poor. I didn't know it was any different either. Until I was six years old, I didn't even realize that I had been abandoned or that I was adopted. I wasn't told that until I made a statement after watching a disturbing television show about a child who ran away after finding she was adopted. "Gee, Mom...I sure am glad I am not adopted!" The reply was, "But you are adopted, David." I was completely shocked, and remember staying in my room for two days trying to figure out why my real mommy didn't want me. Knowing and hearing how I was chosen by my new parents allowed for little consolation when being beaten severely was common and unquestioned. I never had anything else to compare my life with. When a child is in a position where he knows things are bad, that's just the way it is. You just survive and you do what you do. Kids are extremely resilient. They bounce back really well. Once I started realizing what was going on, sure, there were times I was sad or I wished things were different, but it doesn't take very long for even a child to realize that in this harsh world, wishing will get you nowhere. **It's up to you, and only you to change the circumstances within which you may not be happy or satisfied.**

Have you ever had an employee or maybe a co-worker who was always unhappy and constantly wanted more money? This person was likely complaining and just never really had more than a good day now and then. Well, you likely found out that even more money didn't seem to fill the void of this individual's unhappiness. I learned early in my life, that there is only ONE way to get what I want. I have to go get it. There are no magic tricks, and schemes will always eventually backfire. The real secret that every successful person I know lives by, is to **always believe in the future, yourself, and one must always be willing to work for that future.** Regardless of obstructions, changes, and challenges, successful people seem always to be the individuals who won't settle for anything but finding a solution. You simply have to press on. You find something that you're good at or something or someone that you love and you **keep your thoughts and feelings focused on the positive, and on the future.** I also found hard work and studying and things like that usually kept me out from under the stick. So all motivation is not pleasant or fun, but that really doesn't matter. Sometimes the more uncomfortable someone is, the more likely they will do something about it!

Wright

No question!

Rogers

In addition to working hard, studying, and being determined to find solutions for my own discomfort, I began to naturally attempt to anticipate what others wanted and expected from me so that I could please every one as best I could. I learned to listen to, as some say "read" people, and that desire to understand what motivates them and what *else* they are after, led to a life-long search for understanding. The study of people and the way they think and act has not only allowed me to survive, but evolved into an opportunity to help others in understanding these same principals; especially as they relate to personnel management and advertising and marketing. Now I spend most of my time analyzing behavior and response to stimulus, whether it is designing a winning advertising campaign for a small business, or deciding how to best get a critical point of understanding across to a coaching client or a staff member.

Wright

Looking back, we all take courses on profiling to figure that out, DISK and Myers Briggs, but I know that this has not given the normal person 1/10 of the insight you're your experience has ingrained into you. Seeing you operate, whether with your staff, or a stranger, is an amazing thing indeed! People say that after meeting you for the first time, they felt as if they had known you all of your life! Let me ask you another question not totally off the subject, but as you look back to those early years, were there teachers, were there other adults, were there ministers; people that really guided you and helped you along the way?

Rogers

There were people that tried to help. I remember one pastor, for instance, that he was very different, in more ways than one. This man made a profound impact in my young life. We lived in a small, very segregated community in rural, white America. I mean I don't think I'd ever seen a person of any other ethnic origin other than maybe two Hispanics and the rest were all Anglos. This guy was from East India. So he was the darkest person I had ever seen in my 6 long years of life, just black as coal. He really stood out in a crowd and I'd never seen anyone like that before. He was also the kindest, most compassionate, most gentle person I'd ever met in my life. This man actually formed a relationship with me and took me on a few drives and tried to get me to tell him what was going on at home. He knew things were bad, but he didn't know...he couldn't really put his finger on what. Of course, I wasn't telling anybody anything out of a fear of making things worse. This gentleman was very involved in my life for the few years before he was transferred to another area. He was the first example I was given that was worthy of following. Although he was never told what the root of the problem was, he made sure that I was with him or his family as much as possible. It was the only way he could protect an upper-middle class white boy who he sensed was in danger.

I kept my mouth shut, but knowing that there was compassion, and knowing that there were people that were capable of loving other people unconditionally certainly gave me hope and fostered the belief that things would someday be different. It was the beginning of faith and a belief that someday life would be fantastic and that I would someday be safe and secure. This life I was experiencing at the time was more of a temporary glitch, than a fate doomed by misery. There were relatives of my adopted family that were shocked by what was going on and that did have knowledge and could see what was happening from a distance. They were not living in the home, but certainly were closer, and had a clearer understanding of what was taking place than the general public did. And I think their love and their efforts in kindness and consideration for me gave me the idea that life could and would be better someday. The fact of the matter is that I knew I had to press on. What other choice does a child have? Amazingly enough, and a fact that I feel very fortunate about is the fact that I always believed in God. I was born believing in God. Luckily I had that feeling of that faith there all along, and I always knew that He loved me anyway. I also knew that for whatever reason my life was the way it was, I would have a chance to overcome the difficulties and shine some day. I believed in myself, and I still do!

Wright

Everyone has strengths and weaknesses. How have you been able to cash in on your strengths while minimizing your weaknesses?

Rogers

Well having quite literally come from the streets, my instinct for survival and my natural thriftiness helped me immensely. I've heard other people who had difficult upbringings blame their past or their family's economic situation for their own unhappiness and for their difficulty in achieving their goals. I find that despicable and unhealthy. **Just about every traumatic event in my life has either better prepared me, enhanced my compassion for others, or it's paid off,** I mean literally. For instance, had I not been a product of abusive upbringing, I would have never had the experience necessary to help others who came from the same situations and who perhaps did not fare so well. Being in foster and group homes allowed me to counsel and guide employees that were from less than fortunate backgrounds and to provide them with the assurance that they too can become very successful and are not limited by their pasts with the kind of credibility that a normal coach or counselor just doesn't have. I can relate to anyone in any part of society at least for long enough to work together on a project or to understand each other in a conflict. I find the fact that I have made and paid dearly for many mistakes in business, to be a great part of why we are so successful now. I have a broad spectrum of experience to draw from when designing solutions for myself and the business owners who are working with our consulting firm, APM LLC, and the Automated Marketing Group, the one-of-a-kind ad agency we designed to propel small businesses.

Wright

I've seen that a lot down through the years. My wife is a cancer survivor. She almost died, but she made it through. Now we both try to help people that are going through similar circumstances. I'm just a watcher and a listener, but boy when she speaks, they listen.

Rogers

Isn't it amazing when someone shares such a highly personal experience, and their suffering through something of such magnitude. I know I've been confronted with life-threatening trauma with close friends, and even myself, but certainly not a wife in that situation. But I know that to look into someone's eyes that has fought something like that and survived it is to begin to know somebody that's got true character. They are tempered by the realities of life, and are made of solid substance. I think we can all gain a great deal from a chance to meet or listen to people who have overcome such seemingly impossible obstacles and challenges in their lives. I'd welcome any opportunity to listen to someone who has experienced such, speak about survival. It is amazingly inspirational!

Wright

Well said, David. How has your success changed you?

Rogers

Experiencing a greater financial freedom has brought more peace and more patience to my life, along with a greater sense of responsibility. I feel I'm given more time, and therefore the opportunity to work on things that I think are more important, like helping small business owners compete against the large corporate congolomorates. It's essential to me on a very personal level that people get the message that each and every one of us can most definitely become a success. I now get to teach and to speak publicly. Amazingly enough, intelligent and sometimes very successful people will line up and even pay to listen. Most of them may not have listened and certainly wouldn't have paid if I hadn't had the amount of publicity and success that I've been blessed to enjoy. But there again, every day I still have to get up and put my pants on and go to work just like everybody else and I love that. I wouldn't give it up for anything. **My work entails getting to know and understand businesses and people in order to help them overcome problems and issues that create obstacles in their lives.** It still doesn't seem like work to me; it is my passion. To be even a small part of the solution is just the most rewarding feeling I have ever experienced! Seeing a small, family business become everything the family dreamed it could be, or helping a larger company resolve their customer service issues are a couple of great examples. These are real people we are helping! It just doesn't feel like work to me. How have I changed? Not much I guess. I still like my blue jeans and my pick-up truck. I still go fishing and shovel snow for my elderly neighbor ladies. Success has just given me more time to do it, and a better sense of priorities.

Wright

Does your heart and mind go out to the disadvantaged? I mean does it give you a sense of accomplishment when you can help someone that you know has been disadvantaged?

Rogers

Oh, let me tell you, that is exactly what I have been trying to communicate! What benefit exists for any of us if all we are trying to do is fill some empty void with money, material possessions, or some elusive feeling of power or accomplishment? When you asked me the question, "How has success changed you," the first thing that came to mind was how is it different to have money now and be able to go to the grocery store when I want to and other things like that. But truthfully, the biggest thing about it, the greatest thing for me has certainly been that I now have the resources, the time and the influence to make a difference with those who are disadvantaged. I have chosen to recognize a very important principle in my personal and business life. It is this—everyone, to one degree or another, is disadvantaged, has a weakness or handicap, or has the need for help or support. I don't care how smart, how well off, how wealthy, how privileged, how poor, or how abused you are, everyone can be served or supported in some way. I certainly know this is true because I have observed it on both sides of the tracks for myself and in many, many others. This is a key element that weaves itself throughout my personal activities and most definitely in my business activities. I can always find a way to serve, to uplift, to help with a burden, or to teach a better way! Even though it may appear that some individuals are very successful and self-sufficient, I have found that everyone (who is honest with themselves and others) has needs or weaknesses that someone else can help alleviate. For this type of synergy to work, there must be two sides of the relationship. The person who has the need must not allow a "know-it-all" attitude to interfere. No one ever learned anything by refusing help. **On the other side, it takes courage, skill, tact, and commitment to approach another with an offer of help.** In my experience there are far too many times that one party or the other are simply not willing to do their part to accept and facilitate what might have been a beautiful solution to a problem and a resulting life-long friendship!

There are many other ways to serve. We make it a point to find ways to benefit the community, and especially the less fortunate. One example of this is in our yearly Christmas card mailings to our customers and clients. Rather than going and buying cards from a printer creating some nifty design that can (reportedly) subliminally convince people to spend more money with me next year, we buy cards from a group here in Denver called The Gathering Place. It's the only shelter available for impoverished women here, that is open during the day time. So when it's freezing outside and snowing, they can take their children there and get a hot meal. They can do job searches. They help them with job counseling, and help them get cleaned-up. The Gathering Place provides them with clothes, food, whatever they need through donations. The homeless women can actually earn money by working or participating in various programs provided at the center. So we buy Christmas and Holiday cards that homeless people design and paint or draw with anything from a pencil to crayons and water colors. The cards cost one dollar a piece, and seventy-five cents of that goes directly back to the actual homeless person who made the card! And do I feel good about that? I think it's one of the neatest programs ever created! We do food drives at our businesses at least twice per year for the food banks. We also employ struggling youth who are in alternative education high schools as a last resort before they are left to fail or drop out. My entire staff is involved in the mentoring of some of these fantastic kids. There's nothing more important than work like that. You can pile up all the money in the world and it wouldn't do anything for me like it does to know that someone is going to have a better day or a better life because we've gotten involved.

My life has been blessed, and **that blessing is magnified and multiplied every time I choose to share the love and strength that was given to me, with others who need it now.** I will let you in on a little secret. **Money follows happiness; not the other way around!** People choose to do more business with us because they understand what we stand for and represent - not just as successful business people and advertisers, but as people and members of our community and neighborhoods. This kind of business is solid. People who come to you because you offer the cheapest deal will never be loyal. They will always chase a cheaper deal. On the other hand, those who choose to patronize your business because they like who you are or how you do things (be it the actual work or service you provide or sell, or the community involvement and personal contributions of you and your team), will be very grateful and forgiving customers who do not even mind waiting a bit in order to do business with someone they can respect or admire. These are truly the type of people who you can have some confidence in as long-term, loyal customers.

Wright

In my job, I get to talk to people all the time, like you, that have experienced every kind of thing imaginable, such as General Alexander Haig and many other famous people all over the world. They all are very serious about this thing called their job. Depending on which book you read or which psychologist you talk to, there is a general consensus that between 80% and 90% of all the people in America get up, get in their car every morning and go to a place where they do not want to be.

Rogers

That's true!

Wright

On the other hand, as I talk to these people who are so happy and successful, they talk about passion. What is your opinion about having passion and how do you impart it to the disadvantaged? How do you help them understand and lead them to focus on their passion and to keep driving towards that?

Rogers

That's a great little batch of questions. Let me try to respond. The first question: "How do I feel about having passion?" I'll tell you again, when we talk about necessary ingredients, for me there's no need for a j-o-b anymore. My passion is to get out there and make things happen and provide for the families that are helping my businesses, serve the families of our clients, and help other needy families that we find in our path. Passion is the necessary ingredient, I think, that creates the difference between feeling like work is a privilege or like you're being drug in to put another 60 or 80 hours in this week. Where and how do you find that? The first and most important thing is: identify what motivates you and gives you the "fire." What drives you to get up earlier, stay at it longer, and dig much deeper. You must be willing to look at yourself and understand what is it that makes you feel the best. "When have I felt the best in my life?" "When have I been the on a warpath, or in a battle, or on a mission?" I don't necessarily judge that person as unhappy. Sometimes passion includes intensity and confrontation, but it doesn't have to. There are many people who exhibit passion in a personal and sensitive way. The most important factor is to just go out there and discover what it is for you! Find out what really pulls at your heart. **What impacts your feelings and thoughts so greatly that it changes the way you look at and react to the things that happen within that area of your life?** What can you do about that? How can you get more of that or less of that? You must identify yourself and accept who you are and what you need as your own reality! It is even more than that! It is the KEY to your future and to the QUALITY of your life! You may find it in volunteering. Another may find it in a hobby. If you can find something you really care about and you can find a way to get involved through an activity such as volunteering, or something as simple as just being a true friend to someone, or just caring enough to look after your neighborhood, or some of your neighbors, it's amazing how you can find little things that might turn into either a career or perhaps just a great rewarding involvement or relationship that makes everything else in your life meaningful and rich. It's amazing how when you shine a light in the room you see so many beautiful things in addition to the thing you were looking for. Success and happiness in one area of life flows into all other areas of life—including your work!

Wright

So tell me, what's next for you? What is the next mountain you're planning to climb?

Rogers

Well, there are some amazing things in the works. Thanks to a wonderful partnership, we are making available to the public the exact strategies and the techniques we use and have used to make each of our businesses perform, in an incredibly easy and affordable way. Our firm, Automated Marketing Group LLC, is now handling the advertising and the marketing for dozens of other small business owners who are beginning to feel secure and hopeful while putting cash in the bank in spite of the effects of a down economy. We've managed to create a system by which small family businesses can get out and compete with the big boys in a very inexpensive but highly effective format, unlike anything available before. And I'm so excited about bringing this to the business community because we're going to be able to help a lot more people all at once, in a very personal, real, and measurable way! For the first time ever, small business owners can spend pennies on what previously cost dollars! It used to be too expensive for a small business to afford to work with successful ad agencies with proven track records. Our program has completely broken that mold and is just growing so quickly, I can barely believe it myself! I am looking forward to bringing many other family business owners to the same levels of success that I, my family, and our staff have been blessed to enjoy!

Wright

Sounds great! If I were a business owner, I'd stand in line to work with you! What an exciting conversation, David. I really want to thank you for taking this much of your time to talk to me about these important things. I've learned a lot today and I've got a lot to think about, personally.

Rogers

Well, I'm grateful to you, David. Thank you very much for considering me for this project, and for asking some really fantastic questions.

Wright

Today we've been talking to David Rogers, the "Long-Term Growth Guru." By his own admission, his beginnings were very humble, but now we find out what makes David so successful. I suggest that it took more than the usual guts and passion for the job. David is truly a self-made man, and we've really learned a lot from him here today. I hope this chapter will teach the readers lessons that they can use for the rest of their lives. We have David Rogers to thank for it. Thank you so much, David. I appreciate you being with us on *Conversations on Success*.

Rogers

This has been my pleasure, David. Bless you and thank you for having me.

About The Author

David Rogers is the President of Auto Profit Masters LLC, a national consulting and executive coaching firm serving independently owned small businesses. Mr. Rogers is also the President of Automated Marketing Group LLC, a national advertising and marketing agency specifically designed to deliver its inexpensive, easy to manage, and extremely effective advertising program to small businesses.

Mr. Rogers' unique and straightforward approach to understanding, working with and motivating people has received acclaim nationwide from clients, their customers and their employees. His exceptional copywriting and communication skills are highly sought after assets to a significant number of businesses who realize the power of having him project their image and message to their prospects.

Mr. Rogers has built an award winning team of leaders and achievers who deliver results as evidenced by the publicity, testimonials, continued growth, and long-term business relationships he and his staff enjoy.

Mr. Rogers is an active member in good standing of the National Speakers Association, the American Marketing Association, and the Automotive Service Association. Mr. Rogers performs on radio and appears on television regularly as well as providing training classes and speeches for many organizations such as GM, AC DELCO, and NAPA, along with the service organizations such as Rotary Club, Kiwanis, and the Optimists. He has, in the past underwritten many charities including *Project Angel Heart* in Denver, Colorado, an agency dedicated to providing nutritious, home-delivered meals for the terminally ill.

David N. Rogers

Automated Marketing Group LLC.

4845 Pearl East Circle, Ste 101

Boulder, CO 80301

Phone: 1.866.520.3030

Email: David@longtermfix.com

www.LONGTERMFIX.COM

www.AUTOPROFITMASTERS.com